GARDENING WITH
CONIFERS

ADRIAN BLOOM

PHOTOGRAPHS BY
ADRIAN AND RICHARD BLOOM

FIREFLY BOOKS

Dedicated to all those plantsmen who personally inspired my
early interest in conifers and widened my knowledge of
them, most notably Fred Barcock, Maurice Mason,
Jan Dieter zu Jeddeloh Snr, Humphrey Welch, Jean Iseli,
John Bond and Gerard Groenestein

A FIREFLY BOOK

Published by Firefly Books Ltd. 2002

Copyright © Frances Lincoln Limited 2002
Text copyright © Adrian Bloom 2002
Photographs copyright © Adrian and Richard Bloom 2002

First Printing

National Library of Canada Cataloguing in Publication Data

Bloom, Adrian
    Gardening with conifers

Includes bibliographical references and index.
ISBN 1-55209-635-1 (bound)   ISBN 1-55209-633-5 (pbk.)

1. Ornamental conifers. 2. Conifers. I. Bloom, Adrian II. Title.

SB428.B58 2002   635.9'775   C2001-901496-1

U.S. Cataloguing in Publication Data
   (Library of Congress Standards)

Bloom, Adrian
    Gardening with conifers/Adrian Bloom; photographs by Adrian
and Richard Bloom. – 1ˢᵗ ed.
[192] p. : col. photos. ; cm.
Includes bibliographic references and index.
Summary: Guide to using and growing conifers in your garden.
Includes design ideas, sources and directory of 600 different
conifers
ISBN 1-55209-635-1
ISBN 1-55209-633-5
1. Conifers. 2. Ornamental conifers. I. Bloom, Adrian. II.
Title.
635.935 21   CIP   SB428.B66 2002

Published in Canada in 2002 by
Firefly Books Ltd.
3680 Victoria Park Avenue
Willowdale, Ontario M2H 3K1

Published in the United States in 2002 by
Firefly Books (U.S.) Inc.
P.O. Box 1338, Ellicott Station
Buffalo, New York 14205

Edited by Jane Havell Designed by Caroline Hillier

PAGE 1 In late spring, the bright green new shoots of *Abies
balsamea* 'Hudsonia' contrast with older growth.
PAGES 2–3 The author's Norfolk garden in late summer, in
which conifers are mixed with perennials, ornamental grasses
and shrubs. Left to right, the conifers are *Picea omorika*
'Pendula Bruns', *Picea pungens* 'Globosa', *Picea glauca* var.
albertiana 'Alberta Globe', *Picea sitchensis* 'Papoose', *Thuja
occidentalis* 'Holmstrup' and *Cedrus deodara* 'Nana Aurea'.
THESE PAGES Frost on the foliage of *Cupressus arizonica*
var. *glabra* 'Blue Ice'.

CONTENTS

THE MAGIC

OF CONIFERS

'Why should I use conifers in my garden?' is a question that anyone picking up this book might ask. The answer, I hope, will be found in the following pictures, advice and information – conifers can add essential ingredients to a garden not easily or fully replicated by any other plants. I have spent over thirty years creating a garden with, literally, hundreds of conifers that provide interest and color the whole year round. I fully appreciate their value as well as their problems; unfortunately, it is often the latter that are highlighted by members of the gardening media who feel that conifers have little or no place in the modern garden. Gardeners in other parts of the world find it difficult to believe the paranoia that has beome attached in Britain to the Leyland Cypress (× *Cupressocyparis leylandii*); this entirely innocent, fast-growing evergreen has caused costly legal disputes between neighbors simply because people plant it in the wrong places or omit to trim it.

This is not a book about Leylandii, nor is it about the negative sides of conifers, which are no more prevalent than those of any other group of plants (and will of course be covered in the text). Any fast-growing tree – including eucalyptus, poplar or willow – should always be chosen and placed with care. The point to make with this marvelous and varied group of mostly evergreen plants is the same as with other trees and shrubs, even perennials: consider before you buy, plan before you plant, and always take heed of growth rates and likely suitability for purpose.

Far from being dull, to the observant this group of plants can be both awe-inspiring and magical. Conifers come in all shapes and sizes – miniatures may grow less than 3ft (90cm) in a hundred years, while others might reach 130ft (40m) or more in the same period. Conifers include the oldest living plant in the world, the ancient Bristlecone Pine, *Pinus longaeva*, whose 4,500-year-old wind-shattered specimens cling to life over 10,000ft (3,000m) up in

This wind-carved Pinus longaeva, *over 2,000 years old, still survives at 11,000ft/3,350m in Wheeler Park, Nevada.*

the White Mountains of California, as well the tallest, the Coast Redwood, also in California, measuring almost 400ft (120m). If we are lucky, we can marvel at these in nature. It would not, of course, be advisable to plant a Coast Redwood in a smaller garden but, strangely enough, *Pinus longaeva* grows quite successfully at much less elevated positions, even in my garden at Bressingham in Norfolk, UK.

Conifers can be deciduous or evergreen. Among the former, the larches (*Larix*), the Swamp Cypresses (*Taxodium*) and the amazing Maidenhair Tree (*Ginkgo*) have wonderful autumn colors as their leaves turn and fall. In winter, the first two, together with the deciduous Dawn Redwood (*Metasequoia*), exhibit traceries of branches and twigs against the sky, enhanced by frost and water droplets. The evergreens can display a wonderful range of colors. It is magical to see an evergreen like *Pinus mugo* 'Wintergold' transform its green summer needles to a glowing yellow or gold in autumn – such a cheery change can warm the heart during long winter days.

There is great interest, too, in the variety of conifer shapes – weeping trees can take on an ethereal appearance on a misty day; frosted or snow-laden branches can sparkle in low winter sun, their burden later melting in glistening droplets. Winter, when so much else in the garden is dormant, is when conifers really come into their own. But in late

PREVIOUS PAGES *Conifers – most of them 25 to 30 years old – provide structure and a backdrop to perennials and ornamental grasses in the author's garden in Norfolk, England, late summer.*

spring, when the sheathed winter buds swell and burst open on spruces (*Picea*) and firs (*Abies*), smothering them in fresh new leaves, the effect is magical. That in turn can be outdone by the startling red flowers seen on many conifers as the cones begin to develop. The cones themselves can be smaller than a pea or nearly as large as a football; in their young stage, the cones of the Korean Fir (*Abies koreana*) are a rich, deep blue.

The leaves of conifers are by no means uniformly dull, green needles, as many gardeners might believe. The hues of new growth include a brilliant powder-blue, bright grass-green, orange, yellow, cream, even red and crimson. Some conifers, such as junipers, bear both prickly young and quite different coarser mature leaves at the same time; others, such as firs, spruces and pines, have bright silver-blue undersides to their leaves which are gloriously revealed when they turn to face the light.

A further wonderful asset, often overlooked, is the aromatic fragrance given by many conifers, while some junipers have quite a pungent scent.

The awe-inspiring giants of the forest – the ancient, almost prehistoric *Ginkgo*, the *Metasequoia* and the Chilean Monkey Puzzle tree – can all be grown today in gardens. For smaller gardens, however, a further type has added to the range – witch's brooms. These originate as congested growths on much larger trees, and have always been associated with witchcraft. Today, collectors all over the world search forests to find interesting forms that they can propagate and offer us for our gardens.

ABOVE *Juvenile winter foliage on* Chamaecyparis thyoides *'Rubicon'.*

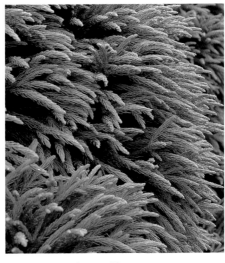

ABOVE *'Ringlets' of leaves on* Cryptomeria japonica *'Globosa Nana'.*

ABOVE *Golden winter needles on* Pinus contorta *var.* latifolia *'Chief Joseph'.*

BELOW *Summer stripes on* Pinus mugo *'Kokarde'.*

BELOW *Frosted winter buds on* Picea abies *'Inversa'.*

BELOW *Exuding resin on cones of* Abies koreana.

CONIFERS AS GARDEN PLANTS

Few gardeners, even professional ones, are aware of how wide a range of conifers is available in most gardening-orientated countries, and therefore they are perhaps not alive to all their possibilities as garden plants. Too often, when conifers are used they are badly chosen and poorly positioned. Whether you want formality or informality in your garden, conifers lend themselves to much wider planting than most people allow.

There is a bewildering list of cultivars available for the garden, but many of them are of interest only to specialist collectors. For most gardeners and garden designers, the best way to choose is with a view to what will suit local conditions. Then, rather than select an inappropriate cultivar on impulse or from a picture in a book, go to a reputable supplier and choose by color, form and type. For example, the Italian Cypress (*Cupressus sempervirens*) is often a popular choice; of Mediterranean origin, it grows well in any similar climate, even in parts of Britain, but it will not survive really cold climates. A more suitable selection might be the bone-hardy *Juniperus chinensis* 'Spartan', or other columnar conifers.

Fast-, medium- and slow-growing conifers can provide structure in any garden, with varying shapes and colors and vital winter interest. Cleverly used, they can make showy specimens in their own right, or be used as foils or contrasts to other plants, deciduous trees, shrubs, perennials or grasses. Some conifers make excellent screens or hedges – for privacy, protection from strong winds, or as backdrops to other plants. The yew (*Taxus*) is as popular as ever for formal hedges against which perennials and other plants can perform, or as a backdrop to statuary. In English gardens, the fastigiate yew plays a role similar to that of the sentinel-like cypress in Italy, but the choice is much broader than these two classical conifers.

A wide range of dwarf, slow-growing and even miniature conifers extends opportunities for the smaller garden. These can be used with other dwarf shrubs, including heaths and heathers (where conditions are suitable), rock and alpine plants, and will flourish in sinks, troughs and containers. Miniature landscapes can be designed with conifers as an integral, or even the whole, part. The choice today seems unlimited: availability is much greater than a few years ago, but decisions can be correspondingly more difficult. Conifers make great container plants, but you do need to take care with selection (see page 71).

Lastly, conifers are friendly to wildlife: some make protective, sheltered houses for birds to nest in, while others provide cones or edible nuts for birds, squirrels and other mammals.

LEFT *In the author's garden in Norfolk, England,* Juniperus communis *'Hibernica' (column, left) provides an accent point,* Picea pungens *(center) a feature specimen and, in the distance, taller conifers act as shelter and year-round backdrop (right). Two Japanese maples add their own summer contrast,* Acer palmatum dissectum *'Crimson Queen' (foreground) and* Acer shirasawanum *'Aureum' (left center).*
RIGHT Berberis × stenophylla *'Corallina Compacta' makes a startling combination with a 10-year-old* Thuja orientalis *'Southport'.* Veronica peduncularis *'Georgia Blue' is in the foreground.*

THE ORIGINS OF GARDEN CONIFERS

The keener you become on gardening, the more fascinating plants seem to be, and it is then a natural development to become interested in the origins of your plants. This can at times be like a detective story. Where did the plant come from? Where is its native habitat? Who discovered it, and when? When was it brought into cultivation, and by whom? Where are the oldest or biggest examples? A plant's origin can provide vital clues as to how well it may grow in other conditions, including not only region but also elevation, rainfall and temperature tolerance. In the directory (page 82), I have wherever possible given details of the background and origin of individual genera, species and cultivars. Conifers are spread widely throughout the world, mostly in temperate or subtropical regions, in both northern and southern hemispheres. They grow from coast to inland valleys and mountains, from boggy, badly drained soils to arid hillsides. Some species are spread throughout Europe as far east as Siberia, including the Scots Pine (*Pinus sylvestris*), despite its common name; others, such as the Monterey Cypress (*Cupressus macrocarpa*), are limited in their natural habitat – in this case, to a small area of the Monterey peninsula in California.

The history of conifers as garden plants is a fascinating one. In the middle ages, conifer forests were seen as dark, magical and threatening; as the population grew, they became increasingly valued, and cleared, for fuel and timber. As the world began to open up through discovery and trade, and greater wealth was created, interest in gardening and landscaping grew. By the eighteenth century, this interest was being fed by the importation into Europe of new species, especially from North America as it opened up to settlers. Two of the earliest foreign conifers to be planted in Britain were the Swamp Cypress (*Taxodium distichum*), introduced by the botanist John Tradescant in 1640 from North America, and the Cedar of Lebanon (*Cedrus libani*) in 1650. North Americans, so rich in natural flora, including conifers, were until the nineteenth century more interested in clearing trees than in planting them.

The nineteenth century saw a real increase in imported exotic plants – this was the century of the professional plant hunter. Botanic gardens and nurseries such as James Veitch and Sons employed plant hunters: David Douglas, Robert Fortune and William Lobb went off specially to find new species in North America, Asia and South America respectively. They risked life and limb to find and collect plants, often in hostile environments that included skirmishes with local populations. David Douglas, discoverer of many conifers in north-west North America, sent valuable seeds and plants back before he met an untimely death in 1834, gored to death in a cattle pit in Hawaii. The Douglas Fir (*Pseudotsuga menziesii*) is named after him. Archibald Menzies, who traveled with Captain George Vancouver up the west coast of the Americas in the 1790s, was the first to spot many conifers; he brought the strange-looking Monkey Puzzle Tree (*Araucaria araucana*) back from Chile in 1795. Robert Fortune introduced such treasures as the Lace Bark Pine (*Pinus bungeana*) and the Golden Larch (*Pseudolarix amabilis*) from his journeys in China and Japan. William Lobb, not to be outdone, was responsible for introducing to Britain *Thuja plicata*, *Abies concolor* and *Abies grandis*. The greatest excitement was created when the true giants of north-western America were introduced into Britain – the Giant Redwood (*Sequoia sempervirens*) in 1843 and the Mammoth Tree (*Sequoiadendron giganteum*) in 1853. For over a century, much to the annoyance of many American horticulturists, the latter was called a Wellingtonia in honour of the Duke of Wellington, the former British prime minister and hero of Waterloo, who had died in 1852.

Great competition existed among estate owners to be the first to have some of these conifers to show off to visiting royalty and dignitaries – much as, these days, garden enthusiasts might vie to have the latest hosta or hardy geranium. It was a boom time for

The famous parterre garden at Drummond Castle, Perthshire, Scotland, borrows from both French and Italian styles. In the foreground, old yews and the taller Chamaecyparis lawsoniana *cultivars (introduced from North America) are clipped; they are silhouetted against the woodland behind, which is planted with many giant species such as* Abies grandis, Sequoia sempervirens *and* Sequoiadendron giganteum.

nurserymen, whose lists of conifers increased rapidly to include, in the latter part of the century, many dwarf and slow-growing types. Early fashions for dwarf conifers in Britain can be tracked in old catalogs and books. J. C. Loudon described only ten in cultivation in 1838, but by 1875 the Lawson Nursery in Edinburgh, introducer of the Lawson Cypress (*Chamaecyparis lawsoniana*), listed around forty for sale. Initially, these were planted as specimens on lawns, but their popularity was limited and did not last; interest in them was rekindled with the advent of the rock garden in the late nineteeth and early twentieth centuries. By 1938, when Murray Hornibrook issued the second edition of his book *Dwarf and Slow Growing Conifers* (the first was in 1923), this special group of conifers was firmly established. The book became a classic for interesting, well-researched, well-observed information and sound advice, in which the author was assisted by the horticultural luminaries Professor C. S. Sargent of the Arnold Arboretum, Boston, and W. J. Bean of Kew Gardens. Amazingly, completely new conifers are still being discovered in the wild – most recently in 1994 in Sydney, Australia, with the large-growing Wollemi Pine (*Wollemii nobilis*), a relation of the ancient *Araucaria* family.

THE CONIFER EXPLOSION

The popularity of conifers reached its height in the period after the 1960s. The economic and social changes which led to the development of suburbia, wider ownership of property and more leisure time also created more people anxious to improve their gardens. Motor cars brought greater mobility, and garden centers, imported from California (where else?), offered container-grown plants, which extended the planting season.

For gardeners wanting low-maintenance, trouble-free plants with year-round color, dwarf and slow-growing conifers seemed to provide the answer, as new selections fueled interest. In North America, native prostrate junipers were planted by the million to landscape the highways. Everywhere in Britain and Europe, conifers were in great demand. During the 1970s year-round color was widely achieved in Britain by planting conifers, often in combination with heathers. In the late 1980s and 1990s enthusiasms moved to other ideas – perennials, ornamental grasses, Mediterranean and tropical plants – but conifers still have a large body of admirers. They are widely available in tremendous variety – from miniatures to trees of different shapes, colors and habits of growth. The very extent of the choice sometimes causes confusion, and because of this perceived complexity they are thought of as a group apart. But the principles of gardening with conifers are straightforward: as with any shrubs and trees, you need to understand how to select, grow and prune them, as well as how to use them to best effect, both immediately and in the long term.

HOW CONIFERS GROW

C olor, shape and size are determined by various factors, such as origin, climate and soil and, with some conifers, cultivation by propagation. It is helpful to have an understanding of how and where these differences occur.

CONIFERS FROM SEED

In nature, most conifers reproduce from seed, and this is the method used by nurseries to produce seedlings for forestry planting or special species for hedging such as *Tsuga canadensis*, *Thuja occidentalis* and *Chamaecyparis lawsoniana*. Other, choicer, trees for garden and landscape use – such as *Pinus bungeana*, *Picea smithiana* and *Abies koreana* – will also be raised from seed. Some are slow-growing, others much faster; seedlings of one species may vary widely. When they do vary, a nurseryman may spot an attractive form and select it as a possible new cultivar. He or she will also raise seedlings of plants to use as "understocks" for grafting – *Picea abies*, for example, is widely used for many spruce cultivars.

NATURALLY ADAPTED FORMS

Presumably anything that arises in nature without the interference of mankind must be natural. Witch's brooms are described as 'mutations', but they are natural; the same term could be applied to the dwarf *Picea glauca* var. *albertiana* 'Conica', which was discovered close to a railway track in Alberta, Canada, surrounded by a forest of tree-like white spruces (see page 131). A more common dwarf adaptation is found in trees that have had to endure harsher climates at high altitudes, or rocky tundra. Many of these – such as hemlocks in the New England mountains and the mountain pine (*Pinus mugo*) in the Alps – will remain reliably dwarf when brought down to more comfortable lowland gardens. Others, which live in a unique habitat – such as the Mendocino Shore Pine (*Pinus contorta* var. *bolanderi*) from Mendocino county in California – will, if moved from their restricted areas, grow into tall trees.

Conifers in their natural habitats can vary considerably. New and interesting plants are continually being sought from the Rockies to New Zealand, from Tasmania to the European Alps. These views show two of Britain's three native conifers (the English Yew, Taxus baccata, *is the other) growing in their natural environments.*
LEFT *Mature Scots Pines (*Pinus sylvestris) *self-seeding in sandy heathland in Suffolk, England.*
ABOVE RIGHT *A varied stand of the Common Juniper (*Juniperus communis) *above Grasmere in the Lake District, Cumbria, England.*

JUVENILE FIXATIONS

Not a term from a book on psychology, but a particular type of conifer! Young conifer seedlings usually have quite different foliage from that of their adult forms, but occasionally a seedling will retain juvenile-style foliage for some years or even for ever. This foliage is usually much more feathery than, say, the coarser adult foliage on chamaecyparis, but more spiny and prickly on junipers. In some cases, as with *Juniperus chinensis* 'Aurea', both juvenile and adult foliage exist together on the same plant; in others, such as *Chamaecyparis pisifera* 'Squarrosa Sulphurea', the foliage is totally juvenile, but occasional adult shoots can develop, which should be cut away. Reversions from juvenile to adult form can occur with many dwarf conifers, including plants that have developed from witch's brooms – if not cut away, these will eventually take over the plant.

SPORTS AND WITCH'S BROOMS

Both these terms refer to genetic mutations, which can be the initial material from which a collector develops a new plant. A sport is a shoot that is different from normal – say, on a green-foliaged

Paler yellow spiky juvenile foliage and adult foliage exist on the same tree, Juniperus chinensis *'Aurea'.*

A golden shoot or 'sport' on the darker purple green foliage of Thuja orientalis *'Purple King'.*

*A witch's broom of dense congested foliage is visible (center) on this Norway Spruce (*Picea abies*).*

plant, one with a gold or white tip. If this remains constant, the shoot can be taken as a cutting and will become a new, wholly golden or part-golden plant. Many variegated chamaecyparis, junipers and thujas have been raised like this and introduced as new plants. Some remain stable, but others may revert to green over time. Usually, these variegated plants have less vigor than their one-color parent.

No one has a certain explanation about why congested growths, called witch's brooms, arise on many conifers such as pines and spruce, seemingly at random. A bud mutation initiates a usually rounded ball of dense foliage, which often hangs rather tantalizingly out of reach at the top of a tree. When stems or even whole growths are detached (they are shot out of trees by some collectors), rooted or grafted, they can become new conifers. Innumerable forms are being raised this way – some would say far too many, and trials ought to be made prior to release to prevent the proliferation of similar cultivars.

CULTIVARIANTS

This strange term is now commonly used; while it is descriptive, it tends to accentuate the apparent strangeness and unpredictability of conifers. In simple terms, it means new types of plant that have been propagated by cuttings or grafts. For instance, with

conifers on which the foliage varies, such as *Chamaecyparis lawsoniana* 'Ellwoodii', two different types of plant will be produced from cuttings taken from the more vigorous top of the plant and from cuttings taken near the base. At least in the early years, the former develops a narrower, faster-growing habit, while the latter is more bushy. *Thuja occidentalis* 'Rheingold' (see page 163) is a classic example of a cultivariant.

In the case of grafting, two aspects can affect growth habits. With *Picea pungens* 'Hoopsii' and other taller cultivars of the Colorado Blue Spruce, the number of semi-erect or upright shoots that can be used as scion wood (cuttings for grafting) are limited, so nurserymen will also use the lower, spreading side branches. What they want to produce is an upright shapely tree, but side branches, understandably, are used to horizontal growth. After grafting (see page 180), they need some years of training to make upright specimens. The scion or cutting is normally grafted on to an understock or seedling of the Norway Spruce (*Picea abies*), which is quite vigorous, so that at least vigor of growth is matched.

Problems can occur when a dwarf conifer is grafted on to a vigorous root stock, which may in time completely change the growth rate and habit of the selected cultivar. *Taxus baccata* 'Standishii', a slow-growing golden-leaved fastigiate yew, can be rooted from cuttings, but because it is very slow to root it is often grafted instead on to a seedling of *Taxus baccata*, which is green. Such a union will induce more vigour, but the understock will often continue to make green shoots which, as with grafted roses, must continually be cut away. It is generally better when possible to have a plant on its own roots, unless it has so little vigour that it will not grow at all. Nurserymen have other reasons for grafting, such as where the understock will increase the hardiness of the plant or make it less susceptible to disease.

Juvenile foliage at the base, adult at the top, on this 5-year-old Thuja occidentalis *'Rheingold' can produce cultivariants when propagated.*

THE NAMING OF CONIFERS

As with all garden plants, the botanical names of conifers are in Latin, the universal language of plants. Common names have their uses, but particularly in the case of conifers these can be downright misleading. Early discoverers of plants often mistook them initially; as a result, many still carry common names that bear no relationship to their true identity. The Western Red Cedar is no cedar at all, but *Thuja plicata*. The Pencil Cedar is also no cedar, but a juniper, *Juniperus virginiana*; neither does it look like a pencil, but got its name because it was used for making pencils. There is room for both common and botanical names, but the botanical name should always be the point of reference. Even if it is not important for the average gardener to have much knowledge of plant taxonomy, when it comes to choosing plants, researching them in books and finding them in catalogs, the botanical names are essential.

The first part of a plant's name belongs to the genus – *Juniperus*, *Cedrus*, *Pinus*, etc. Normally these have several species, distinct but closely related groups found in the wild; in certain cases, such as *Sciadopitys*, there is only one species, *S. verticillata*. Some species have a further climatic or regional variation, a subspecies or variety, to which the taxonomists have attached a further name – such as *Pinus mugo* var. *pumilio*, which, though variable in the wild, has common distinctions from growing at high altitudes which lend it a compactness of growth.

Finally, there is the cultivar. This is the last, often descriptive, name given by the discoverer or owner of a plant that has been selected from the wild or in a garden or nursery. Before 1959, Latin names were generally given to dwarf conifers. If you understood Latin, these were often well described but a bit of a mouthful – such as *Chamaecyparis pisifera* 'Filifera Aurea', which translates into the easier but equally descriptive common name Golden Threadleaf

Chamaecyparis pisifera *'Filifera Aurea', the Golden Threadleaf Cypress – strictly speaking, a False Cypress.*

Cypress, and *Picea abies* 'Nidiformis', which in English became the Bird's Nest Spruce. In 1959 botanists introduced the cultivar code, which forbade the coining of new Latin names for cultivars. Conifer enthusiasts became more adventurous, and names became easier for the less knowledgeable gardener to understand. A witch's broom on *Picea abies* 'Nidiformis' (itself a witch's broom found in 1904 on *Picea abies*), which was discovered in Holland in 1958, could according to the rules have been called *P. a.* 'Nidiformis Minima', but luckily it was named 'Little Gem'. Now the cultivars keep coming with ever more weird and wonderful names – 'Fat Albert', 'Spotty Spreader' and 'Big Tuna'.

It is also part of the international code that names given in the country of origin should be maintained in that language, but this can be a discouragement to gardeners who might already have enough difficulties with the nomenclature. If you are an English speaker, can you imagine a burning desire to obtain the German-raised plant called *Juniperus communis* 'Schneverdingen Goldmachangel'? Of course, this works both ways, but a plea should be made in today's international world of horticulture for succinct names that can be easily translated.

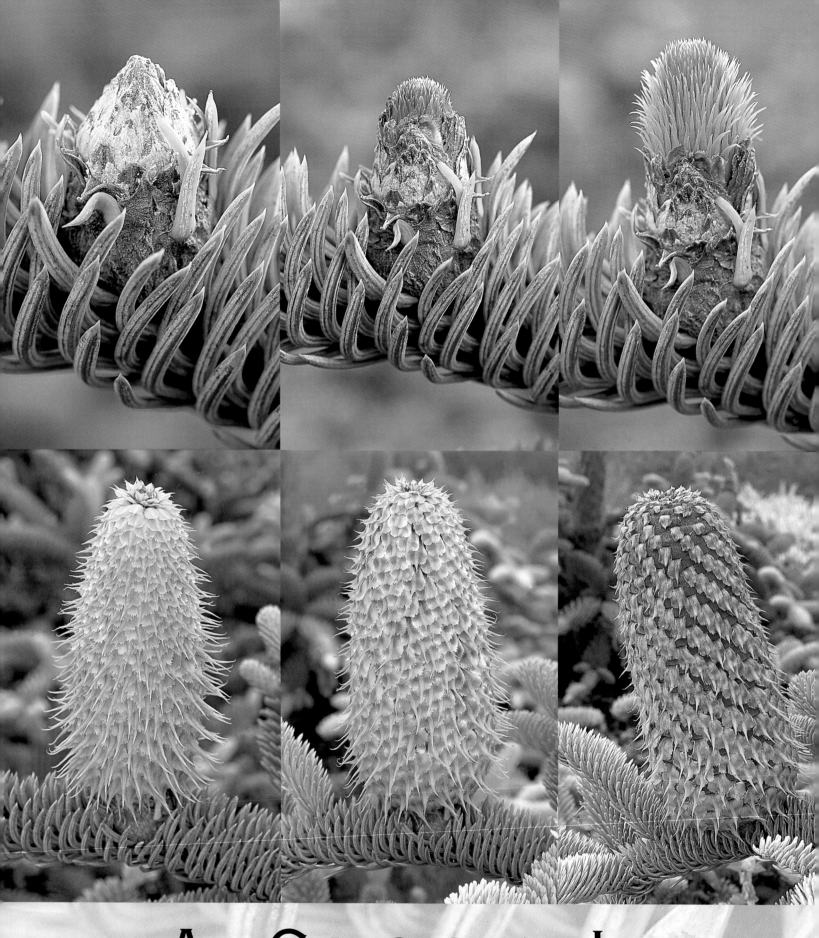

A CLOSE LOOK

AT CONIFERS

FLOWERS AND CONES

Conifers derive their name from the Latin *conus*, a cone, and *ferre*, to bear – all plants within the group bear cones or cone-like appendages (though some are not as easy to recognize as the classic cones of pine and fir trees). Beginning as a tight cluster of female flowers, the cone develops to provide a receptacle to nurture the growing seeds after fertilization. A mature, fertilized female cone is the conifer's fruit – which, in most species, is a woody structure (a pine cone is a good example). Male flowers may also grow in the shape of a cone or a catkin; but though these are often called cones, botanically they remain flowers.

Most species of conifer carry both male and female flowers on the same tree (they are monoecious). In some genera, such as *Juniperus*, *Taxus* and *Podocarpus*, the male and female flowers are borne on different plants (they are dioecious). When the pollen from the male flower ripens, it bursts in a fine dust, often over a wide radius, to be caught and held in any female cones within reach. Fertilization then takes place, producing seeds that are borne within the female cone and ripen in its protective embrace. It can take a year or several years before the seeds are mature; they are then released to drop or be dispersed by wind or birds. Eventually they will germinate, and begin new, young conifers. Some cones, such as the pines, can nurture several

PREVIOUS PAGES *The development and life of a cone on* Abies procera, *England. Top: growth from late winter (16 February) to late spring (26 May). Bottom: growth from early summer (4 June) to maturity in mid-autumn (13 October), at 15cm/6in high (fifth frame). In early winter (14 December), the ripened seeds collapse from the cone (last frame).*
BELOW *The male flower cones of* Abies procera *'Glauca Prostrata'. They appear in late winter (16 February, top left), but develop little before mid-spring (3 April, top center). They then open to shed pollen by late spring (26 May, bottom right).*

seeds, while the junipers and yews can carry only a single seed surrounded by fleshy fruit. Some pine species have cones that will not open at all until they are prompted to do so by the intense heat of a forest fire, with the seeds saved in this way for the regeneration of the forest.

Flowers on conifers? "Surely not," would probably be the reaction of many people. When I first started collecting conifers, I was hardly aware myself that some produce such striking effects with their spectacular displays, usually in late spring or early summer. The male flowers often begin brightly and later fade – for example, on *Abies procera* 'Glauca' and cultivars, the flowers begin crimson and change to yellow, before they disperse their pollen in the wind. Most flowers and cones appear in spring but, as always, there are exceptions. Cedars have flowers that appear in late summer and early autumn, when the males release clouds of yellowish pollen on the wind; the seeds take two to three years to mature after fertilization.

One of the most adaptable of the spruces, *Picea orientalis*, has red flowers and an abundance of narrow, pendulous cones – they are particularly striking on the golden-foliaged selection, *Picea orientalis* 'Skylands'. *Picea abies* 'Acrocona' is known for its bright red male and female flowers, which occur on quite young plants. The female cones protrude from the end of a branch tip, ripening from green to beige and providing interest all year round. A new dwarf selection, a miniature Acrocona called *Picea abies* 'Pusch', is one to look out for if you can find it: its attraction is vivid flowers and cones that are borne when the plant is less than 1ft (30cm) in height.

The *Chamaecyparis* also have colorful flowers, although they are much smaller. The showiest appear on *Chamaecyparis lawsoniana* 'Wissellii' and 'Little Spire', with their masses of small crimson flowers in early spring. Since the cones on these plants are rather small, the flowers are their great attraction, but they do not last long.

On older specimens of Picea orientalis *'Skylands'. masses of crimson flowers appear every spring.*

Pinkish young female cones with pendulous male flowers beneath in early spring on Pseudotsuga menziesii *'Blue Wonder'.*

A miniature cone forming in spring on Larix kaempferi *'Diane'. An old cone is behind.*

The cones of the pines are closely attached to the trees' branches, often in multiples or clusters. Gardeners can have difficulty distinguishing a spruce (*Picea*) from a fir (*Abies*); one sure way is that the spruce always has cones hanging below the branches, while those of the fir stand above. In both cases, the younger, heavier cones often weigh down the spreading branches. Fir cones go through an amazing metamorphosis in the course of a year, from tiny flowers to large cones, particularly in the case of the Noble Fir (*Abies procera*). Toward the end of the autumn and early winter, the hitherto impressive cone will gradually collapse (in strong winds this can happen quite quickly), when its seeds will drop to the ground or be dispersed by the wind. Some firs have the attraction of bearing cones when quite young – the hardy Korean Fir (*Abies koreana*) is an example, its startling deep violet-blue cones ripening to deep blue. The spruce can be pretty colorful, too, but the cones usually do not appear until the plant is at least ten years old. The yews (*Taxus*) and the similar-foliaged podocarpus are an exception to the usual pattern: the fruit or seed is contained not in a cone but in a protective, bright red, cone-like appendage called an aril. This resembles a fleshy goblet and is attractive to birds, who disperse the seeds. On the podocarpus the seed is attached, strangely, to the outside of the aril.

Cones are not only an additional attraction on some conifers, but are of interest in themselves, especially on the larger-growing species. Their sizes and shapes vary greatly. Many can be properly seen only with the help of binoculars, since they form at the top of mature trees. I remember walking under an extensive planting of the Western Yellow Pine (*Pinus ponderosa*) near Lake Tahoe in California, and a heavy ovoid cone 6in (15cm) long narrowly missed me as it fell from a branch 100ft (30cm) above! Some cones can weigh as much as 2.25kg/5lb, as with the Big-Cone Pine, *Pinus coulteri*. Cones can be works of art, and many are well worth keeping as ornaments if you are lucky enough to find them.

Ripened cones on Picea abies *'Acrocona' turn to beige in autumn.*

Upright cones form in dense clusters on Abies koreana *'Horstmann's Silberlocke' in late summer.*

Pea-sized cones on Chamaecyparis obtusa *in mid-summer.*

FOLIAGE

If you have a smaller garden you will need to restrict your choice of conifers to the smaller-growing types, most of which will be unlikely ever to bear cones. But a wide range of attractive foliage more than compensates – the leaves are usually the main attribute of the evergreens as well as the deciduous conifers. Leaves with a narrow or pointed shape are usually called needles, an obvious example being those of the pines. Depending on the species,

these come in bundles of two, three or five; one, appropriately called *Pinus monophylla*, mostly has only one. The firs and the spruces also have needle-like leaves, and there are many others. The other main type of evergreen foliage is a scale-like leaf that usually grows in flattened sprays, as in *Chamaecyparis lawsoniana* and *Thuja*.

Foliage can come in many greens, blue, yellow and gold. Some types have variegated leaf tips, and others

Frost on Chamaecyparis lawsoniana *'Dik's Weeping'.*

Year-round golden-yellow on Thuja plicata *'Irish Gold'.*

Summer blue on Cunninghamia lanceolata *'Glauca'.*

Golden autumn needles on Larix kaempferi *'Diane'.*

change color through the seasons. Many conifers, such as the firs, seem to have entirely green needles, but the undersides have white bands covered in a white waxy coating, which give the branches a silvery appearance. These bands, usually two on each leaf, are breathing pores ("stomata") through which the tree exchanges gases, releasing oxygen after photosynthesis. The waxy coating helps to prevent moisture loss; it is often found on the upper surface, too, creating the blue appearance typical of so many spruces and other conifers. The photographs in this book, especially the close-ups, reveal the tremendous range of color and interest in conifer leaves, even in winter; an arrangement of cut foliage can make an arresting display at Christmas time. A slow-growing conifer like *Thujopsis dolabrata* may be no great beauty from a distance, but just turn over the dark, glossy, green foliage and you are in for a real treat: the undersides are a marvel of nature, a tracery of sparkling silvery-white.

BUDS AND SHOOTS

The most spectacular transformation of conifers takes place in spring, when new growth begins. The spruces and pines are the most noticeable, closely followed by others. These and the firs make one main growth a year, which is mostly finished by the late summer (the inevitable exception to this rule lies in dwarfer types, such as *Picea glauca* var. *albertiana* 'Conica' which can make two or three spurts in certain climates). Then they start the next year's growth by forming buds, which develop and enlarge throughout the winter and early spring; the new shoots are contained in a membrane, preparing for take-off as soon as the time is right. Some buds are strikingly attractive, particularly on the pines – on *Pinus thunbergii* and its cultivars, the elongated buds are sheathed in silky white hairs before the new shoots ("candles") burst. These can be quite spectacular when they are a different color from

Clusters of needles on Sciadopitys verticillata *in summer.*

Frost on winter foliage of the variegated Pinus parviflora *'Ogon Janome'.*

The startling undersides of the lower foliage of Thujopsis dolabrata.

the leaves – white against green on *Pinus thunbergii* 'Thunderhead', and gold against green on *Pinus nigra* 'Aurea' and *Pinus densiflora* 'Taylor's Sunburst'. Spruces also show such color contrasts when their soft new needles burst through their winter sheaths. The Colorado Blue Spruce (*Picea pungens*) has powder-blue new needles that transform the duller, older foliage. New growth maintains this color until it gradually tones down as the needles mature in the summer. *Picea abies* 'Rydal' and 'Rubra Spicata' may look like ordinary Norway Spruces for most of the year, but when new shoots appear in spring they are a deep crimson, which lasts for two or three weeks if the tender new growth is not spoilt by spring frosts. *Picea orientalis* 'Aurea' has bright yellow new shoots against rather drab, deep green older foliage – a few weeks of true glory before it returns to anonymity. These exciting colors allow for a brief fling in spring, even when conifers are planted for the main purpose of providing a regular background green.

Some conifers change their adult or developed foliage as they go into winter. *Pinus mugo* 'Wintergold' becomes brighter, while *Microbiota decussata* darkens from green to bronze without becoming duller. *Pinus sylvestris* 'Aurea' has needles that are bright gold in winter, but light green in summer and so it does not clash with vibrant-colored summer perennials.

Chamaecyparis, junipers and thujas tend to have a longer, more seamless, growing season and can carry on growing into early autumn. Even so, the early summer flush of growth is mostly very noticeable, particularly on some selected forms. The often vigorous forms of *Juniperus* × *pfitzeriana* race away with new shoots in a much brighter color than the old foliage. *Juniperus squamata* 'Holger' is perhaps supreme for its brilliant transformation as butter-yellow new shoots break in early summer, changing the plant from a dullish blue-green to a carpet of creamy-white.

The emerging winter shoots of Pinus thunbergii, *covered in pale silky hairs.*

The next stage, on P. t. *'Yatsubusa', in late spring: the "candles" develop into new needles.*

Spring shoots of Picea pungens *burst through their winter bud membranes.*

THE UNUSUAL

Conifers also have unusual forms which, depending on your level of appreciation, could be described as aberrations, monstrosities, fascinating, intriguing or attractive. Some forms of the Japanese Cedar (*Cryptomeria*) have congested and fasciated foliage; 'Cristata' is an example, a curiosity at best but a must for some collectors. *Cryptomeria japonica* 'Spiralis' has a strangeness about it, too, with twisted leaves and stems. *Larix* × *kaempferi* 'Diane' exhibits misshapen zigzag stems, particularly effective in winter when frost lies on the branches. Some other forms are unusual and often striking, and it is worth knowing the Latin names that describe such appearances: *filifera* and *filiformis* mean threadlike; *coralliformis* also means threadlike, but twisted like coral; *lycopodioides* means like *Lycopodium* mosses, with extended unbranched shoots; *torulosa* means twisted, a term that can apply to stems or, as in *Pinus strobus* 'Torulosa', to needles.

The weird and wonderful can certainly be sought out, but many of these are unlikely to find homes in domestic gardens and will remain collectors' plants.

BARK

When you choose a conifer for your garden, you will probably look at trees when they are young, small, fully clothed in foliage and hardly showing their stems. However, some conifers develop interesting bark, quite a feature in later years. It is worth knowing about this, to avoid mistakes such as the one I made when thinning out some of my larger dwarf conifers: a specimen of the Japanese Umbrella Pine (*Pinus densiflora* 'Umbraculifera') was getting too large, so I dug it up, not realizing that when this plant is 25 years old or so and its lower branches are pruned, their flaking, cinnamon-brown bark is a beautiful feature (now I'll have to start again!). The Lace Bark Pine (*Pinus bungeana*) is very slow, but in time it can compete with the best Paperbark Maple (*Acer griseum*) for interest and beauty. The Californian Redwood (*Sequoia sempervirens*) reveals with age its reddish-brown bark. The ancient Chilean Monkey Puzzle Tree (*Araucaria araucana*) has quite extraordinary sharply pointed leaves on the trunk, enough to deter any monkey. Many other species and cultivars are notable for their attractive bark.

The strange fasciated foliage on Cryptomeria japonica *'Cristata'*.

Pinus densiflora *'Umbraculifera'*.

Spongy, hairy bark on a 40-year-old Sequoia sempervirens.

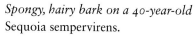

"Lace" bark on Pinus bungeana.

*Armored blades on the Chilean Monkey Puzzle (*Araucaria araucana*).*

FORM

One of the main considerations when making a choice for your garden is the form or shape of the tree, both in its early and later years.
Prostrate plants – such as *Juniperus horizontalis* 'Wiltonii', *Juniperus communis* 'Green Carpet' and *Microbiota decussata* – make excellent ground cover.
Semi-prostrate forms spread to greater width than height, although with age they can reach 6ft (1.8m) high or more. Many junipers come into this category, but so can chamaecyparis, spruces and pines. Some are vase-shaped, others flatter.
Globose, rounded, ball-shaped – these terms all describe the same form, one of the most recognized and popular shapes of dwarf conifers, which can come in different colors and very different sizes.
Pyramidal or upright forms are often just the early stage, with taller kinds, such as the Colorado Blue Spruce, becoming columnar with age.
Columnar, fastigiate, pillar-like, pencil-like – these terms describe narrowly upright forms that vary in width; all are ideal when used as accent plants to create a focal point or to add vertical interest.

So far, so good. But some columnar forms have erect branches (*Juniperus scopulorum* 'Skyrocket', *Cupressus sempervirens* 'Stricta'), while others have branches that are steeply pendulous (*Picea omorika* 'Pendula', *Chamaecyparis nootkatensis* 'Green Arrow'). Pendulous forms can vary from those with secondary hanging branchlets (*Picea breweriana*, *Chamaecyparis nootkatensis* 'Pendula') to those that are actually prostrate unless tied up a stake (*Cedrus atlantica* 'Glauca Pendula') – when trained upward, the branches, with no ground to sprawl along, will naturally grow in a weeping habit. Other pendulous forms may for years be disinclined to take off (although training can help) and then suddenly decide to push up a leading shoot while other branches remain pendulous. *Pinus strobus* 'Pendula' and *Sequoiadendron giganteum* 'Pendulum' are examples and good focal points.

The shapes of conifers often show up best in winter, as here on a misty morning in Norfolk, England. Picea pungens *'Montgomery' (left) and* Thuja occidentalis *'Holmstrup' (center) are the most prominent.*

GROWTH RATES

Conifers can range from the so-called miniatures, such as *Picea mariana* 'Nana', which grow less than 3ft (90cm) high by the same width in a hundred years, to those like *Sequoiadendron giganteum* which grow well over 100ft (30m) high in the same time span (both are shown opposite). In between come those that are less easy to categorize – the dwarf or slow-growing types that you are most likely to find in garden centers; even conifer specialists tend to concentrate on these, since they are more suited to today's gardens. Many are very slow in their early years, but in a time span of twenty, fifty or a hundred years their size may increase dramatically; the broader, more rounded, conifers, like most evergreen shrubs or trees such as rhododendrons and hollies, will expand in all directions. With gardens becoming smaller and people moving home more frequently, most gardeners prefer a more instant effect than is possible with many years of waiting for slower plants to grow. It is often left to the next incumbent to deal with an overgrown garden, but none the less it is important to know how quickly plants are likely to grow and what can be expected of their ultimate size, so that would-be purchasers can make an informed judgment.

Given all the variables of length of growing season, soil, rainfall and climate, it is difficult to estimate growth, but I have attempted to do so in the Directory (page 82) because it is such an important issue. I have listed expected size after ten years, plus a guide to the ultimate size of all the conifers described in this book. Most can be pruned and trimmed without losing all their natural shape, however, so you should not be unduly put off by ultimate sizes – few of us really need to concern ourselves about the possible size a plant may reach in a hundred years or more.

There are now considered to be four main categories of conifer. I have not used these with every description in the Directory as it is more useful to give individual assessments, but a knowledge of these categories is broadly helpful.

Miniature
Growth rate less than 1in (2.5cm) a year
Height after ten years 6–10in (15–25cm)
Ultimate height and spread less than 3ft (90cm)

Dwarf
Growth rate between 1–6in (2.5–15cm) a year
Height after ten years 1–5ft (30cm–1.5m)
Ultimate height and/or spread 10–25ft (3–7.5m)

Intermediate or slow-growing
Growth rate 6–12in (15–30cm) a year
Height after ten years 5–10ft (1.5–3m)
Ultimate height and/or spread 33–50ft (10–15m)

Large
Growth rate 12in (30cm) or more a year
Height after ten years 10–25ft (3–7.5m)
Ultimate height over 60ft (18m)

In addition, with prostrate and semi-prostrate forms, height and width depend on how they are trained.

Conifers do not grow overnight (not even × *Cupressocyparis leylandii* at 3ft (90cm) a year!), and some are very slow indeed. A collection of miniature conifers is unlikely ever to become a nuisance or an embarrassment, but the dwarf and intermediate varieties, if planted too liberally and too closely, almost certainly will do so after a few years. You will then need to consider thinning out – moving some to another part of the garden or pruning. If you start to prune early enough, you can delay thinning for some years (see Pruning, page 174).

Conifers that grow large need not be a problem: they can be used as attractive specimen plants, or structure in the garden around which other plantings can develop. They provide shade, sometimes attractive bark, and colorful summer or winter foliage. Almost certainly some plants will eventually need to go, but if you have enjoyed them for ten, twenty or thirty years, you can soften their departure by looking forward to the new or different plants you can try in their places. A garden must change if it is to develop – in my own garden the chainsaw is in action every winter, thinning and pruning, so that more planting opportunities can be opened up.

Nearly all the conifers in the view below are the same age, give or take a year or two! The taller trees at the back, Sequoiadendron giganteum (15) and × Cupressocyparis leylandii (14), were small when planted in 1964; the remainder were planted in 1967, including the smaller ones in the bed at center left. This association shows more dramatically than words could describe the differences in growth rate between conifers, and why it is so important to understand these when planning your planting.

Miniatures are represented by Picea mariana *'Nana' (8) and* Tsuga canadensis *'Minuta' (2); dwarf by* Chamaecyparis lawsoniana *'Minima Aurea' (3),* Picea pungens *'Globosa' (6) and* Thuja orientalis *'Aurea Nana' (5). Intermediate or slow-growing would be* Abies lasiocarpa *'Compacta' (4), while the* Chamaecyparis lawsoniana *cultivars (9–12) might be intermediate in drier climates but tall in moister ones after 50 years or so.* Chamaecyparis nootkatensis *'Pendula' (13) and* Pinus sylvestris *'Aurea' (1) will both be tall, unless regularly pruned.* Tsuga canadensis *'Cole's Prostrate' (7) remains so except for a reverting shoot.*

1 *Pinus sylvestris* 'Aurea' (pruned)
2 *Tsuga canadensis* 'Minuta'
3 *Chamaecyparis lawsoniana* 'Minima Aurea'
4 *Abies lasiocarpa* 'Compacta'
5 *Thuja orientalis* 'Aurea Nana'
6 *Picea pungens* 'Globosa' (pruned)
7 *Tsuga canadensis* 'Cole's Prostrate' (showing reversion)
8 *Picea mariana* 'Nana'
9 *Chamaecyparis lawsoniana* 'Lutea'
10 *Chamaecyparis nootkatensis*
11 *Chamaecyparis lawsoniana* 'Lane'
12 *Chamaecyparis lawsoniana* 'Green Pillar'
13 *Chamaecyparis nootkatensis* 'Pendula'
14 × *Cupressocyparis leylandii*
15 *Sequoiadendron giganteum*

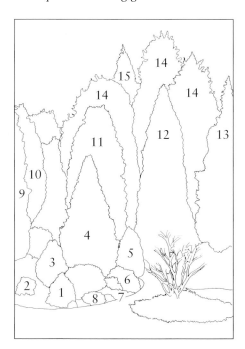

Using Conifers

IN THE GARDEN

Conifers have a wide variety of uses in the garden, but it is important that you find the right fit – the right plant for the right place. You should select for form, color and size, always bearing in mind the rates of growth and the plants' suitability for their chosen site. Are they to be planted in a new garden or an established one? Are they required for a hedge or for screens, as specimens or accent plants, or for containers on a patio?

Having considered what role you think conifers might play, you then have the interesting and challenging part – selecting the right plants for the purpose. In the Directory (page 82), regional climates are denoted by hardiness and heat-tolerance zones – these act as a guide, but remember that many locations within those areas or zones have their own

PREVIOUS PAGES *Conifers in summer, providing structure and contrast to summer-flowering perennials and shrubs, Norfolk, England. Center foreground is a 35-year-old* Pinus pumila 'Nana', *left a* Chamaecyparis lawsoniana 'Golden Pot'. Spanish Broom (Spartium junceum) *offers contrast on the right. Left are a variegated Pampas Grass (*Cortaderia selloana)*, and the tall, silver-gray Scotch Thistle (*Onopordum acanthium).

microclimates. At the bottom of a valley you may be in a frost pocket; close to a lake you may benefit from slightly milder temperatures; hillside or woodland may protect your garden from freezing winter winds; town or city gardens are often a degree or two warmer than those in the countryside. Local gardeners and nurseries can be a fount of good advice on local conditions. Rainfall must certainly be a consideration when choosing conifers, and this can vary considerably within a region.

Even in a small garden, something not classed as hardy by general horticultural references may still be able to thrive. Shelter from trees or a wall, some shade, well-drained soil, sun traps – all can provide a more protected environment for tender plants. Careful soil preparation and annual mulching with a covering of leaf mold, composted bark or pine needles will help to ensure success.

Most conifers are not particularly difficult to grow, nor do they necessarily need special requirements, but it depends on where you live and what you want to grow or achieve. A mild, temperate climate like Britain's almost has the best of both worlds: although

LEFT *Low-lying gardens – such as mine in Norfolk, England, shown here – can act as frost pockets, making plants susceptible to damage in spring when the new shoots are about to emerge. Dwarf conifers are protected by taller ones from the early morning sun, which can damage soft new plant tissue.*

RIGHT *In Jos Flecken's garden in Kerkrade, southern Holland, a high wall protects plants from chill winds. In the foreground, conifers are mixed with summer- and winter-flowering heather, here shown in late summer. Taxodium distichum 'Secrest' in the center, its top grafted and supported by a pole, allows other plants to grow beneath.*

there is a considerable difference between the mild climate of Cornwall in the southwest and that of northeastern Scotland, a wide range of plants will happily succeed in both areas. In North America the climatic differences are much wider; at the extreme ends of this variation – in the more northerly areas of Ontario and Quebec in zone 2, and in the almost sub-tropical parts of Florida or Texas in zone 9 – there will be great limitations on the choices available to gardeners. But zones, which are classified for hardiness alone, can be misleading: Alabama, Georgia and South Carolina all have very hot, humid summers but are classed in zone 8, the same as most of Britain. Conifers that suit cooler climates, such as most spruces and firs, will not generally succeed in such hot summers.

Plants with golden, cream or variegated foliage have particular needs – usually some shade in hot climates, protection from drying or freezing winds in colder regions, with exceptions to every rule, as always. My own garden in Norfolk was a flat meadow with no protection when I first started planting in 1966; being in a frost pocket, many plants, including a few conifers, were lost in such an exposed situation. But as conifers and other plants began to provide structure and shelter, microclimates developed and then I could widen the range grown.

Sometimes the same variety of plant grows much better in one position than another. One example is the golden-needled pine, *Pinus contorta* 'Frisian Gold': I have one which in full sun is brighter and more compact but scorches every winter; another, of about the same age, sited in light shade, is more open and a lighter yellow, but does not scorch. Comparisons between macroclimates in different parts of the world can be a good guide. One would expect the Italian or Mediterranean Cypress (*Cupressus sempervirens*) to grow well in other similar climates, such as California and much of Australia. Likewise, *Juniperus scopulorum* and *Cupressus arizonica* from southeast of the Rockies enjoy good drainage and long dry summers; they adapt well to Italy, Australia and New Zealand, but both, being hardier than the Italian Cypress, also grow well in colder areas.

SOIL CONDITIONS

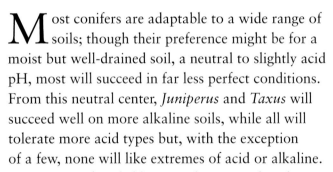

A mature specimen of Taxodium distichum *in the Gotelli Collection at the National Arboretum in Washington, D.C., summer. In this position, with its roots near water, it naturally grows "knees" – hollow aerial roots that assist with breathing.*

A raised mound allows good drainage for some pines, such as Pinus strobus *'Pendula' (center) and the smaller* P. s. *'Blue Shag' (left), shown in Don and Harriet Wild's garden in Ann Arbor, Michigan, summer.*

Most conifers are adaptable to a wide range of soils; though their preference might be for a moist but well-drained soil, a neutral to slightly acid pH, most will succeed in far less perfect conditions. From this neutral center, *Juniperus* and *Taxus* will succeed well on more alkaline soils, while all will tolerate more acid types but, with the exception of a few, none will like extremes of acid or alkaline.

Most conifers dislike poor drainage – but there are, of course, exceptions. The Swamp Cypress (*Taxodium distichum*), as its name suggests, will grow well in boggy, swampy conditions, even actually in water, but it does better in moist soils out of it. The White False Cypress (*Chamaecyparis thyoides*) and the Eastern Arborvitae (*Thuja occidentalis*) both inhabit wet boggy areas in the wild so, although they are better in general garden conditions, they will put up with wetter soils. At the other extreme, many of the pines, junipers, cypresses and yews are tolerant of drought. Within a genus such as the *Chamaecyparis*,

C. lawsoniana from the high rainfall area of the northwest US needs more moisture and suffers much more from drought than the Japanese Hinoki Cypress (*C. obtusa*) from southern Japan, which withstands considerable heat and drought. The origin of plants (covered fully in the Directory) always has a considerable bearing on how they will perform in any given climate or soil.

Natural microclimates or those that, in time, can be created within a garden by shelter and hedges will affect how plants grow. Soil can also be improved to suit particular plants. For example, you can plant *Pinus strobus*, which needs good drainage, on slightly raised mounds or a bank. You can partly remove heavy clay soil, and improve planting areas (either wholly or on a planting hole basis) by adding organic material such as well rotted compost, leaf mold, composted bark or peat, or fertile imported soil. Heavy mulching around the plant when it is first introduced always helps.

SUN, SHADE AND COLOR

Most conifers, including dwarf cultivars, prefer an open situation in an environment that is as close as possible to their natural one. A dwarf Eastern or Canadian Hemlock (*Tsuga canadensis*) may be found in the mountains of New Hampshire or Vermont, normally either in a shady position, or in full sun but protected from cold winds by a rock or tree, or in a gully. Because it is happy in full sun in these cooler, moister conditions does not mean, however, that it will thrive in full sun in, say, South Carolina, but it might grow in half-shade in those climates; hemlocks tolerate some shade very well. Also tolerant of some shade are yews and some junipers. But the price to pay is often that plants become more open, and they can look scruffy in shade, particularly if they are also dry. Conifers with golden or yellow foliage will be much more subdued in shade, the color even turning to green on spruces.

On the other hand, a fully exposed garden can lead to foliage scorch from freezing, desiccating winds, or from severe frosts. Early autumn frosts when leaves are still soft, and late spring frosts, can do equal damage to some gold or variegated forms; spring frosts can also catch soft new shoots as they burst from their buds in mid- to late spring. But these are dangers faced by all plants; careful placing should ensure a minimum of damage except in unusually severe years. Plant tender or brightly foliaged young plants behind taller plants, fences or screens so that they do not catch the early morning sun – this usually does the most damage by striking leaves that are still wet or even frozen. Remember that you can put new or choice younger plants in a small protected area for two or three years before moving them to another position. Most dwarf conifers can be moved successfully if you prune their roots regularly beforehand (see Moving, page 173).

RIGHT Cephalotaxus harringtonii *'Prostrata' is one of the best conifers for shade. It is shown here growing at Longwood Gardens, Kennett Square, Pennsylvania, summer.*

BELOW *The new soft shoots of this choice 6-year-old* Picea abies *'Pusch' may need protection from frost in late spring in some locations, although the plant is hardy.*

WINDBREAKS AND SHELTER

Evergreens, and conifers in particular, are favorites for providing year-round shelter for exposed sites, as well as important structure in a garden. Hedges serve the same purpose, as well as being useful dividers – whether between properties or different sections in one garden. Windbreaks are plantings made deliberately to reduce the effect of wind. There is a wide choice of suitable conifers for this purpose, though without pruning the faster-growing types will get very large in time. Leylandii (× *Cupressocyparis leylandii*) has become so popular precisely because, as well as being highly adaptable (it grows well near the sea and on many difficult soils), it is very fast-growing. In fact, it does everything wanted of it, except to stop growing when told to! If chosen with sufficient knowledge, it is a great plant, offering shelter to birds as well as people.

A windbreak of conifers can be colorful, as seen in this late autumn view in the author's garden in Norfolk. Thuja, spruce, junipers and pine – all about 20 years old – have been allowed to grow into one another to make a patchwork of texture and color. Ornamental grasses and perennials are in the foreground.

For those with larger gardens, a shelter belt planted with a range of forms and colors can be very effective – different cultivars of *Chamaecyparis lawsoniana* would make a good choice. If not suitable, use *Thuja occidentalis* or *Thuja plicata*, the adaptable Serbian Spruce (*Picea omorika*), the Bosnian Pine (*Pinus heldreichii*), the Colorado Blue Spruce (*Picea pungens*), and perhaps cedars and larches, too. Pyramids, columns and conical forms can be selected with blue, green or gold foliage and intermixed. Adequate spacing should be allowed for plants to develop (perhaps they can be staggered in two or three rows), but it will not matter if they eventually grow into each other. These plants do not have the speed of Leylandii, but eventually they will give a more interesting effect. Smaller gardens call for much slower-growing conifers which can be trimmed, such as columnar selections of *Chamaecyparis lawsoniana*, *Juniperus scopulorum* or *J. virginiana*, or *Thuja occidentalis*. In exposed sites where a true windbreak is desired, use younger plants which can establish roots before too much stress is put on them from prevailing winds; larger plants may blow over.

STRUCTURE

The importance of structure can be seen in this autumn view of 15-year-old plantings in the author's garden – originally an open flat meadow. Conifers form the backbone and the backdrop against which other plants perform; they also provide necessary shelter in the exposed situation.

Most garden designers advise the use of foundation planting, or "structure", in a garden, whether from walls, buildings or plants. But in today's smaller gardens, how much plant structure is needed? There are perhaps too many small suburban gardens planted with one Japanese cherry that has grown to enormous dimensions, or with trees and conifers that are now overgrown (such as the ubiquitous Leylandii). In the open-plan gardens of North America foundation planting is a strong feature, with a few trees or conifers often somewhat haphazardly planted, the specimens not necessarily of any great beauty. Structural planting can play an important role, but it should be done with thought and planning, not on impulse.

Trees and shrubs of different forms and habits can add an upper dimension to a garden, like a second story, and they can act as framework and backdrop to show off other plants. Evergreens, including conifers, have an important role to play in the fabric of a garden – visit gardens in winter when deciduous trees and shrubs have lost their leaves, and you will appreciate the true value of the shelter and color conifers provide.

ACCENT PLANTS, FEATURES AND FOCAL POINTS

Accent plants help to map out the design of a garden, drawing the eye to focal points. Vertical conifers, columnar or pyramidal in form, can be planted among deciduous shrubs or trees (remember to give them enough space), or placed in front of or behind them. Cedars, though large-growing if not pruned, are graceful plants which can be kept narrow and shapely by regular trimming. Many pines can also be pruned to keep them narrow, or allowed to grow upright with the bottom branches pruned away so that they can be underplanted. Good positioning of specimen conifers allows them to contrast with brighter flowering plants in summer, and act as an architectural feature on their own in winter. Use color carefully, but in the end this is a matter of personal taste. For example, I prefer not to use golden-foliaged plants for hedging – a darker background is easier on the eye and allows other colors, including golds, to show up against it.

On a frosty winter morning in the author's garden in Norfolk, England, short- and long-distance views are caught through a gap between a cedar and a Blue Spruce, both highlighted by accent conifers. To the left is Picea pungens *'Thomsen', to the right is an irregular* Picea pungens, *and in the middle distance is the columnar* Thuja orientalis *'Collen's Gold'. Deciduous trees grow in the background. Most of these plants are about 25 years old.*

The shapes of most conifers are very definite, which is why they are ideal as focal points. Even in a small garden the eye needs to be directed to something that stands out, or perhaps to several individual specimens to be viewed from different vantage points. I believe it is important to create *changing* points of interest in a garden, by creating plant associations that have seasonal changes around a main selected specimen. Spring bulbs, summer perennials, foliage or flowering shrubs enhance the attraction all year-round. Conifers have more than one season of interest but will always be particularly visible in winter.

Narrowly columnar forms make excellent accent plants, and there are a great many to choose from according to region. A few of the choices in green or blue foliage are the Italian Cypress (*Cupressus sempervirens* 'Stricta') for warmer regions; *Juniperus scopulorum* 'Blue Arrow' or 'Skyrocket' for hot summers and colder winters; *Juniperus communis* 'Sentinel' or *Pinus sylvestris* 'Spaan's Slow Column' for cooler summers and colder winters. Plants with gold or yellow foliage include *Cupressus*

Berta and Nate Atwater's garden in Rhode Island is a classic example of the imaginative use of plants to fit local conditions. The Italian Cypress would not be hardy here; instead, a group of Leylandii, now 7 years old, has been pruned to replicate them. Happy in the maritime climate, they watch like silent sentinels over land and the nearby sea.

sempervirens 'Swane's Gold' and *Juniperus chinensis* 'Aurea'. *Thuja occidentalis* 'Smaragd', so often used for hedging, is not sufficiently appreciated as a single, pleasing, narrow column.

All such vertical plants are best set off by having low, prostrate or semi-prostrate plants growing at their base to emphasize the upright form by contrast. Accent plants can be very effective when planted in threes or more, not too closely, and in even greater number if space allows for a larger informal group. They can create an avenue, or carry the eye along a line or curve. A novel and imaginative use for Leylandii is as a trimmed narrow column, seen to great effect in Berta and Nate Atwater's garden in Rhode Island, USA. Berta carried the garden into the

landscape and the eye toward the distant bay on the edge of the Atlantic by a curving line of well-spaced plants, trimmed to look like Italian Cypresses. Leylandii does well so close to the sea, but the concept requires hard work because pruning must be rigorous and frequent for them to keep this shape.

Specimens can be upright, conical, pyramidal or pendulous, and should have a form or color to contrast with the plants around them. A Blue Spruce (*Picea pungens*), usually with bright silver-blue foliage and spreading branches, makes an arresting specimen, as does the weeping Nootka Cypress (*Chamaecyparis nootkatensis* 'Pendula'); these get very big in time so should be used only in larger gardens. Slower-growing plants, which perhaps can be pruned to keep a natural form, are best for the smaller garden. Traditionally, the conifer specimen has been planted on its own in a lawn, but it is often more effective in a large bed with other lower-growing plants around it. Shrubs, perennials and grasses can enhance its role as a participant in the changing displays of spring, summer and autumn

color. A conifer specimen can be particularly striking if it stands out from a backdrop of deciduous plants, particularly of contrasting color – for example, a blue narrow-leafed conifer against a golden-leafed maple, a purple *Cotinus* or *Cercis*. Alternatively, plant a golden-foliaged conifer against green. Make the most of opportunities to turn an interesting specimen into a striking one by creating a dramatic setting for it.

Select your specimen plants carefully, according to size and suitability. They can become the stars of the garden and you will want them to succeed. Bear in mind that at some point pruning may be not simply an option, but a necessity. Early training of leading shoots is always advisable. If you want a specimen to keep its foliage close to the ground, allow sufficient space around it clear of other evergreens.

Spire-like cypresses dominate the skyline in Lindsay Gray's garden in Melbourne, Australia. Their pencil-like shapes create accent points that draw the eye above the lower-growing plants. None of the conifers shown in this view is native to Australia, but all adapt well to the southeast Australian climate.

HEDGES

Some conifers make excellent evergreen hedges – choose according to local climatic and soil conditions, as well as the eventual size, shape and color you want. The more vigorous the plant, the more clipping it will need. Normally, the choice for a taller hedge would be one of the faster-growing columnar forms, with good vigor and health, well adapted to the situation required. You should select from types with branches that will knit with their neighbors, to add strength against the wind and prevent sections being blown out, as can happen with taller hedges of *Thuja occidentalis* 'Smaragd'. The broader yews, thujas and Leylandii will knit better.

× *Cupressocyparis leylandii* has excellent hedging attributes and is a good choice where it can be grown. Vigorous, bright green in summer and duller in winter, it grows in a wide range of soil conditions, takes well to pruning and can be kept, seemingly without resentment, from as low as 4ft (1.2m) to as high as can be reached. It withstands salt spray to a reasonable extent, a quality inherited from one of its parents, the Monterey Cypress (*Cupressus macrocarpa*). Once the desired height and width has been reached, its growth after a number of years of regular close pruning will be much reduced, but in early years it will grow 3ft (90cm) annually and should be pruned at least twice a year. Whatever you do, beware letting it go for a few years without pruning, because it will be a slow and difficult task to restore it. For those who like golden or yellow hedges, selections of Leylandii fit the bill: × *C. l.* 'Golconda' or × *C. l.* 'Gold Rider' give a bright year-round yellow; × *C. l.* 'Castlewellan' is yellow-brown in winter and more subdued in summer.

Most people prefer uniformity of growth and color in a hedge, for which any single clone or variety, rooted from cuttings or grafted, should be chosen. You can of course create hedges with varied alternating colors, such as green, yellow and blue. but this is seldom restful on the eye, and creates considerable difficulties if you want to plant anything but green in front of it. In France, Italy and Spain where cypresses do well, closely trimmed hedges of the Italian Cypress (*Cupressus sempervirens*) are used, as is the startling blue of *Cupressus arizonica* var. *glabra* 'Fastigiata' – both withstand heat and drought well. If much hardier conifers are required, *Thuja occidentalis* and its cultivars are favorites: *T. o.* 'Pyramidalis Compacta', *T. o.* 'Columna' and *T. o.* 'Nigra' are popular in North America; *T. o.* 'Brabant' is becoming more widely used in Europe. The king of all, especially for the smaller garden, is *T. o.* 'Smaragd' – a handsome specimen on its own with glossy rich green leaves, it has a narrowly pyramidal habit and needs little trimming. Its growth rate is only a quarter to a third of that of Leylandii.

In Britain and northern Europe, the Lawson

TOP *Perfectly manicured* Cupressus sempervirens *act as buttresses at the Generalife Gardens, Alhambra, Spain.*

CENTER Thuja occidentalis *'Smaragd' needs little pruning to form a close hedge at the Ladew Gardens in Monkton, Maryland.*

BOTTOM × Cupressocyparis leylandii *'Castlewellan Gold' makes a good backdrop to* Agapanthus *in Lindsay Gray's garden in Melbourne, Australia.*

Cypress (*Chamaecyparis lawsoniana*) is widely used for hedging; cheap to buy, it is usually sold as variable seedlings, with soft feathery foliage in shades of green and blue. Lawson hedges can be most attractive when well spaced and planted, and given adequate moisture. Take care to avoid the faults that too many of them suffer: avoid dry soils, and do not plant them too closely or the root growth will be restricted, causing them to go bare at the base and develop brown and open patches elsewhere. Selected cultivars are popular in northern Europe, in particular *C. l.* 'Columnaris', which makes an excellent hedge with a lovely powder-blue color in summer. As with all Lawsons, never cut into old bare wood but give it regular light pruning.

The yew is the universal hedge plant, used for centuries in Britain for hedging and topiary in older gardens and estates. Plants raised from seed can be quite variable; ideally, for a 6ft (1.8m) or higher hedge, choose the bushier, upright selections. In Europe the Common or English Yew (*Taxus baccata*) is invariably used, but this species is not sufficiently hardy for the northern US or Canada. There, the choice for similar results is between the Japanese Yew (*Taxus cuspidata*) and the hybrid *Taxus × media*; *T. × m.* 'Hicksii', in particular, is considered a standard hedging form. Yews dislike waterlogging and bad drainage and will soon show their displeasure by going a sickly brown, but once established they will put up stoically with shade and drought. Being malleable to the shears, they can be cut to whatever height, width and shape you want, and they are not as slow-growing as most people think – established plants can put on 12in (30cm) a year, depending on type. Yews have another great attribute – they break freely into growth from older wood or branches, so that if a hedge becomes too wide over time it can be severely pruned, and will eventually fill in with new foliage. Yews are as popular as ever to create dividers or sculptured hedges giving shape and structure to formal and informal gardens; they make a dark and somber background to show off roses, perennials and grasses. Never forget that almost all parts of the yew are poisonous, including the seed (but not the aril), and potentially dangerous to humans and animals.

Another excellent conifer for hedges, and one of my favorites, is the Western Red Cedar (*Thuja plicata*), particularly in its form *T. p.* 'Atrovirens'. Its glossy green foliage, deliciously fragrant when crushed, makes a dense, bright green hedge, slightly duller in winter, which breaks freely into new growth from old wood when cut. It will grow better on moister soils than Leylandii, and is slower-growing.

The hemlocks *Tsuga canadensis* and *T. heterophylla* make graceful informal hedges and take well to pruning, but they succeed only in certain soils and conditions (see Directory, pages 167, 169). The recent spread of the woolly adelgid, *Adelges tsugae*, has discouraged their planting in the US.

Many other conifers will adapt to being kept as hedges. Low hedges can be made with some of the semi-prostrate junipers and yews. Informal, low, lightly trimmed hedges can be created from unusual foliage forms such as *Chamaecyparis pisifera* 'Filifera' or *Cryptomeria japonica* 'Globosa Nana'. In New Zealand, *Podocarpus totara* 'Aureus' is widely used because its prickly foliage makes it resistant to sheep and cattle; deep gold in winter, it breaks easily from old wood so it can be cut back hard when used in the smaller garden.

PLANTING HEDGES

Planning Give thought initially to the ultimate area you want the hedge to take up. Hedges can be kept quite narrow, but only with early and constant pruning – without it, they will become wider every year, and not always amenable to being cut back into old wood to reduce them. *Thuja plicata* and yew will break from old wood, so these can be good choices.
Height Yew can be pruned at almost any height. Generally, the slower-growing the conifer, the lower it can be kept. The faster-growing *Thuja plicata* and Leylandii may resent being kept below 4ft (1.2m).
Preparation The whole length of the planting area for the hedge must be thoroughly dug and prepared, with all perennial weeds removed (for detail, see page 172). A width of 3ft (90cm) is ideal, much wider for a screen, with appropriate additives such as garden

compost or composted bark mixed in.

Planting All hedges, particularly fast-growing ones that are to withstand strong winds, are best if young plants are used, perhaps not more than 3ft (90cm) high, or even smaller in the case of Leylandii. At this height, they will not offer too much resistance to wind until they have got their new roots firmly established. Planting distances may vary, but plants should never be less than 2ft (60cm) and seldom more than 3ft (90cm) apart – they need to be close enough to meet within three years, but not so close that later they will compete desperately for moisture. With young plants no staking should be required. Planting can be done at almost any time of year, with mid-spring to early autumn being the optimum time for planting from containers, spring or autumn for planting rootballed material. It is always best to take advice from a trusted local supplier.

Pruning This is covered in detail later (see page 174), but the main point is to start early in trimming the sides, particularly if a narrow, formal hedge is required. As the hedge matures, always keep other plants away from the base – even strong grass will make the foliage go bare if it is allowed to grow into it. Lawn grass will compete for moisture, too. If you want your hedge to remain green close to the ground, it needs light, air and moisture. Many conifers take moisture from other plants close to them, so plan your planting carefully if the hedge is to be a background to other shrubs or perennials.

Traditionally, a yew hedge makes a dark green backdrop to perennials, shrubs and other plants. Here at Brookside Gardens, Wheaton, Maryland, Taxus × media *'Hicksii' highlights the perennials* Lychnis coronaria *'Angel's Blush',* Eupatorium rugosum *'Chocolate' and a* Kniphofia, *in early summer.*

USING CONIFERS WITH OTHER PLANTS

I believe that conifers work very well with many other garden plants – trees, shrubs, perennials, ornamental grasses and bulbs – and arranging such combinations is a continuing theme of this book. I can well appreciate the value of conifer collections planted with little else, but for most gardeners the best use of conifers is to integrate them within the garden. Conifers can serve many purposes beyond windbreaks, hedging, structure, and focal and accent plants: form, color and texture add to their useful architectural and structural attributes. Always remember that, except for the few deciduous types, conifers provide year-round color so they need to be placed appropriately to play a role in each season,

particularly in winter. The size and rate of growth of chosen plants will have an important bearing on where and how they can be used. Larger, older specimen conifers may cost more money than most people are prepared to pay, but many gardeners will not want to wait ten years for a slow-growing plant such as *Thuja occidentalis* 'Smaragd' to reach 8ft (2.5m), the point at which perennials of 4–5ft (1.2–1.5m) planted around it will seem in scale. Imagine the impact of three or five 'Smaragd' – narrowly pyramidal and rich green – rising out from a planting of deep golden-yellow Black-eyed Susan (*Rudbeckia fulgida* var. *sullivantii* 'Goldsturm') and the brilliant summer blue fescue grass, *Festuca glauca*.

This question of scale is often the greatest problem facing garden designers when using conifers with other plants. If your garden is of restricted size and your budget limited, you should consider the following points when planning to use conifers in new or mature gardens.

CONIFERS IN THE NEW GARDEN

For those moving into a new house with a garden containing few or no plants, planning and planting may seem a daunting task. But it is easier to assimilate conifers in your plan at this stage and plant them alongside other young plants. Inevitably, some trees, shrubs or perennials will grow faster than others, but conifers can be planted in appropriate places with sufficient space left around them to prevent overcrowding later. Low-growing plants – alpine or rock plants, dwarf bulbs, dwarf shrubs and perennials – can be used to give a sense of scale. Each can provide a different aspect or feature for the garden, including a winter feature which should be visible from the house. Slow-growing conifers up to 5ft (1.5m) high can always be moved, particularly if their roots have been pruned (see Moving, page 173). You can do this every two or three years, and move even larger types with professional help. Planning to move conifers from time to time enables them to fulfil several roles – in time they can become specimen or feature plants. Many conifers do change in habit over time, and ideally you should consider this when planting, or adjust to it as you gradually get to know your plants better.

Conifers play an important but changing role in the author's garden in Norfolk, England. Beds with 30-year-old conifers originally planted with heaths or heathers now host perennial grasses and shrubs. Here, in late summer, Picea sitchensis *'Papoose' (center right) is framed by* Spiraea japonica *'Magic Carpet' behind the green mound of* Picea glauca var. albertiana *'Alberta Globe'. These are highlighted by the white* Calluna vulgaris *'Kinlochruel' on the left, the grass* Stipa tenuissima *and perennial* Rudbeckia fulgida var. sullivantii *'Goldsturm' on the right, and* Picea pungens *'Globosa' behind. In the left foregound, a white rose, a golden-leafed* Jasminum officinale *'Fiona Sunrise' and an oak-leafed hydrangea add seasonal interest.*

CONIFERS IN THE MATURE GARDEN

You may already have mature plants – not only trees and shrubs, but conifers. Smaller gardens may be overcrowded, and some plants may be of questionable ornamental value. A garden does not need to be a lifetime commitment, but if it is a lifetime interest or even a seasonal interest it sometimes pays to be ruthless. Cleaning out "root and branch" can be quite appropriate. Tree surgeons or reputable landscape gardeners, although they come at a cost, can achieve such tasks less painfully than you might do yourself, particularly if the conifers or trees are ones you planted! Cleared space offers an opportunity for new plantings. If shady, some of the Eastern Hemlock cultivars (*Tsuga canadensis*) grow very well, particularly those with white or variegated foliage such as 'Gentsch White', as do yews and *Cephalotaxus*.

Dwarf conifers seldom look right planted in the same bed as taller conifers, but you can create a separate adjoining bed and link the two with a pathway: conifers and other plants kept in scale will make this a new stand-alone feature. Brita Johansson, a conifer enthusiast and skillful gardener in Sweden, has somehow managed this difficult task by planting slowish-growing specimens as a backdrop to a natural-looking rock garden planted with dwarf conifers and other plants. In my own garden I have allowed many dwarf and slow-growing conifers to mature, so that at thirty years old they provide focal points and background in alternate seasons to other plants – perennials and shrubs, even trees. I was able to start with an empty field, initially planting small conifers with heaths and heathers (see illustration, page 37). Then, as the conifers developed, I widened the range, replacing some heathers with perennials, shrubs and grasses, always remembering the year-round change and appeal that most of us look for in a garden. Mature conifers can become part of the structure of a garden, able to withstand robust and taller plants around them and becoming a foil for plants such as grasses, later to become the star performer in winter, when the grasses and perennials take second place.

CONIFERS WITH TREES AND SHRUBS

Trees and shrubs fit into the same category as conifers with regard to size and rates of growth, but are seldom broken down into size groupings as conifers are. From the evergreen Eucalyptus, which rivals some of the tallest conifers, to dwarf willows, Berberis and Vaccineum, there are plants that can be categorized as large, intermediate or slow-growing, dwarf and miniature. Just as in a smaller garden it might be difficult to accommodate a Scotch Pine, so might it be equally hard to have an English Oak (*Quercus robur*) or Red Oak (*Quercus rubra*). The first consideration, therefore, in choosing trees and shrubs is to decide what their purpose is and to select them according to the same principles that I have discussed for conifers, of which eventual shape and size are a large part. And, as with conifers, scale is important – trees, shrubs and conifers should look comfortable (if not always natural) in their surroundings. Although there is an enormous range of form and color in individual conifers, there is an even wider range in trees and shrubs. Foliage type and color can vary from the whip-like stems of the brooms (*Cytisus*) to the broad, large-leafed rhododendrons and *Vitis coignetiae*, with shades of green, purple, copper, silver, yellow, blue and variegated, and textures including glossy, matt, woolly or prickly. Many shrubs and trees also have spectacular or fragrant flowers, such as magnolias and rhododendrons, roses and jasmine. There are shrubs that climb, clamber and scramble, like *Hydrangea petiolaris*, wisteria and clematis. This diversity makes shrubs of interest not only in themselves but also in the opportunities they offer of associations with conifers.

Always consider the suitability of trees and shrubs to the proposed site, sun, shade and soil, as well as their rate of growth and eventual size. A magnolia such as 'Jane', a valuable hybrid of *liliflora* and *stellata*, may look small in a garden center but will eventually be of some size – positioning it close to other choice shrubs or conifers may mean that something will have to go in later years. It is better to identify in your early planning the choicer plants you want to see develop as specimens, rather than have them spoil. In between, put less permanent plants, either shrubs or perennials. I am as guilty as anyone in allowing plants to grow into each other – if you love plants and want as much variety and year-round interest as possible, it is easy to give in to the temptation to overcrowd, but you must then be ready to take some tough decisions later.

Conifers make ideal background or foreground plants with broad-leafed shrubs with colorful leaves or brilliant flowers. A golden-foliaged conifer such as *Taxus baccata* 'Repens Aurea' makes a striking contrast to the deep purple-leafed *Cotinus coggygria* 'Royal Purple', both reaching a peak of color in early to mid-summer. Left unpruned, these will become large, but both take well to regular pruning. The versatile shrub *Cornus alba* 'Aurea' makes a colorful backdrop to the weeping bright green *Picea abies* 'Frohburg': from summer into autumn it has bright golden leaves, and in winter it has bright red stems, particularly if pruned.

I find brooms make good companions to conifers, either in the foreground or peeping from behind a contrasting conifer. The buttercup yellow of *Cytisus praecox* 'Allgold' makes a pretty spectacular partnership in early summer with the Blue Spruce, *Picea pungens* 'Montgomery'; when flowering is finished, I cut the *Cytisus* hard back. Brooms are relatively short-lived, and can easily be dispensed with or pruned hard if they get too large. It is important to ensure that other evergreens, or even densely foliaged perennials, do not grow into conifers because this cuts out their light and soon causes them to lose their foliage in that contact area – such bare patches, if they are small, are likely to recover, but larger ones will not.

Rhododendrons and azaleas associate well with conifers, a combination particularly popular in Germany. Rhododendrons, which can get very large, should be chosen with eventual size in mind. A most spectacular sight in spring is a *Rhododendron* 'Amethyst' contrasting with *Abies nordmanniana* 'Golden Spreader'. Rhododendrons, like brooms, make brief and brilliant splashes of color but should

be used with care – they are ideal to light up the garden, but are mostly of limited year-round interest.

Dwarf or prostrate conifers make good partners with dwarf shrubs on a rock or scree garden, interspersed with dwarf perennials or alpines. Colorful conifers, or even darker green or blue, make an excellent contrasting background to shrubs that flower in summer or winter. The yellow- or orange-flowered witch hazels (*Hamamelis*) are even more striking when highlighted against a darker conifer, and grow well on the shadier side.

Climbers are mostly classed as shrubs, though there are a few herbaceous types, and with care they can be used to climb up conifers, particularly if the climber is deciduous. I have seen Boston Ivy (*Parthenocissus tricuspidata*) planted to climb up into a blue-foliaged *Chamaecyparis lawsoniana* 'Alumii', its autumn scarlet and crimson leaves making a spectacular contrasting show. Vigorous climbers should be used with care, however, as they can smother an evergreen conifer. For a larger, established conifer such as the Austrian Pine (*Pinus nigra*) or the

Conifers contribute color, form and a backdrop, as displayed by the dark emerald green hedge in this mixed planting (shown in early summer), in which colorful shrubs and flowering perennials also play their part. The 30-year-old hedge of Thuja occidentalis *'Smaragd' contrasts with* Picea pungens *'Egyptian Pyramid', a broad, irregular Blue Spruce. Between this and the columnar* Taxus baccata *'Fastigiata Robusta' are* Cornus mas *'Aureoelegantissima' and* Berberis thunbergii *'Dart's Red Lady'. The dominant purple-leafed shrub to the right is* Corylus maxima *'Purpurea'.*

Scotch Pine (*Pinus sylvestris*), a *Clematis montana* makes a good companion. *Clematis viticella* and some of the large-flowered hybrids are seldom dense enough to make the semi-prostrate junipers or yews lose their foliage; they need to be planted far enough away for their roots not to get too dry, and can then be allowed to scramble over the conifer to create summer interest. The year-round garden can be enhanced by a wide range of plants – shrubs become focal points when in flower and foliage, then, when their leaves are gone, the stems, bark and winter flowers and, on evergreens, foliage carry on the show.

CONIFERS WITH HEATHS AND HEATHERS

Though heaths (*Erica*) and heathers (*Calluna*) cannot be grown in many situations due to alkaline or dry soils and extreme climates, in cooler, moister locations where they grow well they can make breathtaking displays in both small and large gardens. The *Calluna*, which flower in summer, are acid-loving plants, as are most of the summer-flowering *Erica*, although some of the latter tolerate neutral soils. The winter-flowering heaths can be a real bonus to the winter garden in countries where snow does not cover them for most of the winter – they flower from late autumn to late spring, and are also lime-tolerant. Though they will grow in light shade, they flower best in full sun, but flowers are not their only attribute. A great number of cultivars are now available of both heaths and heathers with colored foliage and brilliant spring shoots – these widen the opportunities for the gardener to create striking plant associations with conifers and other plants.

Most heaths and heathers are relatively low-growing, so vertical or upright-spreading conifers of different shapes and hues can make colorful and contrasting associations – although these might seem static, they can change dramatically with the seasons, yet are relatively restful on the eye and trouble-free. In northern Germany and Holland, the naturally light, sandy, but moisture-retentive soil is ideal for heaths and heathers, and gardens there reflect the more natural look of heathland. Conifers usually take an important, but secondary, role, with the native, vertical-growing *Juniperus communis* making a pleasing contribution.

Over thirty years ago, I planted large groups of over a hundred different heathers, including many golden-foliaged cultivars, interspersed with conifers. The result was a year-round patchwork quilt, amazingly colorful. Many of those aging heathers still flower and perform now but, as the conifers have matured, I have gradually changed the garden by adding shrubs, grasses and perennials. Despite the criticism that many garden writers bestow on this

*This garden in Edewecht, northern Germany, belonging to Kurt Kramer, a well-known breeder of heathers, reflects the natural heathlands nearby. Here, in late summer, cultivars of the Common Heather (*Calluna vulgaris*) mix naturally with various upright selections of the Common Juniper (*Juniperus communis*).*

widely used combination, every garden that can grow them would be enriched by what these groups of plants can add. I have continued to experiment, and recently planted a large new bed of conifers, heathers, some shrubs, perennials and ornamental grasses. The early results are promising!

Regrettably, few parts of North America can successfully grow both summer- and winter-flowering heathers: it is either too cold for some of the summer-flowering types, too hot and humid for the winter heaths, or too dry and desiccating for them in summer and winter. From northern California to Vancouver on the west coast and from Pennsylvania to New England on the east, some varieties can be successfully grown although protection might be needed (suitable microclimates may be elsewhere).

In general, my advice would be not to plant heaths and heathers too close to choice conifers. Winter heaths climbing up into pines – such as *Erica carnea* 'Pink Spangles' into *Pinus mugo* 'Wintergold', or *Pinus contorta* 'Spaan's Dwarf' hosting the clambering *Erica carnea* 'Springwood White' –

will do little harm to either, but the more vigorous types, if allowed to grow into the base of chamaecyparis or thujas, will make them go bare, and this will be all too visible if you ever want to dig up the heather or move the conifer.

Color combinations are inevitably a personal choice. Golden carpets of heath or heather will set off green or blue conifers, and the intense crimson and deep golden winter hues of some of the Callunas in frosty weather are particularly striking. But it is best to widen the palette to include other plants which will add spice and variety. Do not restrict yourself to conifers and heathers – add bulbs, perennials and grasses, and silver, gold, purple or variegated shrubs. Pleasing year-round smaller gardens can always be created by scaling the plants down to fit.

Combined with heaths and heathers in late winter are (center foreground, left to right) Pinus mugo *'Kissen' (30 years old),* Picea pungens *'Moll' (25 years old) and* Thuja orientalis *'Shirley Chilcott' (10 years old). Further behind, to the right, are* Pinus mugo *'Ophir' and* Abies concolor *'Wattezii Prostrate' (both are 30 years old, but pruned).*

CONIFERS WITH BULBS, PERENNIALS AND ORNAMENTAL GRASSES

In associating conifers with bulbs, perennials and ornamental grasses, the principle of scale remains one of the most important considerations. Dwarfer conifers would look ridiculous, and might not even be seen, if planted among the taller *Miscanthus* or *Phlox paniculata*. Every plant has a right to some dignity, after all! Dwarf conifers and dwarf shrubs will be much more appealing with herbaceous plants that are in scale with their woody neighbors. A collection of dwarf or miniature conifers, with year-round interest and color, can be transformed into a broader-interest garden by adding a careful choice of perennials, bulbs, shrubs and grasses.

The brightest colors and most dramatic changes are undoubtedly achieved by interweaving plants whose flowers and foliage make their impact in different ways at different times of year. Among the first plants to flower in the spring are the snowdrops and aconites, followed by numerous other bulbs such as the brilliant dwarf species tulips, the daffodils and

A sloping scree-type garden needs both prostrate and erect plants to give it form. In Don and Jenny Allen's Mast Gully Gardens near Melbourne, Australia, late spring features a 7-year-old Pinus thunbergii *'Yatsubusa' making new growth, its dark green needles contrasting with the gray* Stachys byzantinus *behind, and* Scabious *'Butterfly Blue' in front.*

With perfectly timed flowering, the lilac-purple Allium christophii *forms a pleasing association with* Picea orientalis *'Aurea' at The Victory Garden, Massachusetts, in early summer. This underused but easily grown spruce is dark green most of the year, but its moment of glory is its golden-yellow new growth, which coincides with the blooms of the* Allium.

deep blue muscari. These low-growing bulbs are ideal among dwarf conifers on a scree or rock garden, providing splashes of color as a contrast to the blues, greens and golds of conifers. In my view, large-flowered daffodils and hybrid tulips would look out of scale in this miniature landscape. The pure yellow, large-flowered *Narcissus* 'King Alfred' and other similar types, however, somehow do look natural if planted *en masse* in grass among a background of trees and conifers. Such a planting has been giving pleasure for many years near my house.

Snowdrops and other bulbs close to conifers can look most picturesque, but they may need to be moved as the conifers grow, otherwise they can be smothered. Since the foliage of spring-flowering bulbs soon dies down, they are unlikely to spoil any choice conifer foliage. A crimson *Cyclamen coum* makes a

vivid contrast in the spring if nestled near the base of *Pinus sylvestris* 'Aurea', which in itself is colorful. *Cyclamen hederifolium*, an autumn-flowering species with pink or white flowers, is also attractive through much of winter with its plates of marbled leaves. I have planted *Muscari armeniacum* close to *Pinus mugo* 'Wintergold', and its brilliant deep blue flowers in late spring would make a vivid display against any conifer with golden foliage (it can spread, so do not plant it too close to choice miniatures).

Steve and Maggie Putts's garden in Roydon, Norfolk, England, was planted for year-round interest; it is shown here in early summer. The foreground alpine bed is planted with dwarf conifers and alpine and rock plants, the varieties of blue-and-white Campanula carpatica *making ideal companions to the new conifer foliage. The garden is just 5 years old, and the conifers will eventually require thinning.*

Mature dwarf conifers add structure to the rock garden at Longwood Gardens, Kennett Square, Pennsylvania. Both the Chamaecyparis obtusa *'Repens' (left of center) and the* Picea glauca var. albertiana *'Conica' are about 40 years old, as is the nearly hidden* Chamaecyparis obtusa *'Juniperoides' (center).* Juniperus squamata *'Blue Star' (foreground right) is younger. The low-growing foreground perennials (*Alchemilla, Sedum *and* Campanula) *to some extent outscale the smaller conifers.*

In general terms, alpines or dwarf perennials can be used as edging plants in beds or among dwarf conifers, but you should avoid rapidly spreading types like acaenas and ajuga, which can become weedy. The choice is enormous, and includes the alpine campanulas, dianthus, hardy geraniums, saxifrages, sempervivums, sedums and thymus. With conifers that have grown quickly or developed as mature plants, taller perennials can play an important role. What could be more striking than the brilliant *Crocosmia* 'Lucifer', with its exotic vermilion-flame flowers, against a mature, blue-foliaged *Abies lasiocarpa* 'Compacta'? Perennials add a touch of spice, color and drama that conifers may not always supply on their own. In the formal garden, clipped yew hedges play a supporting but essential role as a backdrop to colorful summer perennials and grasses.

In particular, yew can make a startling contrast in a white garden, which would lack drama without it. Color-themed gardens can also include conifers, shrubs and perennials within the chosen palette. I tend to prefer contrast, but color is not the only consideration: though it is undeniably colorful, I am not sure that *Agapanthus* 'Bressingham Blue' behind *Pinus contorta* 'Frisian Gold' quite works, since the Agapanthus is taller than the conifer, its deep blue flowers rising on arching stems above the foliage.

Low-growing perennials such as bergenias, particularly those with good winter foliage, make successful partners for conifers. The broad, glossy, green leaves of *Bergenia* 'Bressingham Ruby' make a distinct contrast at the base of a blue, fine-needled *Cedrus atlantica* 'Glauca Pendula' in summer, while in winter the bergenia leaves change to ruby red to make an even more striking contrast. Crocosmias, kniphofias and agapanthus, all colorful summer-flowering perennials, associate well (where they can be grown) in the foreground of taller, variously shaped and colored conifers. Richard Ayres has created a wonderful garden near Cambridge, England, showing how well conifers can associate with other plants within a given color range. In my own garden, needing to spice up what I call "the winter bed" (because it is more colorful in winter than in summer), I planted a large group of *Rudbeckia fulgida* var. *sullivantii* 'Goldsturm' with a background of taller conifers, *Picea pungens* 'Hoopsii', *Pinus nigra* and *Picea breweriana*. The effect lasts for many weeks in late summer, and is stunning.

Similar effects can be achieved in the smaller garden by scaling down both conifers and perennials,

Mature slow-growing conifers not only form attractive specimens in their own right, but also provide a foil against which seasonal plants can shine. Here, the blue foliage of a 30-year-old Abies lasiocarpa *'Arizonica Compacta' sets off the leaves and brilliant summer flowers of* Crocosmia *'Lucifer'.*

and selecting those that give a long period of interest. The low-growing *Geranium sanguineum* 'Alan Bloom' or another variety can front a planting of conifers, but this will not flower as long as *Geranium* 'Ann Folkard', *Geranium* × *riversleaianum* 'Mavis Simpson' or *Geranium* 'Rozanne', which flower most of the summer and into autumn. The last will change the scene around the base of a *Sequoia sempervirens* 'Adpressa' once it comes into flower in early summer, its large blue flowers a surprise among evergreen foliage. Choose perennials which suit your plantings, your soil and your climate, and always try to avoid planting those that are too dense and spreading, because they will deprive the base of the conifers of light. With older conifers whose bottom branches have dropped or been pruned away, shade-loving or ground-cover perennials can be planted.

Conifers can be as colorful as any other plant, as shown here in Richard Ayres's garden in Cambridge, England, early summer. The predominantly yellow or golden conifers are enhanced by contrasting and matching perennials. Left of the grass pathway is Taxus baccata *'Semperaurea' with* Juniperus × pfitzeriana *'Wilhelm Pfitzer', both highlighted by* Senecio cineraria *'White Diamond'. On the right, the tall biennial* Salvia sclarea *catches the eye, as do the golden* Chamaecyparis lawsoniana *'Winston Churchill', the matching* Juniperus pfitzeriana *'Aurea' and the spires of* Verbascum *'Anglesey Sunshine'.*

Whereas perennials and bulbs provide color as a contrast to conifers, ornamental grasses add movement and light. These are now going through an unprecedented but deserved popularity. There are many categories to fit different plantings – dwarf, tall, large- and small-flowered (technically, grasses have "inflorescences" but I stick to "flowers" on the basis that you will then know what I am referring to!). Many have blue, gold or variegated leaves, and among them I include sedges and even a member of the lily-of-the-valley family – *Ophiopogon planiscapus* 'Nigrescens', a wonderful ever-black grass-like plant with a great number of uses in all sizes of garden. It has a creeping habit and prefers some shade, but will really show off in contrast to colored dwarf conifers such as *Picea pungens* 'Globosa', *Pinus sylvestris* 'Aurea' or *Calocedrus decurrens* 'Berrima Gold'. The ophiopogon, known as Black Dragon in North America, is an ideal partner to what is perhaps my favorite grass, *Hakonechloa macra* 'Alboaurea' (strangely not yet given a catchy name). You will benefit from a certain one-upmanship in reeling off these names to impress friends! The hakonechloa has gold and green striped leaves with wispy plumes of flowers in late summer. It sets off any blue conifer, such as *Picea pungens* 'Globosa' or *Pinus parviflora* 'Glauca'.

Perhaps completing a trio is another Japanese grass, the stunning *Imperata cylindrica* 'Rubra', sometimes called Red Baron (Red Shogun would be more appropriate!). This Japanese blood grass can be used as a foil to blue-foliaged conifers or planted as a flowing river through conifers, shrubs and other grasses, its summer-long crimson blades setting off all the plants it touches. In a sunny position, the Texan native grass *Stipa tenuissima* looks beautiful for many weeks and often months. Planted among more static conifers, its wispy plumes turn to every summer breeze; they whiten as autumn approaches, shedding light on the darker conifers. It seeds freely but is relatively short-lived and not invasive. It always seems to enhance a planting, wherever it lands. I have used it to create a central scene among established conifers, together with *Kniphofia* 'Bressingham Comet' and 'Cobra', for a period of interest lasting from mid-summer until early the following spring.

Taller grasses come in two categories: those like the *Miscanthus* and *Calamagrostis*, which have many quite dense stems and leaves, with plumes either flowering among or just above the foliage; and those like some *Molinia* and *Stipa* whose foliage is short, but whose flowering stems and plumes rise some way above it, allowing the eye to see through them. Together they create both the substantial and the ethereal. *Miscanthus* can be from 3ft (90cm) to 10ft (3m) in height and should be selected for its size, plumes and color. The variegated, narrow-leafed *Miscanthus sinensis* 'Morning Light' shows up well in front of darker conifers; the taller, ruby-crimson plumes of *M. s.* 'Flamingo' fade to silver and then beige as the flowers ripen, a continuing change against an older, taller, blue conifer such as *Abies lasiocarpa* 'Compacta'.

Miscanthus and many other grasses also act as wonderful backdrops to specimen conifers. An *Abies concolor* 'Compacta' in my garden is backed by various grasses and surrounded in summer by perennials – you notice this blue-needled fir in summer, but it is in winter, when all the life (though not the interest) has gone from the grasses and perennials, that it really comes center stage, highlighted by the whitened foliage of the *Miscanthus*. The blue-foliaged fescue *Festuca glauca* makes a brilliant foil against a golden semi-prostrate juniper like *Juniperus × pfitzeriana* 'Gold Sovereign'. Undoubtedly many of the dwarf, non-invasive grasses make great associations with collections of conifers; all are best used with established dwarf conifers rather than choice miniatures.

Ornamental grasses are close to my heart, and I have been using them for at least twenty years, noting how their popularity has increased and, with it, the new selections from all over the world. The various bronze to reddish, even white-foliaged, *Carex* from New Zealand, being evergreen or ever-colored, are a group that shows conifers off well. *Chionochloa rubra* (not hardy everywhere) is a spectacular foliage plant with long arching stems – it is an almost total antidote, but perfect associate, to conifers.

Lastly, I should mention the once-popular (and perhaps again popular) *Cortaderia*, in particular *Cortaderia selloana*, the Pampas Grass. Conifers, particularly the taller ones with darker foliage, provide a perfect foil for their often stupendous plumes. The tallest, pink-flowered 'Rosea' and 'Sunningdale Silver' are often blown down in the first gale of autumn, but 'Pumila' is valuable for its erect stems and fluffy plumes that remain through winter. A few clumps of these would look great against the bright green background of a hedge of Leylandii. Grasses and conifers make great companions – that's official!

FOLLOWING PAGES *A summer display at Bressingham, Norfolk, England, shows a 25-year-old reverting* Picea pungens 'Prostrata' *(top left; see Directory, page 136), and* Pinus nigra 'Pierrick Bregeon' *(bottom left), in front of* Geranium 'Rozanne' *and the wispy grass,* Stipa tenuissima. *The dark foliage of* Chamaecyparis lawsoniana 'Little Spire' *in the background sets off the variegated* Miscanthus sinensis 'Dixieland'. *In front and to the right of a 30-year-old* Abies concolor 'Compacta' *are* Stipa calamagrostis, Miscanthus sinensis 'Gracillimus' *and* Calamagrostis acutiflora 'Overdam'.

CONIFERS ON THEIR OWN

Gardeners who wish to plant up a bed or even a whole garden with conifers can certainly make their case – after all, there are *Hosta*, *Hemerocallis* and *Sempervivum* (house leek) fanatics all over the world. It should be said, however, that collecting dwarf conifers can present certain problems. Even the largest collections – the National Dwarf Conifer collection at the Savill Gardens, near Windsor, England, and the National Arboretum, Washington, D.C. – in time almost always need more space. I, too, have been faced with the need to thin out, replant and destroy plants; enthusiast that I am, I believe it is as well to be aware of that eventual necessity. A small bed can comfortably accommodate a collection of dwarf conifers for a few years and miniatures for longer, but if they are not to spoil they will eventually need to be thinned out, and some must be moved.

This varied group of conifers in John and Connie McCabe's raised rock garden seems to blend with the distant view in the landscape outside Melbourne, Australia. Yet none of those pictured is native to the Southern Hemisphere. Vertical junipers and cypresses provide accents among the horizontal rocks, over which prostrate junipers and other plants tumble.

The first collector's garden I saw when I was developing an interest in conifers was in 1967 – Ron Corley had an amazing, well laid-out back garden crowded with dwarf conifers, interspersed with dwarf shrubs and alpines or rock plants, with natural stone pathways meandering between. By careful selection of dwarf and miniature varieties, arranged to provide contrast in color and form, he had created a wonderful landscape in miniature (for tips on doing this, see Conifers for the Smallest Garden, page 70). Growth of some conifers may need to be controlled

from an early age by pruning (see page 174). David Ward has created a stunning display, planting not only dwarf and miniature types but taller ones, too. His garden, established twenty years, is never without interest or color, with other trees and shrubs adding further contrast. He has pruned with great skill so that the faster-growing conifers have not lost their natural growth habit, but he will still need to move or thin out his beds in the not too distant future.

A conifer collector will find it hard to resist new plants, but an eventual broad collection may concentrate on favorite groups or types as the main focus, perhaps dwarf spruce or pines. Specialist nurseries are to be found in most countries where interest gardening is strong; it can be fascinating to visit them to see how conifers are propagated and grown and, of course, to bring back a treasure or

This autumn view in David Ward's garden near Leeds, Yorkshire, England, shows a tremendous variety, form and color. A year-round spectacle can be achieved with careful selection, combinations and pruning. Tall, medium and dwarf types are planted here, most between 10 and 15 years old. The tall column at the back is Cupressus arizonica *var.* glabra *'Blue Ice'; at the end of the pathway (center) is* Cryptomeria japonica *'Sekkan'; the deep blue in the foreground left is* Abies concolor *'Violacea'; center left foreground is* Juniperus communis *'Compressa'.*

two. Visiting collections and gardens, and studying books, will add to your knowledge and interest. Those who want to learn more should consider joining the new international American Conifer Society, which is as much for new conifer enthusiasts as it is for the professional. Details, along with lists of gardens and specialist nurseries, are on page 184.

CONIFERS THROUGH THE SEASONS

Picea orientalis 'Aurea' through the seasons. Spring: flowers and new cones.

Mid-summer: purple female cones form, weighing down the branch tips.

Mid-winter: the mature, seed-containing cones are lighter in color and weight.

Conifers always used to have the reputation of being less than exciting, with people thinking they were boring – they were supposed to look the same all year round, except that they were even duller in winter, such as the somber yews seen in British churchyards! But the last forty years has seen a revolution in the development and selection of conifers; now, there are far too many varieties to choose from, and their diversity in size, shape, texture and color is incredible. Even without changing color through the seasons, conifers provide enough shades of color to create year-round interest, particularly if you include the deciduous larches, *Metasequoia*, *Taxodium*, *Pseudolarix* and *Ginkgo*. A garden of carefully selected conifers need never be dull; add the seasonal changes that many exhibit and the opportunity to combine them with other plants and you can create some striking year-round associations.

SPRING

In late winter, as the days get milder, many conifers that have been under stress with cold winds and freezing temperatures lose their extremes of winter color before they break into new growth. *Thuja orientalis* 'Flame' and 'Southport', which are reddish-brown in winter, quickly lighten in color. *T. o.* 'Purple King', named because of its almost purple-black mid-winter guise, changes to green. Buds on the spruce, pine and larch continue to swell and elongate, becoming noticeably larger and brighter. Male and female cones become more prominent on many species and cultivars, the male flowers on the yews among the first to release clouds of pollen. *Cupressus lusitanica* 'Glauca Pendula' has its bluish foliage smothered in male flowers at this time of year.

The build-up to new spring growth seems to sap some plants' energy as they consider procreation, and often in mid-spring the foliage on many conifers seems to be slightly dulled. Undoubtedly, if they have been under stress in recent seasons, particularly through drought, they often flower and bear cones more freely, but there is no certain rule. In mid- to late spring, depending on type, great energy is released in bursts of new growth; the membranes covering the buds of larch and spruce are cast aside to give clusters of bright new needles freedom to grow. This is an exciting period, with flowers, cones, shoots of different shapes and colors, and new growth initially dotted all over the plant as tiny spots of green or blue then enveloping the whole plant. Contrasting new growth is most apparent on some of the dwarfer evergreen firs and spruces, while the deciduous larches soon fill in their bare branches with bright green shaving-brush-like shoots. These plants, and pines with their new candle-like shoots, mostly make one main growth a year; their growing season is shorter, and starts earlier, than the plants that grow throughout the summer, such as the junipers, chamaecyparis and thujas. Considerable variations can occur among species and cultivars.

At the time these changes occur, herbaceous and woody plants are also experiencing exciting seasonal rejuvenation in temperate climates. Because there is so much going on – spring flowers and fresh foliage appearing week by week – conifers can often be overlooked, unless they are a strong feature in the garden. Flowers and cones need acute observation, but foliage growth and color, now at its brightest, are more obvious features, which can be used as main or supporting players against flowering or foliage shrubs, trees or perennials. In early spring, dwarf bulbs can be used in association with dwarf conifers, and daffodils with larger conifers – yellow against green, the blue of *Iris reticulata* or *Scilla sibirica* against golden foliage.

The combination of a blue spruce such as *Picea pungens* 'Globosa' and a golden-foliaged plant such as *Erica carnea* 'Foxhollow' gives a brilliance of blue and yellow in spring and summer that may be too much for some, but remember that in cooler climates where both can be grown this combination gives more subtly changing color at other times of the year. More transitory because it is deciduous, though still summer-long, is a similar combination of *Berberis thunbergii* 'Aurea' beside *Picea pungens* 'Hoto', the bright yellow leaves of the Berberis in late spring contrasting strongly with the blue-needled spruce. I have used two alternative combinations.

Spring: seasonal splendor. From left: Chamaecyparis lawsoniana *'Minima Aurea',* Abies lasiocarpa *'Compacta' (with blue-gray foliage),* Thuja orientalis *'Aurea Nana' and* Chamaecyparis nootkanensis *'Pendula'. Their background form and color set off maples, hostas and rhododendrons.*

One is *Picea glauca* 'F. W. Daisy's White' in front of a deep crimson broom, *Cytisus* 'Compact Crimson', which is mostly green but flowers at the same time as the bright creamy new growth of the spruce, which later tones down to pale green (see page 68). The other combination is a dual planting of the dwarf broom *Cytisus ardoinoi* as a backdrop to *Picea glauca* var. *albertiana* 'Laurin' – again, the peak of the creamy-white spring flowering of the broom coincides with the bright green new growth of the dwarf spruce.

SUMMER

The point at which late spring crosses over into early summer is a time of maximum growth on conifers and most other plants – a busy time for plants and gardeners, when there is seldom time for us to relax and take in all that is happening. Spring frosts and early summer scorching from bright sun can cause damage on some conifers; this is also the time to watch out for aphids and red spider mites on certain conifers (see Pests, page 182). The Colorado Blue Spruce (*Picea pungens*) makes growth in late spring and early summer; one of the latest spruces to shoot is *Picea orientalis* 'Aurea', whose bright golden new leaves and shoots make a startling contrast to the dark green of the old foliage. Some pines also have golden new candle-like growth; *Pinus nigra* 'Aurea' and *Pinus densiflora* 'Taylor's Sunburst' are later in emerging but no less spectacular. Some pines put on tremendous growth in one short season in their youth – the Scotch Pine can grow as much as 3ft (90cm).

In early summer, new growth on golden conifers produces the brightest color – the foliage is soft and bright yellow, lacking in chlorophyll, so it is most susceptible to sunscorch. If this proves a regular problem on a young plant it may be best to find it a position sheltered from morning and midday sun, but many plants are surprisingly resilient. Growth slows later in summer. and needles and leaves toughen, unless secondary flushes of growth occur. With so many golden-foliaged conifers and blue-needled firs and spruce in my garden, June can be a spectacular month – but the conifers form only part

of the picture. The green of the grass and other conifers acts as a softening contrast, further enhanced by the use of purple and golden-foliaged shrubs. These include *Berberis thunbergii* 'Atropurpurea', *Cercis canadensis* 'Forest Pansy' and *Cotinus coggyria* 'Royal Purple', *Cornus alba* 'Aurea', *Physocarpus opulifolius* 'Dart's Gold' and *Spiraea japonica* 'Magic Carpet'. The last is a great plant for providing a carpet of gold; later it has pink flowers that go well with *Picea sitchensis* 'Papoose', whose silvery leaf undersides add a brilliant sparkle.

Cones are particularly striking in their early stage, the seeds developing within solid, somewhat fleshy cones, now at their heaviest. Many are visible only high up on the tops of trees, but the Korean Fir (*Abies koreana*) not only bears cones when quite young, but even when older has abundant cones near its base. And what cones! These are a deep purple-blue for several weeks, standing above the branches. Pines, too, can have cones low down – the Eastern White Pine (*Pinus strobus*) is an example. Some of the slower-growing cultivars such as *P. s.* 'Blue Shag' have free-forming cones appropriately downsized to suit their stature. The cones of the spruce at mid-summer, hanging beneath the branches, are often purple, as with *Picea orientalis*, or green, as with *Picea abies*.

Though conifers are at their brightest in early summer, they cannot easily compete with the multicolored flowers of annuals and perennials; rather, they are a good contrast to them. Roses, rhododendrons and azaleas make a splash against the solid forms and varied hues of conifers, while annuals and perennials can create carpets at the base. Taller perennials – such as the flame-red *Crocosmia* 'Lucifer', the golden *Rudbeckia fulgida* var. *sullivantii* 'Goldsturm' and the blue *Agapanthus* – can contrast with taller blue, green or gold conifers as the summer edges into autumn.

AUTUMN

When does late summer become early autumn? The process is gradual and relative, depending on where you live. In Scotland, autumn-like weather can come

Summer: conifers interplanted with perennials and grasses. Dark green Pinus heldreichii *'Satellit', 30 years old (center foreground), with* Thuja occidentalis *'Holmstrup's Yellow', 20 years old in front of it. The plumes of* Cortaderia richardii *from New Zealand rise between the two arborvitaes,* Thuja orientalis *'Flame' (foreground right) and, in front, the undulating* Juniperus communis *'Horstmann'.*

early. In the whole of Britain, few Indian summers of warm September sunshine are experienced. In New England and the American midwest, however, warm, ripening Septembers are common, yet autumn color on deciduous trees mostly comes earlier and more spectacularly than in northern Europe. Some conifers are at their brightest as the intensity of light increases in early autumn. *Chamaecyparis lawsoniana*

and conifers in moister soils with longer growing seasons put on late growth. Many late summer perennials and ornamental grasses are at their peak, as well as some summer-flowering and foliage heaths and heathers, so conifers can show off among other deciduous plants as they ripen and die back with warm autumn tones. Among perennials there is a late surge of color from the indispensable autumn asters *Aconitum arendsii*, *Cimicifuga* (now *Actaea*) and *Schizostylis*, among others.

But the really spectacular contrasts in autumn come from the dying autumn leaves on trees and shrubs. Brown, yellow, crimson, purple, bronze, gold, scarlet – their colors give brilliant contrast to the blues, greens and golds of conifers. Dark green

Autumn: the morning sun highlights the fast-disappearing leaves on conifers and on Betula utilis var. jacquemontii, Prunus amanogawa *and* Berberis. *The 15- to 20-year-old conifers, interspersed with heathers, are (from left to right):* Taxus baccata *'Dovastonii Aurea' (upright, pruned), in front* Picea pungens *'Globosa',* Picea pungens *'Pendula' (staked to 5ft/150cm), with* Abies procera *behind,* Pinus nigra *'Yellow Parrot' and* Juniperus scopulorum *'Wichita Blue'.*

Incense Cedars (*Calocedrus decurrens*) make a marvelous association with maples (one famous example of such a grouping is in Westonbirt Arboretum, Gloucestershire, England). Perhaps only one of each is needed, as with an inspired coupling of *Acer japonicum* 'Aconitifolium' and *Picea pungens* 'Prostrata' in the Miller garden, northern Seattle.

Though the season of autumn foliage color is transitory, sometimes with only a few days of real glory, it is worth striving for. Plant selection can be scaled down to fit the smaller garden; some of the barberries (*Berberis*) and dogwoods (*Cornus*) are quite small, and can be kept so with pruning to give good autumn color as a contrast to conifers. *Cornus*

sanguinea 'Midwinter Fire' and 'Winter Beauty' have excellent and quite long-lasting autumn leaves, which turn yellow then orange before falling to reveal orange-red stems for winter color. I have placed this behind a blue-foliaged chamaecyparis: half the plant is visible from the kitchen window so that all can enjoy the colorful combination that gradually changes as autumn goes into winter.

Autumn is a time of great change for deciduous conifers. All of them go through beautiful transformations as their leaves prepare to drop. *Pseudolarix amabilis* is known as the Golden Larch simply because of its wonderful autumn color – it is a beautiful tree, though not easy to grow, and its leaves drop early. For most gardeners the true larches are a better choice, particularly since there are now so many dwarfer forms. The change from green to gold takes longer but offers dramatic change among evergreen conifers, whether on taller trees silhouetted against a blue autumnal sky, or on smaller plants in garden settings. The same can be said for the *Metasequoia* and the Swamp Cypress (*Taxodium*) on a larger scale. The latter have vivid russet tones in late autumn, always particularly successful if reflected in water. The branches are naked in winter; bright green leaves in early summer deepen in high summer, then color before dropping in autumn. A real four-season plant, it is a must for any reasonable-sized garden with water. Lastly there is the *Ginkgo*, one of the most unconifer-like looking plants, with simple flattened or cupped leaves. These are bright apple-green in summer, but in autumn the edges turn golden and gradually suffuse the whole leaf until the foliage is briefly a clear, deep, butter-yellow before falling. Most ginkgos are quite slow to become established, but in time will become large; they take well to pruning.

Autumn: the display of orange-gold leaves on Rhus typhina *'Dissecta' is spectacular. Here, it is enhanced by* Juniperus × pfitzeriana *'Compacta' in the foreground, with* Chamaecyparis lawsoniana *'Golden Pot' behind. Also in the background are* Pinus flexilis *and* Picea pungens *'Hoopsii'. All the conifers are 25 to 30 years old.*

WINTER

As autumn descends into winter, for many garden plants the main seasons of color and interest have gone. Not so with conifers. While colors may be more spectacular in autumn, some conifers are quietly changing hue as the days get shorter and the nights colder. Some turn duller or darker, a gradual process that can turn the bright green lacy summer foliage of *Microbiota decussata* to brown and then, in an open situation in frosty weather, to purple-bronze. *Cryptomeria japonica* 'Elegans', *Chamaecyparis thyoides* 'Rubicon' and *Thuja orientalis* 'Purple King' are other examples of conifers whose darker winter color is more striking than their green summer clothes.

The trick in using these is to place them where they can have the most impact – in full sun and associated with other contrasting plants. These could be other evergreen conifers, whose green summer foliage turns to a bright gold or yellow in winter. Sharp-eyed nurserymen and collectors are finding

an increasing number of these in various countries, and some are worth their weight in gold in the winter garden. *Pinus mugo* 'Winter Gold' is one of many forms of the dwarf Mountain Pine that changes to gold, making a brilliant contrast to *Microbiota* at this time of year; in warmer weather in late spring, as new growth is about to emerge, the needles return to a subdued and conservative green.

Other conifers whose golden days are in winter include *Pinus mugo* 'Ophir', 'Carsten' and 'Zundert', *Pinus contorta* 'Chief Joseph', *Pinus strobus* 'Hillside Winter Gold', *Pinus virginiana* 'Wates Golden' and *Pinus sylvestris* 'Aurea'. All of these can be kept small by pruning, even the tree-like golden Scotch Pine (see Pruning, page 174). Among the firs, *Abies nordmanniana* 'Golden Spreader' is light yellow in summer, turning to deep gold even in part shade; despite its name, with age it becomes pyramidal unless a leading shoot is removed. *Abies concolor* 'Wintergold' is a brighter, lighter yellow in full sun; you should give it a sheltered position to prevent sunscorch.

Placing of color is always important, so mix golds with greens and blues and other plants. Do not be tempted to use too many golds, which would be unrestful to look at – just one among other colors provides a better balance and makes each plant an individual, particularly if forms and texture are also taken into consideration. And in winter, many golden conifers are less colorful. Many of the thujas, for example, green and gold in summer, are dull in winter, the Eastern Arborvitae (*Thuja occidentalis*) in particular. Some go yellow rather than gold – for example, *T. o.* 'Sunkist' is a bronze-orange-yellow. Some who see the popular *T. o.* 'Rheingold' in winter are inclined to believe it is dead; others consider that its deep copper-bronze in extreme weather is strikingly attractive. One of my favorite thujas for winter color is *Thuja plicata* 'Stoneham Gold', a selection made in Hampshire, England, of the Western Red Cedar. Slow-growing, it has somewhat thickened foliage; in winter, the leaves are deep golden-yellow-bronze with reddish-brown shoots. *T. o.* 'Holmstrup's Yellow' remains bright in color,

but for this reason beware of its potential to scorch in winter as well as in summer.

Chamaecyparis lawsoniana 'Minima Aurea' or 'Aurea Densa' have bright yellow foliage summer and winter. *Calocedrus decurrens* 'Berrima Gold' is a good yellow color for most of the year, but a richer, copper-tipped orange in winter, most effective against a dark background. In winter the intense summer and autumn blue of *Picea pungens* is toned down, particularly if it is in a semi-shady position, but *P. p.* 'Hoopsii' and *P. p.* 'Thomsen' are among the brightest. The blue-needled firs, on the other hand, keep a good color – *Abies concolor* 'Violacea' is an intense silver-blue, an ideal contrast for green or gold, or as a background to the winter stems of willows and dogwoods, such as *Cornus stolonifera* var. *flaviramea*, *Cornus alba* 'Sibirica' or *Cornus sanguinea* 'Winter Beauty' (syn. 'Winter Flame'). Though both are quite dark, I have planted *Cornus stolonifera* 'Cardinal' next to *Thuja orientalis* 'Flame' – the summer green leaves of the cornus soften the golden foliage of the thuja, while its deep crimson stems blend more closely with the conifer's bronze winter foliage. Blue and yellow always work well for contrast: the intense silver-blue of the vigorous and not always prostrate *Abies concolor* 'Wattezii Prostrate' could not be more striking than when set against the light winter yellow of *Pinus mugo* 'Ophir'.

In winter, many gardens are laid bare. Although deciduous woody plants can be attractive in their own way when leafless, often enhanced by colored stems and bark, I believe all gardens are poorer without the use of evergreens such as conifers to provide structure and color. Form and texture are important in the winter garden, whether formal, informal or mournful. Low winter sun highlights the shapes of conifers, which can be dramatic in half-light or fog when color is less visible. Light and shadow add a new dimension to the winter garden in particular. The weather itself can create drama with even the darkest and dullest of conifers – the appearance of yew hedges is transformed by frost and snowfall. The pendulous branches of *Picea breweriana*, *Chamaecyparis nootkatensis* 'Pendula'

Winter: mid-winter frost adds almost more drama to plants than snow, which often covers them beyond recognition. The tracery of the Betula pendula *(Silver Birch, back) is lined with hoar frost, with the early morning sun filtering through to the low-growing* Pinus nigra *'Hornibrookiana' in the center.* Thuja occidentalis *'Holmstrup' (to the left) and* Abies procera *'Glauca' (right) are strong vertical background plants. A group of three* Picea pungens *'Globosa' rise above the dead flowerheads of* Calluna vulgaris *'Kinlochruel', which flows into the foliage of* Stipa tenuissima, *frozen into wave-like patterns.*

and *Chamaecyparis lawsoniana* 'Dik's Weeping' are striking on frosty, snowy or foggy days.

Snow can be a danger to conifers with erect branching habits, such as chamaecyparis, junipers and thuja – in areas of high snowfall, branches should be tied in to prevent breakage. Pines, firs and spruce are mostly better adapted to carrying snowloads, and can look very picturesque. Layers of pure white on branches; icicles on the tips of shoots caused by melting daytime snow freezing at night; the ghostly effect of hoar frost in moist climates covering needles, shoots and branches – these are some of the pleasures to be gained from living through cold winters. Low winter sun can transform a scene minute by minute, as it strikes frosted foliage to create droplets of glistening water. Such winter days – with the color, form and variety of conifers set off by each other and by other plants – can be magical and more dramatic than almost any summer scene.

67

Seasonal comparisons: who says conifers don't change from one season to the next? By planting different types together or using conifers as a centerpiece to contrasting plants, dramatic and changing scenes can be created, such as these at the author's garden in Norfolk, England.

LEFT, TOP *Cones appear infrequently on young* Abies procera *specimens, but this 20-year-old A. p. 'Noble's Dwarf' surprised us with a magnificent show in late summer. Right: once the snow melted from this wintry scene, some collapsed cones will be revealed.*

LEFT MIDDLE Thuja orientalis *'Flame' is bright golden-yellow in summer, matching* Helenium *'Pipsqueak' in the foreground. It is flanked by a vigorous* Cornus stolonifera *'Cardinal' on the left and* Arundodonax *'Macrophylla' on the right. Right: in winter the background plants,* Pinus heldreichii *and* Betula utilis var. jacquemontii, *are more visible.*

LEFT BOTTOM *In late summer,* Picea glauca *'J. W. Daisy's White' is a light green among perennials and grasses. Right: in late spring, it is transformed by new creamy-white shoots against contrasting foliage and flowers.*

ABOVE *This summer view (left) shows a pruned* Chamaecyparis lawsoniana *'Silberstar', surrounded by* Berberis thunbergii *'Golden Ring',* Geranium *'Rozanne',* Stipa tenuissima *and, behind, the leafy foliage of* Cornus sanguinea *'Midwinter Fire'. The conifer in the background is* Cupressus lusitanica *'Glauca Pendula'. At the end of winter (right), the fiery orange stems of the* Cornus *peek out from behind the* Chamaecyparis, *the two plants making more impact together than either could alone.*

BELOW *It can be an advantage to let conifers grow into each other, especially when they have dramatic seasonal changes in foliage. Here,* Pinus mugo *'Winter Gold', green in summer (left) and golden-yellow in winter (right), is enhamced by* Microbiota decussata, *green in summer and bronze in winter. The lower branches of* Abies procera *remain fairly constant.*

CONIFERS FOR THE SMALLEST GARDEN

Terms such as "small" or "smallest" are somewhat subjective when it comes to defining a garden, rural or urban. An area of 1,076 square feet (100 square metres) may seem small to some people, while others have a patio or balcony no more than a tenth of that. In Japan and many European countries, the front or back doorstep is literally the only area available, yet homeowners manage plants in pots to brighten up their entrances. Many conifers lend themselves well to being grown in containers. They can be used as specimens, a hedge or as garden plants in the small garden as long as the selection is made with care. A slow-growing yew such as *Taxus* × *media* 'Nidiformis' or *Thuja occidentalis* 'Smaragd' can be kept as a small hedge. Narrow upright specimens can give accent points, rising above lower-growing alpines or perennials. Miniature or dwarf conifers, selected for their shape and year-round color, can be kept in scale and shape by pruning; they are ideal for an alpine, rock or scree garden.

If you are a plant enthusiast, you can fit many plants into a small area. Try replicating nature by adding a few rocks or stones, and plant dwarf or miniature conifers and shrubs among alpines, rock plants and bulbs. A bed raised on brick, stone, old railway sleepers or treated wood enables you to garden closer to eye level (raised beds are of course also helpful to wheelchair-bound gardeners). Creating a landscape in miniature can be a fascinating pastime with considerable rewards. Here you do need to use true miniature conifers, which are most likely to be available from specialist nurseries.

Tom de Lange's garden near Eindhoven, Holland, here shown in summer, is a haven for miniature and dwarf conifers. Only 85 square feet/8 square meters, it hosts a varied collection of over 230 varieties. Pruning the lower branches of plants such as Thuja orientalis *'Aurea Nana' allows more space. Other conifers can be top-grafted onto a stem or pruned Japanese-style into "pom-poms" or "clouds" (see page 74). Tom's garden is always of interest at all times of the year.*

GROWING CONIFERS IN POTS AND CONTAINERS

Nearly all conifers grow well in pots and containers – after all, that is how most are grown in nurseries before they are displayed for sale. Dwarfer forms in particular tolerate root restriction better than most plants, often for many years. The variety of shapes and colors – formal, rounded or upright; or informal, weeping, irregular or semi-prostrate – give an enormous choice to the gardener, with sizes and rates of growth to fit any area from a balcony to a park. All sizes can be pruned to create formal pyramids, topiary specimens or bonsai, adding to their versatility. In Italy and France, you will often see conifers in containers being used as "hedges" to mark the area for pavement restaurants.

Container gardening has never been more popular, so just as the choice of conifers is enormous, so is the choice of what to put them in. Clay pots may not be frost proof, so in colder regions you may need to protect them; the more tender plants are at risk of having their roots frozen, since plants are always more susceptible to frost in a container than in the ground. Containers can be wrapped in protective material such as fleece, sunk in the ground in winter, or even brought under cover into a frost-free garage or outbuilding. With larger plants, that is not always practicable, so it is best to play safe and select plants that are even hardier than the zone you live in and keep them in a container that will withstand the expected frost level.

Concrete containers need not be completely utilitarian, and are often used in colder countries in Europe. Treated hardwood and softwood containers are widely used in North America – the latter look more natural, but may not last for ever. Stone troughs and sinks can be hard to obtain and often costly, but good replicas are available at most garden centers. Many plastic, fiberglass and reconstituted materials are on offer, some now looking so close to terracotta that they can be mistaken by the unobservant for the real thing.

Plants in all containers need good drainage, especially if the pots are plastic or concrete, and regular watering is essential to preserve health. Clay or unglazed pots are likely to dry out twice as fast as plastic, so plants in these may need watering once or even twice a day, or whenever the compost feels dry. Evergreen foliage transpires in winter and summer, so the water supply must be matched to the demand to prevent foliage from drying out. In summer, containers can be stood on a dish or tray or be watered by an automatic device. Mulching the top surface of the compost with 1–2in (2.5–5cm) of chipped stone, gravel or composted bark chippings will help prevent surface water loss.

Taller conifers, unless weighted down by a heavy container, may catch the wind and blow over, especially if the compost is allowed to dry out. Adding as little as 10 percent extra loam will provide useful extra weight. Stones in the base of the container help with drainage as well as weight.

Conifers can remain for several years in the same container, or can be potted on as they increase in size. If the container is unchanged, an annual feed of slow-release fertilizer should be given in early spring or late summer. You should avoid overfeeding (or overwatering) because you will not want the plants to grow too quickly. Some conifers, however, such as *Chamaecyparis lawsoniana* 'Snow White' and *C. l.* 'Nana Albospica', will only perform at their best if pushed to their ultimate growth and color, so these may be better avoided. Most just need reasonable care and attention to stay in good condition. This may include pruning, trimming and, on some plants such as *Picea glauca* var. *albertiana* 'Conica', precautionary sprays of insecticide (see Pests and Diseases, page 182).

You can also use containers or window boxes for short-term interest. If you cut strong stems of foliage in late autumn from firs, spruces, pines or thujas, and plunge them into compost, most will last the whole

RIGHT *Two specimens of* Thuja orientalis *'Aurea Nana' make perfect twins in Lindsay Gray's garden near Melbourne, Australia. They contrast well with the broad leaves of* Agapanthus *lining the steps.*

BELOW LEFT *Despite the overcrowded look of this stone trough in Kas Koeman's small garden in Boskoop, Holland, several conifers happily co-exist there. Prostrate* Juniperus communis *'Corielagan' (left) and* Juniperus procumbens *'Nana' (right) cascade to the ground. The taller pyramid is* Picea glauca *var.* albertiana *'Laurin', and left of it* Chamaecyparis obtusa *'Nana Lutea'. In front is* Juniperus communis *'Berkshire', and right at the base is* Pinus heldreichii *'Smidtii'. The silver-blue is* Juniperus horizontalis *'Blue Pygmy' and the bright yellow* Chamaecyparis obtusa *'Fernspray Gold'. Planted 5 years, they need frequent watering in summer and will soon need pruning and thinning.*

BELOW RIGHT Cedrus deodara *'Cream Puff' makes a good container plant, given ample fertilizer and water. It is improved by pruning in early spring to promote creamy-white new shoots.*

winter without drying out. They can then be removed to make way for spring or summer plantings.

When choosing plants, consider not only the size of your container but also the position it will be placed in, whether full sun or half-shade. In general terms, go for plants that are hardy in your region and reasonably drought-resistant. Some yews and pines, particularly *Pinus strobus* and its cultivars, need good drainage and will also tolerate drought. *Thuja orientalis* cultivars generally make great container plants – they withstand drought well and are hardy outside in Britain in winter, but they would not survive cold northerly Scandinavian or American winters. *Chamaecyparis lawsoniana* cultivars will not withstand drought as well as *Chamaecyparis obtusa*. See the Directory (page 82) for clues on genera and species, even if not all cultivars are individually included. If you have a frost-free greenhouse or conservatory, you can enjoy experimenting with the less hardy warm temperate or subtropical species in containers. Wonderful examples include the Norfolk Island Pine (*Araucaria heterophylla*), the Kashmir Cypress (*Cupressus cashmeriana*) and *Cupressus macrocarpa* 'Goldcrest' – all of these can be house or conservatory plants which can be taken outside in summer. *C. m.* 'Goldcrest' is hardy in much of

Britain, but susceptible to frost damage in a container in more severe winters.

Conifers can be grown either as single specimens in a container with no other plants, or perhaps underplanted with some non-competing annual, perennial, bulb or ornamental grass; or they can play their part in an association in a big enough container. The objective is to create seasonal changes and contrasts. A blue Campanula comes into flower just as a *Thuja orientalis* 'Aurea Nana' puts on its new golden yellow shoots in early summer. The always useful *Ophiopogon planiscapus* 'Nigrescens' creates extra drama at the base of *Calocedrus decurrens* 'Berrima Gold' for year-round contrast. Always ensure that there is not too much competition among the plants for space, moisture and light.

BELOW LEFT *A raised concrete trough (resistant to freezing) in this Connecticut garden borrows from Japan with a single dwarf* Pinus parviflora, *one stone and low-growing alpines.*
BELOW CENTER *This 8-year-old* Sciadopitys verticillata *at Iseli Nurseries in Oregon seems happy in its restricted environment, serving as a backdrop to* Chamaecyparis pisifera *'White Pygmy',* Taxus cuspidata *'Aurescens' and a creeping thyme.*
BELOW RIGHT *The colorful* Calocedrus decurrens *'Berrima Gold' makes a striking contrast with the black-leafed* Ophiopogon planiscapus nigrescens *in early spring.*

JAPANESE GARDENS AND BONSAI

Through their unique and distinctive garden culture, the Japanese have given the rest of the world at least two widely copied garden forms in which conifers are an important ingredient – the Japanese garden and its diminutive art form, bonsai. The first is a distinctive garden design, and the second (literally meaning "to plant in a tray") a creation that reflects the beauty of nature in a pot or container.

Much of Japanese garden philosophy is based on the creation of something that not only replicates nature but is a part of it, blending wherever possible into the surrounding landscape. Both garden plants and bonsai are artfully contrived, usually to look much older than they are; they become places and objects that create scenes of tranquillity and shrines to nature. In gardens, this includes the careful placing not only of plants but also of stones, rocks, gravel and water. Japanese gardens are seldom gaudy, but are colorful in spring and autumn and more restful in the heat of summer. Color comes from new foliage and bright flowers such as azaleas in spring, while brilliant autumn foliage is carefully mixed in among evergreens.

Conifers such as the Japanese Black Pine (*Pinus thunbergii*) and the Japanese White Pine (*Pinus*

The Flat Garden in the renowned Portland Japanese Garden in Oregon was designed by Professor Takuma Tono and planted in the early 1960s. Raked Shirakawa sand, imported from Japan, represents the sea, with dwarf Pinus mugo *on the island. Other pines are carefully trained* Pinus thunbergii *and* Pinus contorta *var.* contorta, *a restful green in autumn against the colored leaves of Japanese maples and* Cornus kousa. *In spring the garden is brilliant with Japanese azaleas.*

parviflora) and their cultivars have long been the obvious choice for main structure plants, the former with its often craggy outline and fissured bark a favorite for the selected specimen tree or focal point. Pruning and training young plants to look older than they are, both in gardens and for bonsai, calls on the same traditional practices and is a skilled and time-consuming task. Training canes are used for positioning and tying the branches, and unwanted shoots and branches are thinned out. This process continues through much of the tree's life after it is moved to a garden. Ancient Japanese gardens, if well planted, adapt and change over the centuries as any garden must – they are living entities and their plants will continue to grow, although control is achieved by pruning. Those gardens that have not changed are primarily the Zen Buddhist and dry landscape gardens, where raked gravel and rocks are used to represent lakes and islands.

We cannot all visit Japan to see the great and revered gardens there, but some excellent examples have been created by professional Japanese gardeners and designers in many other parts of the world, including those in the botanic gardens in Missouri

In this garden near Aomori, northern Japan, spacious for that country, most of the plants are severely pruned, not only to create pleasing forms but to retain their scale and to prevent crowding. The mature pines are thinned and shaped to look even older than they are: representing old specimens in nature, they are intended to dominate the landscape. Pruned shrubs and conifers hang close to the rocks, and the wooden bridge is adorned with the spreading tentacles of Juniperus procumbens.

and Chicago, one in Portland, Oregon, and Kew Gardens, England. The home gardener can create a Japanese corner, scaling it down in size. Japanese gardens are meant to look natural, but this look is man-made and it is a lot of work – plants have to be trained to develop the natural look, then maintained as they grow. Not everyone will want a perfect replica of a Japanese garden, nor the work involved in achieving it.

Pinus parviflora 'Glauca' and *P. p.* 'Negishi', with their spreading branches, can be pruned to resemble older trees, and the Tanyosho Pine or Japanese Umbrella Pine (*P. densiflora* 'Umbraculifera') develops attractive bark with age. Other conifers often used are the Sawara Cypress (*Chamaecyparis pisifera*), *Juniperus chinensis*, particularly the form *J. c.*

In this garden in northern Japan, a mature Pinus thunbergii *has been bent and shaped early in life. Its lower branches have been removed to reveal the fissured bark, while other branches have been individually trained to sweep downward so that the tree resembles an ancient one in a wild landscape. Its height and spread tower above the controlled garden below, where rounded shrubs and conifers are pruned annually.*

'Kaizuka', and *Sciadopitys verticillata* (also the Japanese Umbrella Pine). These are Japanese natives, but it is not always necessary or even advisable to use only Japanese plants. *Pinus thunbergii*, for instance, is not always available in Europe and may not grow as well as *Pinus sylvestris*, which with age has an equally craggy, irregular growing habit and attractive bark. If you are gardening in, say, the northwest US, you could equally well create a garden using native American plants, and prune them to mimic nature in the traditional Japanese way. However, you will then be making something different, in the local idiom. It will not be a Japanese garden, any more than Japanese whiskey is Scotch!

For both the Japanese garden and bonsai, correct pruning is the ultimate key. In bonsai, both the top growth and the roots are pruned. The plants are made to mimic mature older specimens by exposing their roots and bark, thinning out their branches and pruning new growth before it can develop. Root-pruning on established specimens takes place every three years or so, and enables certain types such as *Pinus parviflora* to live as perfect replicas of nature for two or three hundred years.

The idea of growing trees in containers is thought to have originated in India, and was then picked up by the Chinese, who were the first known practitioners. The Japanese, who learned much from Chinese culture, adapted and developed the practice as an art form at least as early as the twelfth century, though the term "bonsai" was not used until the early eighteenth century. The pines were among the first conifers chosen, *Pinus thunbergii* and *Pinus parviflora* in particular. Some of the most revered bonsai plants were originally collected from rocky, windswept hills, cliffs and mountains where their roots were exposed and they were bent by the prevailing wind. These were root-pruned and trained in a container.

Most bonsai these days originate from nursery-grown plants, seedlings, cuttings or grafts. At its highest level, creating bonsai is a very specialized craft – specimens are developed by accredited bonsai masters, and plants originating in the wild in Japan command vast sums of money. But interest and appreciation are widespread and bonsai is extremely popular among hobbyists and general gardeners throughout the world. At the annual Chelsea Flower Show in London there are many displays of bonsai, and do-it-yourself kits and specialist books are available in most garden centers. Miniature, dwarf and slow-growing conifers are the perfect subjects for this treatment. If you want to buy a ready-made bonsai, go to a reputable or specialist garden center – many plants offered as bonsai may not be genuine, but simply rather crudely pruned plants put into pots or trays.

It is amazing what can be grown in these relatively small, shallow trays with very little soil. Usually this is a loam-based, free-draining soil which for conifers can be given an annual slow-release fertilizer. The contained plant will soon become rootbound, so watering is essential, usually on a daily basis from spring to autumn. But avoid overwatering, especially

Three magnificent bonsai specimens at Iseli Nurseries, in Oregon, are displayed on special stands on a damp autumn day. Left is a 30-year-old Pinus parviflora, *grafted onto the lower stem of* Pinus thunbergii, *so that later in life the latter's attractive bark will add an appearance of age. Center is a 40-year-old* Juniperus chinensis *'Shimpaku', its bark revealed by careful pruning and shaping. Right is a dwarfed 30-year-old* Ginkgo biloba, *its autumn leaves contrasting with the* Picea pungens *'Procumbens' to the rear. Behind and to the left is* Acer shirasawanum *'Aureum'.*

with pines. Fast-growing plants such as larches may need root-pruning every year, others every second or third year. Repotting may be necessary as plants grow. Bonsai conifers, unless they are subtropical species, should be grown in an outside natural environment, ideally displayed at eye level on shelves or raised platforms. Most plants will need some protection in winter from freezing winds and severe low temperatures, and in summer from prolonged exposure to full sun.

Bonsai is sometimes regarded as a rather cruel way to grow plants, but in fact the pruning and training is no different in principle from the treatment of other shrubs and conifers such as roses and yews. An art form that can be practiced by those with small gardens, a patio or balcony, it can become an absorbing and satisfying pastime – even an obsession!

CONIFERS AS GROUND COVER

Among the wide range of prostrate and semi-prostrate spreading conifers are many that make excellent ground cover for garden and landscape. Though there are forms of fir, spruce and tsuga that are prostrate and very effective, the juniper and yew cultivars are most widely used. Thirty to forty years ago, ground-cover junipers were used extensively alongside US highways, but with low maintenance they have not always stood the test of time. For garden use, careful consideration should be given to likely growth rates and the need for early pruning. Ground-hugging plants such as *Juniperus horizontalis*

Some prostrate and semi-prostrate conifers make excellent ground cover, most preferring good drainage. Juniperus, Taxus *and* Cephalotaxus *are among the most commonly used, but lesser-known types are also worth considering. Shown here are* Microbiota decussata *with its bright green summer foliage, and* Pinus mugo *'Wintergold' with* Erica cineria *growing through it. The winter foliage of this combination can be seen on page 69.*

'Wiltoni' and 'Emerald Spreader' make carpets of color, but these are sometimes not dense enough to prevent weeds coming through. Low-growing forms such as *Juniperus procumbens* 'Nana' make excellent ground cover for a bank or over a wall, and need good drainage.

A range of semi-prostrate plants, in different heights, shapes and colors, is perhaps the most effective choice, since between them they will block out light entirely. *Juniperus × pfitzeriana* 'Aurea' is one of the most vigorous; *J. × pfitzeriana* 'Gold Sovereign' and 'Saybrook Gold' are more golden. Different heights and textures can be achieved with the steel-blue *Juniperus squamata* 'Hunnetorp'. *J. communis* 'Green Carpet' is one of the most ground-hugging of the species, though the rather somber *Juniperus communis* 'Repanda' is more vigorous and widely used. Some cultivars described as semi-prostrate will actually reach well over 6ft (1.8m) after not too many years, particularly if planted in a semi-

In the Miller garden, Seattle, the dwarf prostrate Tsuga canadensis *'Cole's Prostrate' has been imaginatively used as ground cover to line a pathway in semi-shade. This plant is slow-growing in early years, but gradually builds up into a mound, particularly if it is pruned from the side, so that the branchlets cascade downward. Autumn leaves should not be allowed to accumulate for long on conifer foliage, as in time they may create bare patches.*

shady position. Check the Directory (page 82) for an indication as to rates of growth and eventual size.

Other conifers can be used alone or with other plants for ground cover. Most prefer sun or at least no more than semi-shade to maintain a dense habit. Yews and their close relation cephalotaxus do best in shady spots; in dry areas, they may need strict attention to watering until they are well established. *Taxus baccata* 'Repandens', dark green in summer and almost black-green in winter, is a good selection. Other prostrate green-foliaged selections include the hardier cultivar *T.* × *media* 'Cross Spreading'. Those

with golden foliage are not always bright in summer in the shade, let alone in winter; the brightest semi-prostrate form in winter is perhaps *T. baccata* 'Corley's Coppertip'.

One of my favorite ground-cover conifers is *Microbiota decussata*, with lacy foliage that changes color with the seasons; coming from Siberia, it is very hardy. The spreading dwarf pines are also suitable: *Pinus mugo* 'Corley's Mat' stays reliably low, as does *P. sylvestris* 'Hillside Creeper'. I hesitate to recommend the Prostrate Blue Spruce (*Picea pungens* 'Prostrata' or 'Procumbens') since, despite its name, without pruning it is anything but prostrate. *Picea abies* 'Repens' makes a pleasing spreader, with green foliage. More dramatic is *Picea abies* 'Inversa'; more often seen trained up a stem, it will make a rope-like carpet if left untrained, but it is not totally weedproof. *Tsuga canadensis* 'Cole's Prostrate' is a choice form for semi-shade.

In general, there are only a few rules to follow when planting conifers for ground cover. Check the rates of growth and ultimate size before selecting and planting. Ensure that no perennial weeds exist where you propose to plant. Space the plants sufficiently so that they do not meet for, say, three or four years; in the meantime, you can plant low-growing perennials between them to keep down the weeds, or mulch the ground with composted bark or other weed-free material. Be prepared to weed and prune if necessary. Perhaps consider including some vertical plants, conifers or others, to add structural interest. If you have only limited space, but want a spreading plant for its effect on the corner of a pathway, remember to prune it from an early age to improve its density.

And a few warnings. The prostrate forms may look like a carpet or a lawn you could walk on, but they will not tolerate much trampling. When conifers get very dense, they can hide small rodents in winter; these can chew the bark, revealing dead shoots the following spring. Some junipers are susceptible to dieback caused by *phomopsis* (juniper blight; see Pests and Diseases, page 182).

CONIFERS FOR TOPIARY, LIVING SCULPTURES AND UNUSUAL FEATURES

Like bonsai, topiary is at its best an art form – sculpture created from living plant material. The practice dates back to Roman times; today, many topiary and sculpted plants are grown in Italy and exported to the rest of Europe. Topiary gardens or features have long been fashionable in Britain – one of the oldest living examples, at Levens Hall in Cumbria, consists mostly of box and yew over three hundred years old, cut and closely manicured in shapes and forms as attractive in close up as from a distance, with dark and golden yews silhouetted against the sky and casting long shadows in summer and winter. In North America, one of the outstanding examples is at Ladew Gardens in Maryland, the depicted hunt with horse and hounds as amusing as it is imaginative. Most larger garden centers offer a

Shown here are some creative topiary examples from Berta and Nate Atwater's garden in Rhode Island. Taxus × media 'Hatfield', 30 years old, have been pruned to make a hand and pointing fingers. In the corner, Cedrus atlantica 'Glauca Pendula' has been given an unusual form suited to its position. Cedrus deodara 'Silver Mist' is on the left. Pruning is done twice a year, at mid-summer and in early autumn.

wide range of specimen and "starter" topiary, using different types of plants but strongly featuring conifers, particularly yew.

Topiary is the art of training, then clipping, plants to desired shapes – balls, pyramids, animals, birds. In older properties, traditional shapes are often chosen, but topiary is increasingly coming to include other plants and other influences, particularly from Japan. Terms like "cloud-pruned" (*hindu-pan*) and "pom-pom" are beginning to appear, denoting certain forms and shapes. Larger plants, such as *Pinus thunbergii* or *Pinus sylvestris*, are pruned to show the branching system, the foliage closely cropped at least every year. Cloud pruning creates branches that terminate in foliage in the shape of clouds. The Iseli nurseries in Boring, Oregon were pioneers of unusual topiary.

Not only are Japanese-style pruned specimens now available, but the art of *dantsugi* is also practiced – that of grafting two or three different cultivars onto the same rootstock. One eye-catching combination uses *Chamaecyparis obtusa* 'Nana Lutea', *Juniperus squamata* 'Blue Star' and *Thuja occidentalis* 'Rheingold' – colorful, if not exactly natural. Many nurseries turn unwanted specimens of *Chamaecyparis pisifera* 'Boulevard' or *Picea glauca* var. *albertiana* 'Conica' into cloud-pruned, tiered or pom-pom shapes, skilled work that greatly increases the value and saleability of the plant in a short space of time.

The Jean Iseli Memorial Garden at the Iseli Nurseries, Oregon, planted in 1982, was named after its charismatic founder. BELOW LEFT *A grouping of three* Picea glauca var. albertiana *form a display of living statuary. The tiered 'Conica' in the center are encircled by the dumpy 'Hobbit' and 'Jean's Dilly'.* BELOW RIGHT *Nearby is a* Chamaecyparis pisifera *'Squarrosa Intermedia', its birds sculpted from dense, pruned side growths.*

In Europe, Italian and Dutch nurseries are at the forefront of creating unusual specimens and topiary. Many ball-shaped or pendulous plants are top-grafted onto a stem, an ideal way to show off weeping plants that would otherwise be prostrate. Such specimens can be grown in containers or in open ground in the garden. A conifer widely used in this way without top grafting is *Cedrus atlantica* 'Glauca Pendula'. Trained up, it can form an arch or almost anything you want – perhaps a monster-like plant leading in several directions. It can be as successful in the small (but not miniature) garden as in a larger one; as with bonsai and topiary, a combination of training and pruning can allow the gardener to be in control, even though it might not look like it.

This is an exciting new area of gardening, in which devotees are experimenting with ever more unusual and extreme plant combinations. It may have only minority appeal, but demand for it is increasing. Living sculpture and topiary fit gardens both new and old, in town and country, with a choice of plants to suit each. Yews may still be the favorite for topiary, but a great many other plants can be used to create different effects, and not all require constant attention. As always, it is important to select those that are reliably hardy in your area.

SOME OF THE

Best Conifers

From the vast range of conifers, the following is a varied selection that, while concentrating on the dwarf and slow-growing conifers more suitable for smaller and average-sized gardens, gives important background information on genera and species, including origins. Most will be available from general and specialist sources (see page 184) although some may be specific to certain countries; new types are always being made available on a regular basis in Europe, North America, Japan and Australasia. Wherever possible, alternatives or comparable cultivars are briefly described.

Growth rates Because mature size and growth rate are among the most important considerations when making a choice, some arbitrary categorization is necessary. However, climate, aspect and soil conditions

PREVIOUS PAGES *The new "All Seasons" bed in the author's garden has been planted with a flowing river of Japanese Blood Grass (Imperata cylindrica 'Rubra') between conifers and heathers. Left foreground is* Cedrus deodara 'Feelin' Blue', *behind* Tsuga canadensis 'Elizabeth', *left of* Cedrus deodara atlantica 'Glauca Pendula' *in the distance. The white plumes of* Pennisetum villosum *are in the center, with a large 25-year-old* Pinus koraensis 'Winton' *on the right, and a dwarfer 20-year-old* Pinus heldreichii 'Smidtii' *on the extreme right.*

vary, and all have a bearing on growth rate, form and, to some extent, color – so use these categories as a guide only. With selections made available only recently, ultimate heights can only be guessed at.

Zoning, cold and heat tolerance Most North American gardening reference books and catalogues give guidance by indicating hardiness zones on a map denoting low temperature tolerance. This can be used only as a guide, since other factors are also important (see pages 32, 33) – in particular, tolerance of heat and humidity. In this book we have widened the definition somewhat by giving low and high figures after the Z. For example, it is suggested that *Abies balsamea* 'Piccolo' (below) is hardy to Zone 2, and happy in warmer climates to Zone 6; beyond this its heat tolerance may be limited.

See zone map on page 186.

Abbreviations Measurements given are for the plant named in the main heading of each section, unless indicated otherwise.

H	Approx. 10-year height, without pruning
W	Approx. 10-year width, without pruning
UH	Ultimate height
UW	Ultimate width
G	Indicates that a plant is likely to have been propagated by grafting (see page 180).
Z	Zones to indicate hardiness

ABIES

The Silver Firs are a genus of about 50 species originating in cooler temperate zones of the northern hemisphere. Conical or columnar in habit, most make imposing forest trees, too large for gardens, but there are several excellent dwarf, even miniature, selections. The attractive silver of the undersides of the leaves is more pronounced in certain cultivars.

Though generally of easy cultivation with few pests and diseases, they prefer cooler temperate zones with a cold winter period and moister soils; highly alkaline soils, particularly dry chalk, are less suitable. Cones are held erect above the branches but, with a few notable exceptions, they are borne only on mature plants; most dwarf cultivars will not bear cones at all.

ABIES BALSAMEA

Abies balsamea 'Nana'. Popular dwarf selection of the Balsam Fir, discovered in the White Mountains of New Hampshire. It makes a rounded bush of dark green foliage, its brown winter buds opening to bright green shoots in late spring. Very similar, particularly in early years, are *A. b.* 'Hudsonia' and the rarer *A. b.* 'Prostrata'.

H 12in (30cm), W 12–18in (30–45cm)
UH 30–36in (75–90cm), UW 4–5ft (1.2–1.5m), Z 2–6

Abies balsamea 'Piccolo'. Attractive ball–like miniature with small, dark green leaves, densely packed branches and reddish-brown buds in winter. Ideal for alpine gardens and troughs.

H 10in (25cm), W 10in (25cm)
UH 24–30in (60–75cm), UW 30–36in (75–90cm), Z 2–6

ABIES CONCOLOR

The Colorado White Fir originates in Western North America up to Utah

A 12-year-old dwarf Balsam Fir, Abies balsamea *'Nana', England, autumn.*

and down to northwest Mexico. A large pyramidal or columnar tree, it often has striking gray-blue or silver-blue foliage. Tolerant of drier soils than many firs, it is not susceptible to aphids. Plants from seed vary, but several faster-growing selections have been made, as well as some dwarf and slow-growing forms, all of which are cold-hardy.

H 13–20ft (4–6m), W 6–10ft (1.8–3m)
UH 85–150ft (25–45m), UW 26–33ft (8–10m), Z 4–8

Abies concolor 'Compacta'. An excellent slow-growing conifer with somewhat stiff and irregular branches clothed in widely spaced needles, the older season's deep blue-green, the new a brighter blue-gray. An excellent specimen to contrast with other plants.

G; H 24–30in (60–75cm), W 24–30in (60–75cm)
UH 10–16ft (3–5m), UW 10–16ft (3–5m), Z 4–8

Abies concolor 'Archer's Dwarf'. Another slow-growing selection that gradually forms a dense upright bush of thin, curving, blue-gray needles.

G; H 3–4ft (90–1.2m), W 18–24in (45–60cm)
UH 16–26ft (5–8m), UW 8–10ft (2.5–3m), Z 4–8

Abies concolor 'Violacea'. Perhaps the bluest of the larger-growing selections most readily available, this is a conical tree with striking silver-blue needles. *A. c.* **'Candicans'**, whose needles are a paler gray-blue, has a similar growth rate. Ideal as a specimen plant or a backdrop in a larger garden, it should be given room to develop. Leading shoots may need training up a cane in early years.

G; H 13–16ft (4–5m), W 6–10ft (1.8–3m)
UH 50–80ft (15–25m), UW 23–33ft (7–10m), Z 4–8

Abies concolor 'Wintergold'. A relatively new introduction found as a

Abies koreana, *England, in early summer. The cones appear when the plant is quite young.*

seedling by the Horstmann nursery in northern Germany, this has narrow needles which in summer are grayish-green, sometimes tinged with yellow, but in winter brighten to a deep golden-yellow. It will eventually form a leading shoot.

G; H 30–36in (75–90cm), W 24–30in (60–75cm)
UH 16–33ft (5–10m), UW 10–13ft (3–4m), Z 4–8

ABIES KOREANA
The Korean Fir is an outstanding species of great ornamental value. Slow-growing, it forms a narrow symmetrical pyramid of glossy, dark green foliage, the needles bright silver

beneath. Most seedlings produce startling bluish-purple cones within ten years of age, often clustered together along the branches like blue candles. An almost bewildering number of selections and witch's brooms have been put into cultivation by collectors and specialists

H 6–10ft (1.8–3m), W 4–5ft (1.2–1.5m)
UH 26–40ft (8–12m), UW 16–23ft (5–7m), Z 5–7

Abies koreana 'Luminetta'. One of several seedling selections with golden foliage (many of the earlier ones are called 'Aurea'; this was first called 'Lutea'). Attractive pyramidal plants, their pale golden-yellow leaves may scorch in bright sun. Like the species, they produce cones (normally much paler in color), when quite young. **A. k. 'Goldener Traum'** ('Golden Dream') is an excellent new cultivar.

G; H 4–5ft (1.2–1.5m), W 3–4ft (90cm–1.2m)
UH 10–16ft (3–5m), UW 6–8ft (1.8–2.5m), Z 5–7

Abies koreana 'Silberlocke' (Silver Curls). Introduced by Gunter Horstmann (and originally named 'Horstmann's Silberlocke'), this distinctive slow-growing conifer has needles that curl upwards, clearly showing their silver undersides. Often slow to make a leading shoot unless pruned and kept as a bush, it will eventually make a medium pyramidal tree. Older plants cone freely, and on some branches the curled leaves are less pronounced. **A. k. 'Silver Show'** is similar.

G; H 5–6ft (1.5–1.8m), W 4ft (1.2m)
UH 33–40ft (10–12m), UW 6–8ft (1.8–2.5m), Z 5–7

Many miniature selections, most originating in Germany, have recently been introduced. They have stubby, densely packed branches, with the needle tips around the terminal buds exposing their silvery undersides. They include **A. k. 'Silberperl'** (Silver Pearl), **'Silberzwerg'** (Silver Dwarf) and **'Silberkugel'** (Silver Globe); all have merit for miniature collections, troughs or scree gardens.

G; H 12in (30cm), W 12in (30cm)
UH perhaps less than 3ft (90cm), UW 3ft (90cm), Z 5–7

ABIES LASIOCARPA

Abies lasiocarpa 'Arizonica Compacta'. This is among my top ten garden conifers. Slow-growing at first, it gradually forms a shapely specimen of dense, soft, gray-blue foliage. Its prominent, beige, resin-coated winter buds burst into bright silver-blue shoots in early summer, startling in their intensity. It is a good form of the species, the Alpine Fir, which originates in the mountainous regions of western North America. Very hardy, it will retain its lower branches well in an open position; best in cooler climates on good deep soil. Plant it where in future years it can stand alone as a specimen, because you will not want to part with it.

G; H 3–4ft (90cm–1.2m), W 24–36in (60–90cm)
UH 26–40ft (8–12m), UW 10–16ft (3–5m), Z 3–7

ABIES NORDMANNIANA

The Caucasian Fir or Nordmann Fir, although eventually large, has great ornamental value and is fast replacing the Norway Spruce (*Picea abies*) as a favorite Christmas tree, since it retains its attractive needles much longer after cutting. Native to the Caucasian mountains, it varies widely from seed although most assume a pyramidal, later a conical, habit; branches are horizontally arranged in tiers, and clothed to the ground in open situations. Luxuriant, glossy dark green needles are marked beneath by two bright silvery bands; the winter buds are an attractive reddish-brown.

H 16–20ft (5–6m), W 7–10ft (2–3m)
UH 100–130ft (30–40m), UW 23–33ft (7–10m), Z 5–7

Abies nordmanniana 'Golden Spreader'. An outstanding slow-growing conifer for cooler climates which arose as a seedling in Holland. Although it is flat-topped and spreading in early years, it will eventually produce a leading shoot that must be pruned away if it is not to grow pyramidal. For year-round color it is superb, its deep golden-yellow needles being particularly

Abies nordmanniana *'Golden Spreader',* 15 *years old, England, spring.*

bright in winter; the color dulls somewhat when bright yellow shoots appear in spring. It needs cooler temperate climates; best in full sun or, in areas of summer heat, in half-shade to prevent leaf scorch.

G; H 24–30in (60–75cm), W 24–36in (60–90cm)
UH 16–20ft (5–6m), UW 5–8ft (1.5–2.5m), Z 5–7

ABIES PINSAPO

The Spanish Fir originates in southern Spain and is distinctive for the way the rigid, blue-gray needles radiate outwards from the branches at right angles, quite sharp and prickly to the touch, giving it its other common name of Hedgehog Fir. Adaptable and surprisingly hardy, it tolerates better than almost all other firs hotter and well-drained conditions, including chalky and free-draining soils. Eventually it makes a broad pyramidal or conical tree, varying considerably from seed. Older specimens produce vivid red male flowers and cylindrical purple-brown cones. A particularly good blue-needled selection, *A. p.* **'Glauca'**, was introduced in France as long ago as 1867 and propagated by grafting.

H 10–16ft (3–5m), W 5–6ft (1.5–1.8m)
UH 80–115ft (25–35m), UW 26–40ft (8–12m), Z 7–8

Abies pinsapo **'Horstmann'**. A first-class selection for the smaller garden, although in time it will make a large, spreading bush. It develops an irregular form which may vary according to soil and situation, in time often developing stronger shoots that should be cut away to keep it compact.

G; H 18–24in (45–60cm), W 24–30in (60–75cm)
UH 10–16ft (3–5m), UW 10–16ft (3–5m), Z 7–8

ABIES PROCERA

In its native habitat in Washington, Oregon and northern California, the Noble Fir makes a magnificent large tree of up to 250ft (75m). It needs cool winters and moist conditions, and will not succeed in drier, chalky soils. A vigorous, narrow, conical tree, it is branched to the ground in open situations, clothed with soft, bluish-green needles. Once it has reached 20ft (6m) or more, impressive cones appear, often in clusters – these can

be as much as 12in (25cm) high and 3in (7.5cm) wide, greenish with yellowish bracts (see illustration, pages 18–19). Often the species and some cultivars have a mass of bright crimson male flowers in spring. Selections with more intense silver-blue foliage are usually found under the name *A. p.* **'Glauca'**.

H 16–26ft (5–8m), W 6–8ft (1.8–2.5m)
UH 100–250ft (30–75m), UW 26–33ft (8–10m), Z 5–7

A 20-year-old Abies pinsapo *'Horstmann', Norfolk, England, summer. It is the centerpiece to surrounding shrubs, grasses and perennials, giving structure and contrast in color and form.*

Abies procera 'Glauca Prostrata'. A most attractive and desirable conifer with brilliant silver-blue needles and, when mature, crimson male flowers in spring. Its prostrate habit is the result of grafting rather than any long-term tendency to remain low-growing. Although initially flat in habit, its upward shoots must be regularly pruned away if it is not to develop into an irregular, spreading bush determined to head for the sky. It makes a striking specimen among heathers or in a larger rock garden.

G; H 18–24in (45–60cm), W 30in–4ft (75cm–1.2m)

UH, UW controlled by pruning, Z 5–7

Abies procera 'Noble's Dwarf'. This little-known compact variant, more reliably prostrate than *A. p.* 'Glauca Prostrata', was selected from the old Noble Collection in Strybing Arboretum, Golden Gate Park, San Francisco. It will remain prostrate for some years unless a leading shoot is trained upwards; cones occasionally form on older plants.

G; H 12in (30cm), W 18–24in (45–60cm)

UH (variable, controlled by pruning) 16–26ft (5–8m),

UW 5–16ft (1.5–5m), Z 5–7

ARAUCARIA ARAUCANA
The Monkey Puzzle or Chile Pine, which originates from Arauco Province in Chile, can make an unusual, prehistoric-looking specimen, particularly when relatively young. It is the hardiest of several species native to South America and the southwest Pacific which include the Norfolk Island Pine (*A. heterophylla*; a beautiful tree which in cool temperate zones can be grown only as a house or conservatory plant). Initially slow-growing, it has an open habit when young, the trunk and branches densely clothed in radially arranged sharp, spiny, dark green leaves that point forward along the stems. Young trees

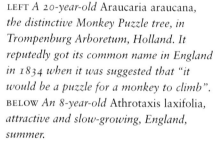

LEFT *A 20-year-old* Araucaria araucana, *the distinctive Monkey Puzzle tree, in Trompenburg Arboretum, Holland. It reputedly got its common name in England in 1834 when it was suggested that "it would be a puzzle for a monkey to climb".*
BELOW *An 8-year-old* Athrotaxis laxifolia, *attractive and slow-growing, England, summer.*

make handsome specimens for some years as container or patio plants. With age, the tree becomes pyramidal and the lower branches drop to reveal a base and stem resembling an elephant's trunk; the downward-sweeping branches curve sharply up at the tip, each terminal shoot resembling a monkey's tail. Large rounded cones the size of coconuts are quite showy on older trees, turning from green to russet-brown over three years as the seeds ripen. Best grown on moist soils with room to develop and ideally protected from persistent cold winds, the Monkey Puzzle can live for hundreds of years.

H 5–10ft (1.5–3m), W 4–5ft (1.2–1.5m)
UH 65–100ft (20–30m), Z 7–8

ATHROTAXIS LAXIFOLIA

The Tasmanian Summit Cedar is the hardiest of just three species native to western Tasmania, well worth garden space if the climate allows. It forms a conical bush of light green with scale-like leaves pressed to the branches; in a sunny situation, the new growth in early summer is bright yellow. It remains dwarf or slow-growing for some years, particularly on drier soils, but given the moist conditions it prefers, it will grow more quickly. With age, small, light yellow cones appear freely, turning brown as they ripen; older trees also develop attractive reddish-brown bark, which becomes deeply fissured and peeling.

H 5–8ft (1.5–2.5m), W 3–4ft (90cm–1.2m)
UH 50–100ft (15–30m), UW 16–26ft (5–8m), Z 8–9

CALOCEDRUS DECURRENS

The Incense Cedar, one of only three species in the genus, is a distinct and very beautiful conifer, native mostly to higher elevations from central California to Oregon. The best

selections form a single main trunk with short, upward-curving branches that carry flattened foliage sprays of rich, glossy, green, scale-like leaves. Other plants may fork near the base with several stems to make a broader column. Older trees develop red-brown fissured bark. The wood has long been used for building and for making pencils; like the foliage, when crushed it is pleasingly aromatic. As a garden plant it is pretty adaptable: it makes a superb specimen for the larger garden and is also effective planted in a group. The form **C. d. 'Pillar'** seems reliably narrow in habit.

H 13–20ft (4–6m), W 3–5ft (90cm–1.5m)
UH 80–130ft (25–40m), UW 6–25ft (1.8–8m), Z 5–8

Calocedrus decurrens
'Aureovariegata'. You will either love or hate this selection, which has splashes of gold in variable amounts all over its green foliage – try to find a plant with even color distribution. It should be pruned to improve density; growth rates may vary considerably.

G; H 6–10ft (1.8–3m), W 2–4ft (60cm–1.2m)
UH 40–80ft (12–25m), UW 6–16ft (1.8–5m), Z 5–8

Calocedrus decurrens **'Berrima Gold'.** A recent introduction from Australia, this fully golden plant is already proving an excellent choice for the garden. Pale yellow-green in summer, it is deep gold in winter with almost orange shoots lighting up the garden; best color will be achieved in full sun or light shade. Light pruning of side branches to increase density will help it to form a broad column.

G; H 5–8ft (1.5–2.5m), W 24–36in (60–90cm)
UH 33–50ft (10–15m), UW 6–10ft (1.8–3m), Z 5–8

Calocedrus decurrens 'Berrima Gold', 6 years old, in winter when its color is at its brightest, Norfolk, England.

CEDRUS

The common name of Cedar was bestowed by early plant explorers on several conifers, but there are only four closely related species of the genus Cedrus, the true Cedars, which spread from north Africa and the eastern Mediterranean to the western Himalayas. Most eventually form large trees, densely foliaged and pyramidal in early years, some characteristically flat-topped with age. The needle-like leaves are spirally arranged in clusters along the branches and branchlets, some quite sharp to the touch. On established trees, male cone-like flowers and female cones stand above the branches; the flowers soon shed pollen, and the cones take two years to ripen. From the species have come some excellent garden conifers, adaptable to a wide range of soils, though there is a limit to their cold

hardiness at or below Z 6. They withstand pruning well.

CEDRUS ATLANTICA

Cedrus atlantica 'Glauca'. The Atlas Cedar originates in the Atlas mountains of Algeria and Morocco, where it makes a massive tree; it was introduced to Britain around 1840. The selection *C. a.* 'Glauca', which was found in the wild in 1845, will in the right place make an imposing and beautiful specimen, but it is suitable only for large gardens. Open, ascending branches become more horizontal with age, the side ones

Cedrus atlantica *'Glauca Pendula', a remarkable plant, here trained as an arch to make a feature in Kas Koeman's garden in Boskoop, Holland. Without training it would remain prostrate. This plant is 20 years old.*

sweeping gracefully downwards. The needles are a brilliant, intense silver-blue; older trees develop masses of yellow cone-like flowers which shed their pollen in late summer, and pale green barrel-shaped cones which ripen to brown in their second year. This is a hardy, adaptable conifer, tolerant of heat and drought; it can be pruned to restrict its size or espaliered along a wall.

Mostly G; H 13–20ft (4–6m), W 6–10ft (1.8–3m)
UH 110–150ft (35–45m), UW 33–80ft (10–25m), Z 6

Cedrus atlantica 'Fastigiata'. Although its blue-gray foliage is less striking in color than that of 'Glauca', this columnar cultivar makes a fine accent plant, gradually forming a densely branched pillar, with almost vertical branches, that broadens with age. Much more suitable for the

smaller garden than 'Glauca'.

G; H 10–16ft (3–5m), W 24–36in (60–90cm)
UH 50–80ft (15–25m), UW 6–10ft (1.8–3m), Z 6–9

Cedrus atlantica 'Glauca Pendula'. This fascinating blue-needled weeping conifer is so adaptable to being trained that it can be all things to all gardeners. Leave it to its own devices and it will sprawl unevenly across the ground or, more picturesquely, over a wall or down a bank. Train its main branch upwards for 7–10ft (2–3m) and its branches will cascade down like a fountain. It can be made to form an archway or even a pergola; for both smaller and larger gardens it is a living sculpture. Once established, it grows at the rate of 8–16in (20–40cm) per year, and should be trained and pruned as required.

G; Z 6–9

CEDRUS BREVIFOLIA

The Cyprian Cedar (syn. *Cedrus libani* subsp. *brevifolia*) is found in the wild only in Cyprus, and is quite distinct from other cedars as it has much shorter needles. It is slow-growing at first but eventually of some size; its branches arch out from the main stem, pendulous at the tips, with foliage of deep green. It should be more widely grown for its slow growth and picturesque outline; cones on older trees are a bonus. It withstands heat and drought better than *C. deodara*. Two dwarf cultivars of note are *C. b.* 'Kenwith' and *C. b.* 'Epsteinianum'.

H 6–10ft (1.8–3m), W 6–8ft (1.8–2.5m)
UH 50–65ft (15–20m), UW 13–23ft (4–7m), Z 7–9

CEDRUS DEODARA

The Deodar originates from Afghanistan to the western Himalayas. Although considered the least hardy of the species, it has variations in form, color and hardiness according to region. Grown from seed, the plants

Regular pruning can keep Cedrus deodara *small, as here in Suffolk, England.*

generally have attractive bluish-gray young foliage that goes greener with age. Its pyramidal habit is enhanced by graceful, weeping branch tips. It becomes large in time and wide-spreading, losing its lower branches, so space should be allowed for development. Male cone-like flowers appear on older trees; ovoid female cones occur later and more seldom. Many selections are suitable for the garden, from tall to miniature. Most are propagated by grafting; those rooted by cuttings will be slower-growing. Some early shoots are susceptible to spring frosts. It is quite adaptable to pruning and to a wide range of soils where it is not too dry.

H 10–16ft (3–5m), W 6–10ft (1.8–3m)
UH 80–110ft (25–35m), UW 33–40ft (10–12m), Z 7–9

Cedrus deodara 'Aurea'. The plants that used to be sold under this name, from the original selection introduced in 1866, have mostly been superseded by more recent introductions, all with golden-yellow foliage. All need full sun to reflect their best color, which is more intense when they are young. 'Aurea' itself may gradually fade to light green; *C. d.* 'Gold Mound' is more golden and probably more vigorous. Pruning for some years will improve density and restrict size; growth rates are similar.

G; H 10–16ft (3–5m), W 6–8ft (1.8–2.5m)
UH 50–80ft (15–25m), UW 26–33ft (8–10m), Z 7–9

Cedrus deodara 'Blue Dwarf'. A seedling discovery in Holland, this is ideal for the smaller or alpine garden. Like all other cultivars produced from grafts it is initially slow-growing, later making a globular bush with grayish-blue foliage. *C. d.* 'Pygmy' is similar.

G; H 12–18in (30–45cm), W 18–24in (45–60cm)
UH 3–4ft (90cm–1.2m), UW 4–5ft (1.2–1.5m), Z 7–9

Cedrus deodara 'Cream Puff'. Perhaps the best of several cultivars with cream or white foliage, this is one of many selected at Alan Goddard's nursery in Victoria, Vancouver Island, which are improvements on *C. d.* 'Albospica'. Though not widely available, they are attractive and worth growing, but the conditions must be right – all are susceptible to cold winds, spring frosts and sunscorch from extreme heat. 'Cream Puff' is the most vigorous, making a small pyramid of creamy-white foliage, brighter in summer. Prune to enhance density. Dwarfer white-needled forms, worth trying if you can find them, are *C. d.* 'Silver Mist', 'Snowsprite' and 'White Imp'.

G; H 5–6ft (1.5–1.8m), W 3–4ft (90cm–1.2m)
UH 23–33ft (7–10m), UW 10–16ft (3–5m), Z 7–9

Cedrus deodara 'Feelin' Blue'. An outstanding selection made in Boskoop, Holland, in 1987. A hardy, spreading, prostrate plant with densely furnished blue-gray needles, its branches are pendulous at the tips. It is ideal for any garden, attractive on a mound or over a rock. It does not seem to make a leading shoot.

G; H 12–18in (30–45cm), W 3–4ft (90cm–1.2m)
UH 4–5ft (1.2–1.5m), UW 13–23ft (4–7m), Z 7–9

Cedrus deodara 'Golden Horizon'. A vigorous cultivar from Holland with bright golden-yellow needles in summer, lighter yellow-green in winter. It varies considerably in habit, perhaps because of the influence of grafting; low and prostrate initially, it can become semi–prostrate. Upright branches must be cut out to prevent a tall, upright tree. It is difficult to estimate growth since pruning is undoubtedly necessary.

G; H 18–24in (45–60cm), W 5–6ft (1.5–1.8m)
UH 3–6ft (90cm–1.8m), UW 23–33ft (7–10m), Z 7–9

Cedrus deodara 'Karl Fuchs'. One of several selections introduced from Germany from seed collected in Paktia Province, Afghanistan, all considered hardier than the type. A distinctive plant, it makes a narrow pyramid of striking silver-blue-gray foliage, with deeper blue-green inner needles; 'Eisregen' is similar.

G; H 10–16ft (3–5m), W 5–6ft (1.5–1.8m)
UH 50–65ft (15–20m), UW 10–13ft (3–4m), Z 7–9

Cedrus deodara 'Nana Aurea'. This may be an illegitimate name, but it is an excellent Deodar, though dwarf it is not. In early years it makes a compact pyramid of bright golden-yellow, brighter in summer than winter. If pruned early it can be kept relatively dwarf, with pendulous tips like a cascading waterfall. Let it go and it will eventually become large. Several other golden-foliaged forms exist.

G; H 10–13ft (3–4m), W 5–6ft (1.5–1.8m)
UH 50–65ft (15–20m), UW 16–26ft (5–8m), Z 7–9

CEDRUS LIBANI

The Cedar of Lebanon, closely related to *C. atlantica*, is seldom planted in Britain these days, having been overtaken by *C. a.* 'Glauca', which is considered more ornamental. Its needles are shorter and greener than *C. atlantica*. A narrow pyramid when young, it eventually makes the typical flat-topped tree seen in large gardens and churchyards throughout Britain. The dwarfer and slower-growing selections described below are more suitable for average gardens.

H perhaps 10–16ft (3–5m) in ten years
UH 100ft (30m) or more, Z 5–9

Cedrus libani 'Green Knight'. A desirable but very slow-growing dwarf, with clusters of short, deep green needles and an irregular

branching habit. *C. l.* 'Green Prince' is less compact, in time making an open-branched pyramid. Both are somewhat bonsai-like in habit and ideal for pots and miniature gardens.

G; H 12in (30cm), W 8–12in (20–30cm)
UH 6–10ft (1.8–3m), UW 24–36in (60–90cm), Z 6–9

Cedrus libani 'Sargentii'. A first-class selection with a prostrate, eventually mounded, habit and bluish-green needled branches. If given the opportunity, these will cascade down a bank or over a wall. Much slower than the large-growing *C. l.* 'Pendula', it is ideal for a rock garden. New growth can be struck by spring frosts.

G; H 12–18in (30–45cm), W 24–30in (60–75cm)
UH 24–30in (60–75cm), UW 10–13ft (3–4m), Z 6–9

CEPHALOTAXUS

A small genus closely related to the yew (*Taxus*), originating in China, Japan and Korea. They resemble large-leafed yews and, like them, are adaptable to sun or shade and quite tolerant of alkaline soils. Unlike yews, it is happy on moist soils, but it must not be waterlogged. The species make small, upright, bushy or spreading trees, useful and decorative as background or ground cover, with good heat tolerance.

CEPHALOTAXUS FORTUNEI

The Chinese Plum Yew, variable in habit, usually makes a large bush or a small tree with erect stems, with glossy green leaves on widely spaced branchlets. Male and female flowers appear on separate trees. The female fruit, resembling pale green olives ripening to brown, contains the seeds – enclosed in a fleshy, plum-like capsule, these turn from green to purplish in autumn.

Growth rate perhaps 6–10 (15–25cm) in a year, Z 2–9

CEPHALOTAXUS HARRINGTONIA

The Japanese Plum Yew makes a broad, variable but mostly spreading bush, with soft dark green needles, light green beneath. It is hardier and slower-growing than *C. fortunei*.

Growth rate variable, c. 4–6in (10–15cm) a year, Z 6–9

Cephalotaxus harringtonia 'Fastigiata'. Perhaps the most gardenworthy form is this upright plant, first a fastigiate, later a vase-shaped plant with deep green needles. It is a good accent plant. Good low-growing, spreading forms, excellent for shade, are *C. h.* 'Duke Gardens' and *C. h.* 'Prostrata'.

H 4–5ft (1.2–1.5m), W 12–24in (30–60cm)
UH 10–16ft (3–5m), UW 5–8ft (1.5–2.5m), Z 6–9

Cephalotaxus harringtonia *'Fastigiata', 35 years old, Holland, summer.*

CHAMAECYPARIS

The False Cypress is one of the most popular groups of garden conifers, with multitudes of cultivars raised and selected from seed and sports. The species originated from North America, Japan and Taiwan; the trees are closely related to the true cypress (*Cupressus*) and were for many years listed under that name. Species and cultivars grow successfully where there is adequate moisture, although *C. obtusa* is pretty resilient to heat and drought. None except *C. thyoides* will tolerate wet or waterlogged conditions for long. Most dislike open positions exposed to cold, drying or freezing winds, particularly when young, so they need protection from open ground after transplanting. The smallest cultivars are suitable for troughs and sinks, while the larger-growing trees give background and shelter, providing form and foliage color all year round.

CHAMAECYPARIS LAWSONIANA

The Port Orford Cedar, or Lawson Cypress, is native to the Siskyou mountains of northern California and Oregon where it makes a large forest tree up to 165ft (50m). After its discovery in 1854, the first seed sent to Europe went to the Lawson nursery near Edinburgh, Scotland, where the first plants in Britain were raised, giving the species its name. With its enormous range of ornamental cultivars, it has become the most popular of garden conifers in Britain – so much so that many of the selections are simply called "Lawsons". With so many to choose from, including many tall conifers with blue, green or golden-yellow foliage, the species itself is seldom used as a garden or landscape plant. However, mixed seedlings are often sold for hedging, since their variation can be more attractive than a single variety hedge. They need care and regular pruning; as young plants they are susceptible to windburn and roadside salt spray. Culturally, both species and cultivars prefer moist soils with good drainage; plants in higher rainfall areas grow more quickly than those in drier climates, although some drought is tolerated. *C. lawsoniana* is not as adaptable to extremes of heat, drought and cold as *C. obtusa*.

It is somewhat ironic that this North American native species is now far more popular in other countries, particularly northern Europe, than in its own. In its native California and Oregon, nurseries are reluctant to grow the cultivars because of their susceptibility to the fungal disease Phytophthora, which is prevalent in warm, moist conditions and attacks the roots; sadly, it has now probably spread from nurseries back to infect the native plants. Though most cultivars are hardy to zone 6, golden and cream-foliaged forms need some shelter from cold winds and intense sunlight in their early years; dessication of foliage can occur in severe winters. Some are less tolerant of heat and cold. There is room to describe only a few of the most distinctive types here.

Chamaecyparis lawsoniana 'Aurea Densa'. One of three seedlings selected and introduced between the two world wars by the nursery of W. H. Rogers at Chandlers Ford, Hampshire, England, this is among the finest dwarfs for year-round color. Though slow, it soon makes an attractive specimen; in a sunny position it will be almost brighter yellow in winter than in summer. It forms a round-topped cone of rather rigid branches, the foliage stiff to the touch. Another of the Rogers three, *C. l.* 'Minima Aurea', is almost identical but slightly more pyramidal in habit when young.
H 12–18in (30–45cm), W 12in (30cm)
UH 6–8ft (1.8–2.5m), UW 3–4ft (90cm–1.2m), Z 6–8

Chamaecyparis lawsoniana 'Bleu Nantais'. A cultivar introduced by the French nursery of Renault Frères in 1967, it is similar in habit to the popular but overused *C. l.* 'Ellwoodii'. It has bright silver-blue juvenile foliage, dense at the base, more open at the top. Rather similar is the

Chamaecyparis lawsoniana *'Minima Aurea', which is very similar to 'Aurea Densa'. A 10-year-old plant in Yorkshire, England.*

slightly bluer *C. l.* **'Chilworth Silver'**, raised in England. *C. l.* **'Blue Surprise'**, a seedling raised in Holland, makes a more narrowly columnar bush of startling blue. All fulfil a role as colorful slow-growing conifers, good for containers and combinations with other plants.

H 4–5ft (1.2–1.5m), W 12–24in (30–60cm)
UH 16–26ft (5–8m), UW 3–4ft (90cm–1.2m)
All sizes approximate, Z 6–8

Chamaecyparis lawsoniana **'Broomhill Gold'**. Distinctive in its cone-shaped form, this has erect branches and deep golden-yellow foliage, especially when young, becoming yellow-green with age. Unlike the similar *C. l.* **'Golden Pot'**, it does not hold its color in winter.

H 8–10ft (2.5–3m), W 18–24in (45–60cm)
UH 33–50ft (10–15m), UW 5–6ft (1.5–1.8m), Z 6–8

Chamaecyparis lawsoniana **'Columnaris'**. One of the most popular and widely grown selections, with bluish-gray flattened foliage sprays, much brighter on new summer growth than in winter. Habit may vary according to soil and situation: it grows narrower on drier, thinner soils, and broader on heavier types. A superb accent plant, it is also used widely in northern Europe for hedging. Plants of equal merit and similar habit are *C. l.* **'Grayswood Pillar'** and *C. l.* **'Pelts Blue'**; both are narrower than 'Columnaris', and the latter a deeper blue.

H 6–10ft (1.8–3m), W 12–18in (30–45cm)
UH 33–50ft (10–15m), UW 24–36in (60–90cm)
All sizes approximate, Z 6–8

Chamaecyparis lawsoniana **'Dik's Weeping'**. Unusual and dramatic, its narrow upright form is suitable for the smaller garden. A leading shoot should be trained upwards, and its long branches and branchlets of bright green foliage will cascade down.

H 10–13ft (3–4m), W 4–5ft (1.2–1.5m)
UH 50–65ft (15–20m), UW 10–13ft (3–4m), Z 6–8

Chamaecyparis lawsoniana **'Ellwoodii'**. This popular plant, although sold by the million as a pot plant, is not a dwarf, although it and similar forms are suitable for tubs and containers. It has a neat bushy habit when young, with several upright leading shoots and dark blue-green feathery foliage that eventually forms a cone. Plants can vary in habit depending on what part of the parent tree the cuttings were taken from. It has produced many sports and mutations.

H 6–8ft (1.8–2.5m), W 24–36in (60–90cm)
UH 23–33ft (7–10m), UW 5–6ft (1.5–1.8m), Z 6–8

Chamaecyparis lawsoniana **'Ellwood's Gold'**. The first sport with golden foliage, but the color is pronounced only in summer on new growth, and is more evident on younger plants; the foliage turns green in winter. It had a further mutation on a plant in Surrey: a white-tipped sport which, when propagated by cuttings, made a new variegated cultivar called *C. l.* **'Silver Threads'** with golden-yellow foliage flecked with creamy-white.

H 5–6ft (1.5–1.8m), W 18–30in (45–75cm)
UH 20–26ft (6–8m), UW 24–36in (60–90cm), Z 6–8

Chamaecyparis lawsoniana **'Ellwood's Pillar'**. Introduced from Holland in 1977 (but possibly originating from the US), this makes a tight, narrow column of blue-green foliage – a miniature 'Ellwoodii', it takes its time

Chamaecyparis lawsoniana *'Ellwood's Pillar', 20 years old, winter, England.*

exceeding 10ft (3m). It produced a gold sport, discovered in Bedfordshire in 1990 and called *C. l.* **'Ellwood's Gold Pillar'**, which is slower-growing, similar in habit, and a better, deeper gold than 'Ellwood's Gold'.

H 3–4ft (90cm–1.2m), W 12in (30cm)
UH 10–13ft (3–4m), UW 18–24in (45–60cm), Z 6–8

Chamaecyparis lawsoniana **'Golden Pot'**. One of the brightest yellow Lawsons, this is a sport from *C. l.* 'Pottenii', with similar soft, feathery upright-branching foliage but much slower in growth. It maintains its color all year round. It may be prone to sunscorch in hotter climates. Use it as a focal point with contrasting foliage, perennials, grasses or heathers.

H 4–5ft (1.2–1.5m), W 24–30in (60–75cm)
UH 20–26ft (6–8m), UW 10–13ft (3–4m), Z 6–8

Chamaecyparis lawsoniana **'Golden Wonder'**. One of the most popular and one of the hardiest medium to large

Chamaecyparis lawsoniana *'Golden Pot', 15 years old, shown in winter with* Erica carnea *'Springwood White', Norfolk, England.*

A perfect Chamaecyparis lawsoniana *'Lane', 15 years old, in Yorkshire, England, contrasting with the autumn colors of Japanese Maples.*

golden-yellow Lawsons, introduced in Holland in 1963. Pyramidal in early years and more conical with age, it maintains a deep golden-yellow all year round. Good as a specimen plant if there is space, also as background.

H 10–13ft (3–4m), W 3–5ft (90cm–1.5m)
UH 33–50ft (10–15m), UW 10–13ft (3–4m) Z 6–8

Chamaecyparis lawsoniana 'Grayswood Feather' . A narrow, flame-shaped cultivar more suitable for the smaller garden, with dark green feathery foliage on upright, somewhat flattened branch sprays.

H 6–8ft (1.8–2.5m), W 18–30in (45–75cm)
UH 26–33ft (8–10m), UW 5–6ft (1.5–1.8m), Z 6–7

Chamaecyparis lawsoniana 'Green Globe'. Discovered as a seedling in New Zealand, this true miniature is now found all over the world.

It slowly makes a dense cushion of rich green foliage that visitors seem impelled to stroke. A perfect dwarf for rock gardens, troughs and sinks. It is more rounded and compact than the otherwise similar **C. l. 'Gnome'.**

H 6–8in (15–20cm), W 8–12in (20–30cm)
UH 12–18in (30–45cm), UW 24–36in (60–90cm), Z 6–7

Chamaecyparis lawsoniana 'Green Pillar'. I recommend this rich green conifer as among the best of the medium Lawsons. It is almost a green counterpart to the bluish-gray **C. l. 'Columnaris'** and, with its narrower form, a better garden plant than **C. l. 'Erecta Viridis'**, which eventually gets large with open branches. Both this and another deep green cultivar, **C. l. 'Green Hedger'**, can be recommended for hedges; all are also ideal as foils to forms with blue or golden foliage.

H 8–10ft (2.5–3m), W 24–36in (60–90cm)
UH 33–50ft (10–15m), UW 6–10ft (1.8–3m), Z 6–8

Chamaecyparis lawsoniana 'Ivonne' (syn. 'Yvonne'). Distinctive recent Dutch introduction of conical habit with pale yellow, somewhat laminated, foliage sprays, brighter and deeper yellow in summer. Like all golden forms, its color is best in full sun.

H 8–10ft (2.5–3m), W 3–4ft (90–120cm)
UH 25–40ft (8–12m), UW 8–10ft (2.5–3m), Z 6–8

Chamaecyparis lawsoniana 'Lane' (syn. 'Lanei'). This popular taller-growing Lawson has golden-yellow leaves in summer, turning a brighter, clearer yellow in winter. Pyramidal when young. it eventually makes a broad column and will need space.

H 8–10ft (2.5–3m)
UH 50–60ft (15–18m), UW 10–16ft (3–5m), Z 6–8

Chamaecyparis lawsoniana 'Little Spire'. A distinctive and useful conifer introduced by the late Don Hatch in Devon; 'Little' has proved to be a misnomer! Considered a hybrid between *C. l.* 'Fletcheri' and *C. l.* 'Wissellii', it looks more like a smaller edition of the latter, making a similar show of bright crimson flowers on dark blue-green, somewhat congested, fern-like foliage in late spring. Its narrowly columnar form makes it a good accent plant.

H 6–10ft (1.8–3m), W 18–24in (45–60cm)
UH 33–40ft (10–12m), UW 4–5ft (1.2–1.5m), Z 6–7

Chamaecyparis lawsoniana 'Minima Aurea'. See *C. l.* 'Aurea Densa' (page 93).

Chamaecyparis lawsoniana 'Minima Glauca'. Widely grown dwarf making a compact, broadly pyramidal bush, with fan-shaped sprays of bluish-green foliage. These are quite soft to the touch but, like *C. l.* 'Aurea Densa', the plant has a rigid branching system.

H 18–24in (45–60cm), W 18–24in (45–60cm)
UH 10–13ft (3–4m), UW 5–6ft (1.5–1.8m), Z 6–8

Chamaecyparis lawsoniana 'Nidiformis'. Still the most widely grown of the prostrate or semi-prostrate Lawsons, it gradually forms a spreading bush of somewhat arching branches, carrying sprays of bright green fern-like foliage that droop gracefully at the tips.

H 24–36in (60–90cm), W 3–4ft (90cm–1.2m)
UH 5–6ft (1.5–1.8m), UW 13–20ft (4–6m), Z 6–8

LEFT Chamaecyparis lawsoniana *'Little Spire', Norfolk, England. The 25-year-old specimen, resembling its parent 'Wissellii' with age, dominates the plants around it in late summer. The main conifers to the left are* Picea mariorika *'Machala' and the blue* Picea pungens *'Prostrata'.*

Chamaecyparis lawsoniana 'Oregon Blue'. Appropriately, there is at least one good Port Orford Cypress raised in Oregon (and named after it), where the species originated. This forms a large tree with a strong leading shoot; the leaves are deep blue and the branch tips slightly pendulous.

H 10–13ft (3–4m), W 5–6ft (1.5–1.8m)
UH 50–65ft (15–20m), UW 10–16ft (3–5m), Z 6–8

Chamaecyparis lawsoniana 'Pembury Blue'. Undoubtedly one of the best of the taller Lawsons, with rather open early upright growth that soon develops into a broad column – it is bright silver blue, particularly on new growth tips in summer. It is ideal as a specimen plant, or colorful background plant mixed with other tall golden and green cultivars. Allow it space to develop. *C. l.* 'Spek', with foliage of a more grayish-blue, is also an excellent selection of similar growth rate.

H 8–10ft (2.5–3m), W 4–5ft (1.2–1.5m)
UH 33–50ft (10–15m), UW 8–10ft (2.5–3m), Z 6–8

Chamaecyparis lawsoniana 'Pottenii'. Introduced in 1924, this makes a narrow cone of dense, soft, feathery, light-green foliage. With age, it has a tendency to fall open, particularly in snow, heavy rain and wind: tie it in winter to prevent whole branches from coming out.

H 8–10ft (2.6–3m), W 24–36in (60–90cm)
UH 50–65ft (15–20m), Z 6–8

Chamaecyparis lawsoniana 'Pygmaea Argentea'. Though limited to relatively few climates or microclimates, this showy dwarf, first introduced over a hundred years ago, is at its best a real gem. Very popular in Britain, it slowly forms a bush with bluish-green inner foliage. In the right spot, the tips appear to have been splashed with cream or paint. In the shade it will stay green, however, so site it in sufficient sunlight, though not extreme or its foliage tips will scorch. It also needs protection from cold winds.

H 12–18in (30–45cm), W 12–18in (30–45cm)
UH 3–4ft (90cm–1.2m), UW 3–4ft (90cm–1.2m), Z 6–8

Chamaecyparis lawsoniana *'Pygmaea Argentea', 30 years old, in Norfolk, England, late summer.*

Chamaecyparis lawsoniana 'Wissel's Saguaro'. Six 6-year-old plants make a striking feature in Holland, late summer.

Chamaecyparis lawsoniana 'Summer Snow'. This slow- to medium-growing cultivar has the same characteristics of Lawsons, with light or pale green foliage in winter and, where conditions are right, creamy-white new growth in summer. It needs sun and good moist soil to perform regularly. *C. l.* '**Silver Queen**', an old variety more open in habit, and the Dutch introduction *C. l.* '**Luna**', are considered improvements, both making taller, narrower trees.

H 6–8ft (1.8–2.5m), W 3–4ft (90–120cm)
UH 23–33ft (7–10m), UW 8–13ft (2.5–4m), Z 6–8

Chamaecyparis lawsoniana 'Wissel's Saguaro'. A Dutch nurseryman selected this unusual mutation on a *C. l.* 'Wisselii'. It varies somewhat in its habit, but mostly makes a narrow, erect, irregularly branched specimen with dark blue-green congested foliage. Its similarity in appearance to the saguaro, the giant cactus, inspired the name. Slow, in time it makes a good accent plant for the smaller garden; a group of three or five is even more dramatic.

H 4–5ft (1.2–1.5m), W 8–12in (20–30cm)
UH 16–20ft (5–6m), UW 18–24in (45–60cm), Z 6–8

CHAMAECYPARIS NOOTKATENSIS

The Nootka Cypress, native from Oregon, north through British Columbia to Alaska, is a handsome, extremely hardy species. It looks similar to a *C. lawsoniana*, in the wild growing to over 100ft (30m), but has coarser foliage with a distinctive pungent smell when crushed (*C. lawsoniana* is more fragrant). The species grows in a broad cone shape, with erect branches, often sharply pendulous at the tips, carrying mostly light to mid-green foliage. Suitable only for the larger garden, it has produced relatively few distinctive garden forms. It is more vigorous in areas of high rainfall.

H 10–13ft (3–4m), W 3–4ft (90cm–1.2m)
UH 85–100ft (20–30m), UW 13–16ft (4–5m), Z 5–8

There are two or three selections with colored or variegated foliage, all with the species' columnar habit and pendulous branch-tips, but slower-growing. *C. n.* '**Aurea**', though somewhat dull in winter, has new growth of a deep golden-yellow, becoming greener with age. This is especially true of young plants in a

98

sunny situation. *C. n.* **'Aureovariegata'** has foliage splashed with cream to golden-yellow. *C. n.* **'Variegata'** has green foliage tipped with white. These are not perhaps in the first rank of ornamental conifers, but offer a good choice in places where *C. lawsoniana* may not be hardy.

Cultivars mostly G

H 8–10ft (2.5–3m), W 3–4ft (90cm–1.2m)

UH 50–65ft (15–20m), UW 8–10ft (2.5–3m)

Sizes approximate, Z 5–8

Chamaecyparis nootkatensis **'Green Arrow'.** One of several selections with a narrow, pillar-like form, with downward-sweeping branches close to the trunk and sometimes wider at the base (it is quite distinct from what is usually sold as *C. n.* 'Pendula', below). Quite fast-growing, it makes a highly dramatic sculptural conifer, even more so if planted in threes or fives according to space. Other selections worth considering are *C. n.* **'Jubilee'** and *C. n.* **'Strict Weeper'.**

G; H 10–13ft (3–4m), W 18–36in (45–90cm)

UH 33–50ft (10–15m), Sizes approximate, Z 5–8

Chamaecyparis nootkatensis **'Pendula'.** Under this name come some beautiful conifers with weeping foliage which need to be at least 10 years old before they can be appreciated. Young plants may need a leading shoot to be trained up a cane, but will soon develop their own. There are two main types: one with widely spaced arching branches and somewhat open habit, the branchlets of deep green foliage cascading beneath like streamers; the other denser and more columnar, with shorter branches and weeping branchlets. Allow room if they are to become specimens.

H 8–10ft (2.5–3m), W 5–6ft (1.5–1.8m)

UH 50–65ft (15–20m), Z 5–8

CHAMAECYPARIS OBTUSA

The Hinoki Cypress from Taiwan and Japan is considered sacred by followers of the Shinto faith. The large-growing species itself is seldom grown these days as a garden or ornamental conifer, but it has produced a wide selection of miniature, dwarf and slow-growing forms, many with golden or yellow foliage. The species makes a broadly conical tree with short, flattened sprays of glossy green leaves which have distinctive silver markings on the undersides; the foliage is pleasantly aromatic when crushed. Some of the dwarfer varieties, well manicured or trained, feature in typical Japanese gardens and also in bonsai culture. *C. obtusa* and its cultivars prefer a moist but not waterlogged soil, and tolerate drought better than any other Chamaecyparis species. Used to extreme heat and humidity in their natural environment, they are less happy in drier, colder climates and resent freezing winter winds and spring frost, particularly when young. They are excellent for containers. Some are genuine miniatures, with minimal annual growth of 1/2in (1.25cm). Cultivars are best obtained as plants on their own roots; grafting can distort growth in time.

H 8–10ft (2.5–3m), W 3–4ft (90cm–1.2m)

UH 50–65ft (15–20m), UW 10–16ft (3–5m), Z 5–8

Chamaecyparis obtusa **'Bess'.** A good slow-growing plant, selected by Joseph Reis in Long Island, New York, this forms a dense column of dark green.

H 8–12in (20–30cm), W 6–8in (15–20cm)

UH 5–6ft (1.5–1.8m), UW 18–24in (45–60cm), Z 5–8

Chamaecyparis obtusa '*Bess*', 9 years old, in Holland, summer; an ideal plant for the smaller garden.

Chamaecyparis obtusa **'Chilworth'.** This is one of many fine miniature selections raised at the W. H. Rogers nursery at Red Lodge, Hampshire, England, early in the twentieth century from seed of *C. o.* 'Nana Gracilis'. Some of these were sent to collectors in the US, where they grew very well. This has light green recurved foliage sprays; it is hummock-like when young, and broadly pyramidal with age. Other seedlings from this source, **'Bassett'** and **'Flabelliformis'**, have darker green foliage. All reach perhaps 36in (90cm) or less in thirty years. More compact and rounded are the 'tennis ball' types, **'Caespitosa'**, **'Intermedia'** and **'Juniperoides'**; they are ideal for troughs and miniature gardens, but need protection from frost and scorching sunlight.

Growth rate 1/2–1in (1.25–2.5cm) a year, Z 5–8

Chamaecyparis obtusa 'Crippsii'. This is one of the most beautiful of the medium-growing conifers, its rich golden-yellow foliage borne on wide-spreading branches, pendulous at the tips. A leading shoot should be trained up a cane when planting, and uneven sideshoots pruned away. Eventually, it will be broadly conical. Similar, but denser in habit, is *C. o.* 'Goldilocks', an excellent medium grower. *C. o.* 'Confucius', a selection from New Zealand, is more compact with bright golden-yellow foliage; both have prominent brown stems.

H 10–16ft (3–5m), W 5–6ft (1.5–1.8m)
UH 33–50ft (10–15m), UW 8–13ft (2.5–4m), Z 5–8

Chamaecyparis obtusa 'Golden Fairy'. One of several seedlings raised in 1966 by the noted collector Joel Spingarn, then of Baldwin, Long Island, from seed of *C. o.* 'Nana Gracilis' and *C. o.* 'Gracilis Aurea'. These new types have considerably increased the range of dwarf Hinoki Cypresses, and most are excellent plants for the smaller garden, for troughs, sinks and patios. Faster-growing than 'Golden Sprite', this forms a dense pyramid and, later, a conical specimen of golden-yellow. An attractive cultivar, with newer, more vigorous stems a bright coppery red. 'Golden Nymph' is similar. Joel Spingarn also introduced dwarfs and miniatures with green foliage – notably 'Elf', globe-shaped with tiny bright green leaves, and 'Ellie B', a later selection with densely packed sprays, initially flat-topped, later developing a more upright habit. They grow ½–1in (1.25–2.5cm) a year.

H 12–18in (30–45cm), W 6–8in (15–20cm)
UH 6–8ft (1.8–2.5m), UW 24–30in (60–75cm), Z 5–8

C. o. 'Golden Sprite' is a true miniature, making a ball of dainty

Chamaecyparis obtusa *'Kosteri', one of the most attractive dwarf forms. This is a 10-year-old specimen in Oregon, USA, autumn.*

golden foliage sprays; it can scorch so it needs shelter.

H 6–8in (15–20cm), W 6–8in (15–20cm)
UH 18–24in (45–60cm), UW 24–30in (60–75cm), Z 5–8

Chamaecyparis obtusa 'Kosteri'. One of my favorites, this is appreciated more with age, although it soon makes a pleasing plant. Its tiered branches and lacy foliage sprays develop into a broad, bright green column, bronzing somewhat in winter, often flat-topped when young. It is worth considering for an eventual specimen, so give it space when planting.

H 18–24in (45–60cm), W 12–18in (30–45cm)
UH 10–13ft (3–4m), Z 5–8

Chamaecyparis obtusa 'Lycopodioides'. This and similar forms are distinguished by their unusual foliage. They make rather open, erect bushes with thick stems bearing congested, often twisted, dark green foliage; some stems becoming fasciated, giving a cockscomb appearance. Slow-growing for some years, the plant benefits from pruning to make its branches more compact. **C. o.** 'Lycopodioides Aurea' is more attractive, with bright yellow new shoots, yellow-green by autumn with bronze stems.

H 3–4ft (90cm–1.2m), W 18–24in (45–60cm)
UH 10–16ft (3–5m), UW 5–6ft (1.5–1.8m), Z 5–8

Chamaecyparis obtusa 'Mariesii'. A choice, very slow-growing cultivar, introduced just a century ago. At its best, it forms a rounded, eventually broader, conical bush with all the foliage tips creamy-white and brighter in sun. It needs an open position but must be sheltered from freezing winds, spring frosts and intense midday sunlight which can scorch the foliage. Prune it lightly to improve density in its early years.

H 10–12in (25–30cm), W 12–18in (30–45cm)
UH 6–8ft (1.8–2.5m), UW 5–6ft (1.5–1.8m), Z 5–8

Chamaecyparis obtusa 'Nana'. The true form of this was introduced in 1867, and has had many imitators since; specialist nurseries should ensure you an authentic plant. Very slow to form a flattened bun of dark green, its delicate fan-shaped foliage sprays are cupped and slightly tiered; after some years it becomes a more rounded, but irregular, globe. It is ideal for troughs and miniature rock or alpine gardens.

H 4–6in (10–15cm), W 6–10in (15–25cm)
UH 12–24in (30–60cm), UW 24–36in (60–90cm), Z 5–8

Chamaecyparis obtusa 'Nana Gracilis'. The Dwarf Hinoki Cypress is one of the most popular dwarf conifers, with good reason. It forms a dense, often globe-like bush when

Chamaecyparis obtusa *'Nana Gracilis'*,
25 years old, Seattle, autumn.

Chamaecyparis obtusa *'Nana Lutea'* shows
its bright winter colour in Yorkshire, England.

young, becoming more broadly conical with age; its glossy, dark green foliage is held in thick bunches of shell-shaped sprays with silvery markings beneath. Growth will be slower in plants that are rooted from cuttings, but these are to be preferred over those that are grafted as the latter often produce more open bushes with vigorous shoots that distort the shape. Allow it space to develop; it makes a very good contrast to golden plants.

H 24–36in (75–90cm), W 24–30in (60–75cm)

UH 13–19ft (4–6m), UW 5–6ft (1.5–1.8m), Z 5–8

Chamaecyparis obtusa 'Nana Lutea'.

A sport from *C. o.* 'Nana Gracilis', this has proved a valuable garden conifer with good year-round color although, like others with golden-yellow foliage, it is prone to sunscorch in exposed positions when young. It forms a rounded, then more conical, bush of densely held golden sprays,

becoming a whiter yellow in winter in open situations. The occasional strong growths on older plants should be cut away. An older selection, **C. o. 'Nana Aurea'**, is faster-growing, more open in habit and has foliage of a deeper gold, but in my view 'Lutea' is a better plant. **C. o. 'Verdon'** (syn. 'Verdonii') is similar to 'Nana Lutea' but faster-growing and a deeper golden-yellow; it is an excellent plant and less prone to sunscorch.

H 18–24in (45–60cm), W 12–18in (30–45cm)

UH 8–10ft (2.5–3m), UW 4–5ft (1.2–1.5m), Z 5–8

Chamaecyparis obtusa 'Pygmaea'.

The name is something of a misnomer, for this plant eventually makes a large spreading bush unless it is trimmed. It has bright green foliage in summer, held in flattened sprays with prominent orange-brown shoots spreading outwards, the whole plant slightly bronzing in winter. Grafted

plants will be more vigorous and should be avoided.

H 18–24in (45–60cm), W 24–36in (60–90cm)

UH 5–6ft (1.5–1.8m), UW 8–10ft (2.5–3m), Z 5–8

Chamaecyparis obtusa 'Rigid Dwarf'.

This excellent, very slow-growing selection has an unimaginative name, but it is at least descriptive of its habit. It has stiff, upright branches clothed in rich, glossy, dark green foliage; these slowly form a narrowly pyramidal to conical shape. Very hardy, it is worth allowing it space to develop as a specimen.

H 18–24in (45–60cm), W 12–18in (30–45cm)

UH 10–16ft (3–5m), UW 5–6ft (1.5–1.8m), Z 5–8

Chamaecyparis obtusa 'Tempelhof'.

More widely available, easier-growing and reliable, this was raised by the conifer specialists Konijn in Holland. It is relatively quick to form a leaderless bush, and is later a densely foliaged conical plant. It has light green, fan-shaped sprays on almost horizontal branches, bronze-green in winter in more exposed situations, with the bonus of attractive orange-brown stems.

H 3–4ft (90cm–1.2m), W 18–24in (45–60cm)

UH 16–25ft (5–8m), UW 5–6ft (1.5–1.8m), Z 5

Chamaecyparis obtusa 'Tsatsumi Gold'.

This is an unusual, slow-growing dwarf conifer, with contorted, thread-like foliage. Its twisted shoots are a bright golden-yellow, while the foliage beneath and inside the plant is greener. With age it throws out thick protruding branches, and these are best pruned or shaped. It needs full sun, but some foliage scorch can occur.

H 18–30in (45–75cm), W 18–24in (45–60cm)

UH 8–16ft (2.5–5m), UW 4–5ft (1.2–1.5m), Z 5–8

CHAMAECYPARIS PISIFERA

The Sawara Cypress in its native Japan reaches an imposing 170ft (50m) but is seldom planted as an ornamental conifer these days. It has given us a wide range of valuable garden cultivars, most of which, however, bear little resemblance to the species. Green, blue, yellow and variegated forms exist, some with adult foliage like the parent species, others with juvenile or semi-juvenile leaves, and several with thread-like foliage. On some dwarfer forms there is a tendency for plants to revert by throwing up vigorous adult shoots, and these need to be pruned away as soon as they are noticed. Generally easy to please, they prefer some moisture at the roots and will succeed better in moist climates than dry ones although they will not tolerate waterlogging (good cultural practices can overcome some of these problems). Some will not thrive on dry chalk or highly alkaline soils. Most have pleasantly fragrant foliage when rubbed.

Chamaecyparis pisifera 'Boulevard'. Deservedly popular worldwide since its introduction in 1934 by Boulevard Nurseries in Newport, USA, this makes a dense bush of juvenile foliage, brilliant silver-blue in summer and duller in winter. Pyramidal when young, it eventually makes a broadly conical specimen of some size. At its best, it is an eye-catching plant; at its worst, if left unpruned, it can be quite dreadful! 'Boulevard' prefers a neutral soil, fertile with adequate moisture. Like many *C. pisifera* selections, it is improved by pruning and it looks stunning when quite closely pruned as a narrow pyramid; it makes an excellent container plant. It has produced several sports, but they need some years of testing before their stability as separate forms can be evaluated. *C. p.* '**Baby Blue**' is a dwarfer selection: when young, it makes a rounded, ball-like shape; later it is pyramidal and lighter in hue. *C. p.* '**Curly Tops**', similar in habit, color and growth to 'Boulevard', has leading outside shoots that grow in a spiral twist. All are best in full sun or very light shade, and provide excellent contrast to other plants.

H 5–6ft (1.5–1.8m), W 24–36in (60–90cm)
UH 16–26ft (5–8m), UW 5–8ft (1.5–2.5m), Z 5–8

Chamaecyparis pisifera 'Filifera Aurea' (sometimes wrongly named *C. p.* 'Filfera Aurea Nana'). The eventual size of the Golden Threadleaf Cypress (as given below) should not deter those with smaller gardens, since it is an excellent and showy cultivar, slow in early years and quite amenable to control by pruning without its

Chamaecyparis pisifera *'Curly Tops',*
10 years old, Holland, summer. It arose in
Australia as a sport on C. p. *'Boulevard'.*

effect being spoiled. It forms a low spreading bush when young, eventually developing into a broad pyramid of bright, golden-yellow thread-like pendulous foliage that maintains its color all year round. The side branches should be pruned to encourage leading shoots to develop, and the whole plant pruned to the size you want. It makes a superb specimen plant, especially against a dark background. *C. p.* '**Filifera Aureovariegata**' is another slow-growing threadleaf cypress, this time with dark green whipcord branches and scale-like leaves; the ends of the branches are irregularly splashed with gold and yellow. Similar to *C. p.* 'Filifera Aurea', but slower in growth.

H 3–4ft (90cm–1.2m), W 3–4ft (90cm–1.2m)
UH 23–33ft (7–10m), UW 16–23ft (5–7m), Z 5–8

Chamaecyparis pisifera 'Filifera Nana'. The common name of Dwarf Threadleaf Cypress indicates that this is much smaller, and more suitable for the average garden. It makes a low spreading mound of overlapping mid-green foliage, pendulous at the tips.

H 18–24in (45–60cm), W 24–36in (60–90cm)
UH 4–5ft (1.2–1.5m), UW 10–16ft (3–5m), Z 5–8

Chamaecyparis pisifera 'Gold Spangle'. One of the brightest golden-foliaged conifers, which arose as a sport from *C. p.* 'Filifera Aurea', with a real mixture of its parents' thread-like foliage and more adult fern-like sprays all on the same branch. The effect is unusual and striking, as is its color – few brighter plants exist in the winter garden. It may scorch as a young plant from exposure, so site it where it will be shaded for part of the day and give it shelter from freezing winds. Slow to develop a leading shoot, it is eventually pyramidal with pendulous shoot tips.

H 3–4ft (90cm–1.2m), W 24–30in (60–75cm)
UH 16–26ft (5–8m), UW 10–13ft (3–4m), Z 5–8

Chamaecyparis pisifera 'Nana'. This cushion-shaped plant, a selection introduced before 1890, has short, somewhat coarse, light-green sprays of adult foliage with silvery markings beneath; it is often suffused with gold in the summer. Less reliable, more open in growth and less stable in habit and, in my opinion, best avoided are **C. p.** 'Compacta' and **C. p.** 'Compacta Variegata'. Good garden choices include **C. p.** 'Nana Aureovariegata', with small flecks of yellow on light-green foliage, which exhibits a golden sheen on the leaves, particularly in winter; the similar **C. p.** 'Gold Dust'; **C. p.** 'Nana Albovariegata' (syn. 'Nana Variegata'), with deeper green leaves and occasional specks of white on the foliage tips, and the almost identical **C. p.** 'Silver Lode'. All of these should be reliably miniature, and will suit troughs, sinks and miniature gardens;

in 30 years they are unlikely to become higher than 12in (30cm) or wider than 24in (60cm).

H 6–8in (15–20cm), W 8–12in (20–30cm)
UH 12in (30cm), UW 18–24in (45–60cm), Z 5–8

Chamaecyparis pisifera 'Plumosa Aurea Nana'. The foliage on the Plumosa types is much softer and more feathery than on the species; it is termed 'semi-juvenile' foliage, though the real miniatures in the group have wholly juvenile foliage. C. p. 'Plumosa Aurea Nana' may be somewhat variable in habit but normally forms a bright yellow, feathery, broadly conical bush, its color in full sun held throughout the year. Similar in size and texture is **C. p.** 'Plumosa Flavescens', with lighter sulphur-yellow foliage, duller in winter. **C. p.** 'Plumosa Aurea' is much faster-growing, with a duller color not held in winter. All tend to open up with winter snow. Cut out stronger shoots and trim the plant as necessary.

H 3–4ft (90cm–1.2m), W 3–4ft (90cm–1.2m)
UH 8–13ft (2.5–4m), UW 6–8ft (1.8–2.5m), Z 5–8

Chamaecyparis pisifera 'Plumosa Compressa'. One of the dwarfest of conifers, this arose as a sport on C. p. 'Squarrosa', which accounts for its wholly juvenile foliage. Tightly compressed, diminutive leaves are densely packed into a cushion, light gray-green in winter, sulfur-yellow in summer. Not consistent in growth, it needs pruning to prevent it becoming uneven; cutting away stronger growths will maintain a tight, moss-like ball, ideal for sinks or troughs.

H 4–6in (10–15cm), W 8–12in (20–30cm)
UH 18–24in (45–60cm), UW 24–30in (60–75cm), Z 5–8

Chamaecyparis pisifera 'Snow'. An eye-catching dwarf conifer in summer, this has feathery foliage of a brilliant snow-white that tones down in winter. It is hardier than it looks, but needs placing in a light, sheltered position; it can scorch in the midday sun of hotter climates, and in winter frost. It gradually makes a rounded ball; occasional strong shoots should be cut away to maintain its dwarf habit.

H 10–12in (25–30cm), W 12in (30cm)
UH 3–4ft (90cm–1.2m), UW 2–3ft (60–90cm), Z 6–8

Chamaecyparis pisifera 'Squarrosa Sulphurea'. Probably the most popular garden conifer of the Squarrosa group, this has soft, fully juvenile foliage. Easy-growing, it makes a compact pyramidal bush with stronger shoots protruding; dull in winter, it is transformed in summer by fresh, bright, sulphur-yellow foliage. *C. p.* 'Squarrosa Intermedia' is best trimmed once or twice annually to make a dense tight ball of bright blue in summer; it will be quite different if

Chamaecyparis pisifera *'Nana', a true 15-year-old miniature, in Michigan, USA, planted with dwarf ornamental grasses.*

allowed to develop its open, somewhat undistinguished, natural habit.

H 3–5ft (90cm–1.5m), W 3–4ft (90cm–1.2m)

UH 16–26ft (5–8m), UW 10–13ft (3–4m), Z 5–8

Chamaecyparis pisifera 'Tsukomo'. A true miniature introduced by Joel Spingarn in Long Island, New York, which can be relied upon to remain a compact bun (though occasional reversions need to be pruned away), so it is ideal for troughs and sinks. It has minute, dark green leaves. **C. *p*. 'Pygmy'** is almost identical; **C. *p*. 'White Pygmy'** is a pleasing variation with light gray-green inner foliage and creamy-white tips. They all need good light in a sheltered position.

H 4–6in (10–15cm), W 4–6in (10–15cm)

UH 12in (30cm), UW 18–24in (45–60cm)

Sizes approximate, Z 5–8

CHAMAECYPARIS THYOIDES

The White False Cypress in its native habitat spreads along the eastern side of the US from Florida to Maine. Unlike all other species, it is tolerant – in fact it enjoys boggy and wet conditions, summer heat and winter cold. It has given some plants of ornamental value, and more selections are being made from the wild because of their adaptability. All the cultivars are easy to grow; they are best on moist soils, less happy on heavy clay or highly alkaline, chalky soils.

Chamaecyparis thyoides 'Andelyensis'. Slow-growing columnar form with many upright branches carrying short sprays of bluish-green adult foliage which turns a deep bronze in winter; a good accent plant.

H 3–4ft (90cm–1.2m), W 12–18in (30–45cm)

UH 10–16ft (3–5m), UW 3–5ft (90cm–1.5m), Z 5–9

C. *t*. 'Andelyensis Nana' is a dwarf

Chamaecyparis thyoides *'Rubicon'*, *10 years old, winter.*

This 8-year-old Cryptomeria japonica *'Elegans' turns purple-bronze in winter.*

form with adult foliage that makes an irregular mound-shaped bush. **C. *t*. 'Little Jamie'** and **C. *t*. 'Meth Dwarf'** are more desirable with semi-juvenile foliage, making tiny pyramids, green in summer, bronzing in winter.

H 24–30in (60–75cm), W 12in (30cm)

UH 5–6ft (1.5–1.8m), UW 18–24in (45–60cm), Z 5–9

Chamaecyparis thyoides 'Ericoides'. Of the many good dwarf selections of the White False Cypress bearing juvenile foliage this is by far the oldest, dating back to 1840 when it was introduced in France. It soon forms an oval bush with soft, feathery foliage, grayish-green in summer, turning deep purple in winter. It can be prone to frost damage and dessication where sun and freezing winds occur in winter, but it is safe sheltered from these and makes a striking plant. Other good selections – more compact but with equally intense

winter color – are **C. *t*. 'Rubicon', 'Purple Heather'** and **'Heatherbun'**. With age, they need tying in in winter to protect against snowfall.

H 24–36in (60–90cm), W 12–18in (30–45cm)

UH 5–6ft (1.5–1.8m), UW 24–36in (60–90cm)

Sizes approximate, Z 5–9

CRYPTOMERIA JAPONICA

The Japanese Cedar is the only species in the genus *Cryptomeria;* native to Japan and southeast China, it makes a tree of up to 150ft (45m). Too large for most gardens, it is seldom planted these days. It is pyramidal to conical in habit, with a strong central trunk which in mature years has beautiful red, peeling bark. The foliage is distinctive, with bright green spirally arranged leaves closely adpressed to the branchlets which resemble ropes or cords; most leaves bronze somewhat in winter. The many cultivars, often with accentuated winter bronzing, include dwarf and miniature types. Most Cryptomerias are easy to accommodate, preferring well-drained, moist soils. Some dwarf or colored foliage forms tolerate some shade; in exposed positions they need shelter from spring frosts and cold, desiccating winds.

H 13–20ft (4–6m), W 6–10ft (1.8–3m)
UH 100–150ft (30–45m), UW 25–40ft (8–12m), Z 6–8

Cryptomeria japonica 'Elegans'. A medium to tall selection, whose main attraction is soft, feathery, juvenile foliage which turns from light green in summer to deep purple bronze in winter. It can be leggy when young, with quite flexible stems; it must be pruned to maintain a bushy habit. A sunny situation will give the best winter color, which can be spectacular, particularly when associated with blue or golden conifers. It is less hardy than the species and need shelter from strong, cold winds. The lesser known **C. *j.* 'Elegans Aurea'** is bushier and a bright green in summer, with a pleasing yellow-green cast in winter.

H 7–10ft (2–3m), W 4–5ft (1.2–1.5m)
UH 50–70ft (15–21m), UW 13–23ft (4–7m), Z 7–8

Cryptomeria japonica **'Globosa Nana'**. A distinctive and attractive dwarf conifer with bright green leaves pressed to short, rope-like branches, which gradually builds to an irregular dome of some stature. The leaves are similar to C. *j.* 'Spiralis' but are not twisted around the stem; they turn a light bluish-purple in winter.

H 24–36in (60–90cm), W 3–4ft (90cm–1.2m)
UH 10–16ft (3–5m), UW 16–23ft (5–7m), Z 6–8

Cryptomeria japonica **'Sekkan'** (syn. 'Sekkan–sugi'). At its best, this cultivar, introduced in Pennsylvania,

Cryptomeria japonica *'Sekkan', 9 years old, in Yorkshire, England, autumn.*

is a superb foliage plant, whose summer growth is a brilliant creamy-white, a beacon among contrasting foliage plants such as the purple-leafed Japanese maples. In winter it turns a light greeny yellow. It must be sited with care, sheltered from spring frosts, desiccating winds and extreme sunlight, all of which lead to scorching of its delicate foliage. Where it is happy, it will become large, but it takes pruning and could make an excellent container plant for some years. **C. *j.* 'Barabits Gold'**, which arose in Hungary, is similar and reputedly hardier.

H 6–10ft (1.8–3m), W 4–5ft (1.2–1.5m)
UH 33–65ft (10–20m), UW 13–23ft (4–7m), Z 7–8

Cryptomeria japonica **'Spiralis'**. Peculiar to some, attractive to others, this makes an unusual specimen, its rope-like branchlets clothed with bright green leaves, twisted spirally around the stem. Unusually for the species, it maintains its color all year round. Bushy or wide-spreading, it is very slow-growing in early years, but without pruning it is likely to form one upright leading shoot and eventually attain some size. Pruning is highly recommended.

H 3–4ft (90cm–1.2m), W 18–24in (45–60cm)
UH 10–26ft (3–8m), UW 10–16ft (3–5m), Z 6–9

Cryptomeria japonica **'Tansu'** (sometimes listed as C. *j.* 'Yatsubusa').

This is an attractive dwarf that deserves to be more widely known. It slowly forms a broad pyramid of mid-green juvenile foliage, all shoots nodding at the tips and turning bronze in winter. For a real miniature gem, look for **C. j. 'Tenzan Sugi'**, perhaps the smallest Cryptomeria, which makes a tight ball of congested deep green leaves, bronzing in winter; it is hardy but needs protection from early morning sun in spring frost areas. The latter is excellent for troughs, and for miniature gardens and bonsai.

H 18–24in (45–60cm), W 12–18in (30–45cm)

UH 4–5ft (1.2–1.5m), UW 4–5ft (1.2–1.5m), Z 6–9

Cryptomeria japonica 'Vilmoriniana'. Imported from Japan and introduced in France over a hundred years ago, this is still a popular dwarf. Slow at first, it soon makes a globular bush of tightly packed, rigid, deep green foliage, which turns a russet-bronze in winter. **C. j. 'Compressa'** is similar, but its foliage is more tightly held and redder in winter; **C. j. 'Birodo'** is more conical. There have been a few recent selections of similar habit and growth rates, with different colored foliage: **C. j. 'Tilford Gold'** is light yellow in summer, pink-tinged in winter; **'Golden Promise'** and **'Vilmorin Gold'** have creamy-white new shoots. All are attractive, but susceptible to scorching in open situations.

H 12–18in (30–45cm), W 12–18in (30–45cm)

UH 3–4ft (90cm–1.2m), UW 3–4ft (90cm–1.2m), Z 6–9

CUNNINGHAMIA LANCEOLATA
Cunninghamia lanceolata 'Glauca'. The Chinese Fir makes a large forest tree in its native central and southern China, but is not normally considered for garden use except in this selection, 'Glauca'. At best it makes a very handsome specimen, hardier than the

Cunninghamia lanceolata *'Glauca', near Seattle, USA, autumn. Regular pruning keeps it small and promotes new growth.*

species, but it needs shelter from strong, cold and dessicating winds, and from severe or spring frosts. It is best in light shade, on acid, moist, free-draining soil. With most of these requirements, you may be rewarded with a spectacular specimen, a broad pyramid of blue-green branches and slightly pendulous foliage like a large-leafed yew or Cephalotaxus; its new growth is a startling powder blue. By nature large, it can be kept compact by hard pruning. One or two dwarfs or miniatures of rounded habit provide a texture different from most: **C. l. 'Bánó** (syn. 'Compacta') and **C l. 'Little Leo'** are green, bronzing in winter.

H 10–16in (3–5m), W 5–6ft (1.5–1.8m)

UH 33–50ft (10–15m), UW 10–16ft (3–5m), Z 7–9

× CUPRESSOCYPARIS LEYLANDII
This hybrid, commonly called the Leyland Cypress or simply Leylandii or Leyland, could be termed *the* plant of the twentieth century, so great has its effect been on our gardens and landscape. Although several intergeneric hybrids are listed under *Cupressocyparis leylandii*, the best-known are those that have come from various accidental crosses between *Cupressus macrocarpa*, the fast-growing Californian Monterey Cypress, and *Chamaecyparis nootkatensis*, the much hardier northwest American Nootka Cypress (which even now is under a possible reclassification as a *Cupressus*, a true cypress). The first seedlings were collected from a Nootka Cypress in England in 1888 and other selections followed until 1940, but it was not until the early 1950s that the plants began to be fully assessed for their value and introduced more widely into cultivation. Since then, over 60 million plants are estimated to have been sold in the UK alone, mostly for hedging.

× *C. leylandii* fulfils the wishes of most gardeners looking for quick results. It is versatile and adaptable to a wide range of growing conditions, including chalky soils and coastal regions, and it is fast-growing, to 3ft (90cm) a year. But once it has got away from the reach of pruning equipment, it is difficult to hold back, much to the dismay of those whose neighbors have planted a hedge and left it untrimmed until it eventually blocks out their light. It does, in fact, make an excellent hedge and screen (see page 40), but in its various clones it also makes an imposing columnar tree, likely to reach well over 100ft (30m). It is becoming widely grown around the world and has given several forms with golden or variegated foliage but, at the time of writing, only one dwarf. The most commonly grown clone is × **C. leylandii 'Leighton Green'**, a vigorous form with rich green foliage, now almost synonymous with the name Leylandii. All forms are best planted young without staking, to establish good roots to support the rapidly growing plant against strong winds, which can snap the branches.

H 26–33ft (8–10m), W 6–8ft (1.8–2.5m)

UH 100–130ft (30–40m), UW 10–16ft (3–5m), Z 6–9

× *C. leylandii* '**Castlewellan**' (syn. 'Castlewellan Gold'). This widely used cultivar with golden foliage arose in Northern Ireland in 1963, from seed of *Cupressus macrocarpa* 'Lutea' which had accidentally crossed with *Chamaecyparis nootkatensis*. It has the habit of the latter, with soft, feathery foliage and a dense columnar habit. Bright yellow in summer, it turns a rather dull greeny yellow in winter, touched with bronze in colder temperatures; as a hedge in shadier positions it will be quite green in winter. Other golden selections of note are × *C. l.* '**Gold Rider**' from Holland, a brighter gold the year through, as is the highly rated × *C. l.* '**Golconda**', which makes a narrow column of bright golden-yellow foliage; both are prone to some foliage damage in exposed situations. A few selections have been made from sports or variegated shoots, such as × *C. l.* '**Harlequin**' from England and × *C. l.* '**Silver Dust**' from the USA, but they are not of great garden value and can become large very quickly.

H 20–26ft (6–8m), W 5–8ft (1.5–2.5m)

UH 65–80ft (20–25m), UW 10–16ft (3–5m)

Sizes approximate, Z 6–9

CUPRESSUS

Originally, this genus (the cypress) of about 25 species also included all the chamaecyparis (False Cypress) species, but in 1842 the taxonomists

× Cupressocyparis leylandii *'Golconda'. One of the brightest golden Leylandiis, this 6-year-old plant in Norfolk, England, makes an eye-catching centerpiece to other conifers, grasses and perennials;* × C. l. *'Gold Rider' is similar. Both become large in time unless they are pruned.*

separated them. The true cypress has a sparser, almost scale-like foliage, with leaves closely pressed to the stem and much larger cones, which are very hard and last on the tree for some years. The species vary in habit. Some are native to western North America, others are from North Africa across to China. Most are tolerant of hot, dry conditions, aided by a tap root that goes down for moisture. This is not always an ideal attribute for a garden plant: in areas of higher rainfall the growth can be rapid, causing plants to blow over in strong winds. There are some excellent selections for garden use, although many are not hardy in colder temperate zones. On some species, canker is a serious problem. Cupressus are best planted young and in their final positions; if you do have to move them, prune the roots well a year or two beforehand.

CUPRESSUS ARIZONICA

The Arizona Cypress is also known as the Tough-Barked Cypress, after the fissured bark on old trees. It is seldom planted in gardens, most of the garden cultivars having been selected from

C. arizonica var. *glabra*, the Smooth-Barked Cypress. (Various closely related forms of *C. arizonica* occur in the wild from northern Mexico through Texas to Arizona, which has led to some confusion in their naming.) Hardier than most species, *C. a.* var. *glabra* is tolerant of drought and dry chalky soils, so it is a first-class choice for Mediterranean and hotter climates. With age, the bark becomes attractive, olive-green to purple-green, smooth and flaking to reveal circular silvery-white patches. An increasing number of good cultivars are available.

Cupressus arizonica var. glabra 'Pyramidalis'.

This perhaps best represents the species, making a tall, conical tree with blue-green winter foliage, bright silver-blue in summer. It is often grafted, but plants on their own roots are preferable.

H 13–20ft (4–6m), W 5–6ft (1.5–1.8m)
UH 50–65ft (15–20m), Z 7–9

Cupressus arizonica var. glabra 'Blue Ice'.

This outstanding selection from New Zealand, a great accent plant, has a narrow columnar habit and foliage of a striking silver-blue. '**Silver Smoke**', also from Duncan and Davies nurseries in New Zealand, is more blue-gray, fast-growing and more open with pendulous branch tips. '**Blue Streak**', of a similar growth rate, makes a conical to pyramidal accent plant. Two weeping forms from Australia are worth looking for: the gray-blue '**Raywood Weeping**', irregular in form unless a leader is trained, its branchlets cascading beneath; and '**Blue Spire**' (considered to be synonymous with 'Angaston') whose leading shoot also needs training in early years and whose

bright silver-blue foliage sweeps vertically downwards, making it a great choice for the smaller garden. All are usually grafted, but plants on their own roots are preferable.

H 13–16ft (4–5m), W 4–5ft (1.2–1.5m)
UH 50–65ft (15–20m), UW 6–10ft (1.8–3m), Z 7–9

Cupressus arizonica var. glabra 'Sulphurea'.

A form with densely held foliage, slow to make a column of light creamy-yellow in winter, brighter sulphur-yellow in summer. It is best in full sun, and will eventually be tall, so it is an excellent choice for the larger garden. '**Aurea**', also large, is more of a mustard-yellow and broader in habit. '**Chaparral**' has more juvenile foliage, which is creamy-white all year round and does not scorch even in full sun. 'Sulphurea' is often grafted.

H 7–13ft (2–4m), W 3–4ft (90cm–1.2m)
UH 50–65ft (15–20m), UW 6–10ft (1.8–3m), Z 7–9

CUPRESSUS LUSITANICA

Cupressus lusitanica 'Glauca Pendula'
This form of the Mexican Cypress has wide-spreading branches, with plume-like pendulous branchlets of a bright glaucous blue in summer, deeper blue in winter. It can be open when young, so pruning will improve density and restrict its size to fit the smaller garden. Quite tender, it needs protection from cold winds, but it is a beautiful specimen that should be planted more widely. It is best in full sun with good drainage.

H 10–16ft (3–5m), W 8–10ft (2.5–3m)
UH 40–50ft (12–15m), UW 13–20ft (4–6m), Z 8–9

CUPRESSUS MACROCARPA

The Monterey Cypress was the × *Cupressocyparis leylandii* of the late nineteenth and early twentieth centuries – it and its cultivars were renowned for their fast growth. The

Cupressus arizonica *var.* glabra *'Blue Spire', a graceful, 15-year-old specimen near Melbourne, Australia, in spring.*

species, though it provides one of the parents of Leylandii, is now much less used for gardens or windbreaks. *C. macrocarpa* originates from a very small area on and surrounding the Monterey peninsula in California; inland it makes an upright tree with wide-spreading branches, while near the coast it is contorted and bends away from the prevailing salt-laden winds, like a natural bonsai. It has coarse, scale-like, dark green foliage and older trees freely produce nut-brown cones. Distributed across the world, it has settled in well in marine and milder areas. Seedlings and sports have arisen to create a number of cultivars – most, like the species, eventually large. The species and cultivars prefer moister climates and will freeze or desiccate in drier, colder regions; they are less hardy than *C. arizonica* cultivars but better as coastal plants. *C. macrocarpa* is variable from seed.

H 16–25ft (5–8m), W 8–10ft (2.5–3m)
UH 80–110ft (25–35m), UW 16–33ft (5–10m), Z 8–10

Cupressus macrocarpa 'Goldcrest'. One of the most attractive of golden-foliaged columnar *C. macrocarpa* cultivars, this will thrive only in conditions suitable for the species. Often sold as a houseplant, it has fine semi-juvenile foliage, making a dense column of bright golden-yellow, toning down in winter. For the smaller garden, the slower-growing *C. m.* 'Golden Pillar' is more suitable, making a narrow, compact cone. Both of these supersede the much taller but generally hardier *C. m.* 'Donard Gold' and *C. m.* 'Lutea'. Good accent plants, they are suitable for seaside locations.

H 13–20ft (4–6m), W 3–5ft (90cm–1.5m)
UH 40–65ft (12–20m), UW 7–10ft (2–3m), Z 8–10

Cupressus macrocarpa 'Greenstead Magnificent'. From Australia, this makes a prostrate bush of gray-blue, turning brilliant silver-blue in summer, the reddish-stemmed branchlets pendulous at the tips. It is vigorous in warmer climates but can be pruned to keep it to size; it can make a good container or patio plant. It is often sold top-grafted on to a stem of *C. macrocarpa*. It can be tender.

Mostly G; H 24–36in (60–90cm), W 4–5ft (1.2–1.5m)
UH 6–10ft (1.8–3m), UW 16–26ft (5–8m), Z 8–10

CUPRESSUS SEMPERVIRENS
The Italian Cypress or Mediterranean Cypress is so much a part of the Mediterranean landscape, with its narrow, vertical, pencil-like form, that few realize that in nature it is quite variable from seed; broader, bushy and spreading forms exist. It occurs from the Mediterranean to Iran and the Himalayas. Few plants are better at creating an imposing and dramatic accent than the pillar-like selections, with their dark green foliage and narrowly erect form. The most

Green and gold columnar cypresses make accent plants in Lindsey Gray's garden in Australia. Cupressus sempervirens 'Swane's Gold' (left) and C. s. 'Stricta' are both about 8 years old.

common, **C. s.** 'Stricta', comes fairly true from seed but will give variations; other selected cultivars are mostly grafted. All are best in well-drained soil and planted young; they prefer hot, dry climates but will adapt to cooler ones if they are given shelter from strong and cold desiccating winds. In hotter climates, canker is a problem, so nurserymen are seeking canker-resistent varieties. Selected cultivars include **C. s.** 'Gracilis', 'Green

Pencil' (syn. 'Greenspire') and **'Totem Pole'**. They are tighter in habit in hotter, drier climates; in cooler, wetter regions branches sometimes fall out.

H 10–13ft (3–4m), W 12in (30cm)
UH 33–50ft (10–15m), UW 24–36in (60–90cm)
Sizes approximate, Z 8–10

Cupressus sempervirens 'Swane's Gold'. Introduced by Swane's nursery near Sydney, Australia, around 1960, this superb accent plant is still the only golden-foliaged form that is widely grown. It has quite soft, feathery foliage held on erect branches and soon makes an attractive pillar of bright golden-yellow, which in sunny situations is held quite well through the winter. Slightly less hardy than most green forms, it could be used as a container or patio plant, brought under glass in winter in cooler climates.

H 7–10ft (2–3m), W 8–12in (20–30cm)

UH 26–40ft (8–12m), UW 18–24in (45–60cm), Z 9–10

GINKGO BILOBA

The Maidenhair Tree or Chinese Maidenhair Tree hardly resembles most people's idea of what a conifer should look like – this ancient plant, proved by fossils to have been growing over 150 million years ago, is both broad-leafed and deciduous. Slow-growing initially, the species becomes

a large tree, normally upright and branching but often variable from seed. It has simple fan-shaped leaves, a fresh apple-green in summer, turning a beautiful clear gold in autumn. Both male and female trees exist but they are difficult to tell apart when young. The female fruit is edible but its fleshy green skin, when it ripens to the color of an apricot, has a distinctly unpleasant, pungent smell, so male clones are preferred, particularly for street planting. For best growth, Ginkgos prefer climates with high summer temperatures but are otherwise quite adaptable, preferring deep, well-drained but not dry acid or alkaline soil, tolerating atmospheric pollution and proving no problem with pest or diseases. Many selections have been made from seed in North America, Europe and Australasia, adding some excellent forms that must be propagated by grafting. Pruning is best done in spring; Ginkgos take well to pruning but may throw out vigorous shoots if pruned hard.

H 10–16ft (3–5m), W 3–4ft (90cm–1.2m)

UH 33–65ft (10–20m), UW 26–33ft (8–10m), Z 4–9

Ginkgo biloba 'Autumn Gold' and 'Saratoga'. These are both upright-branching selections from the Saratoga Horticultural Institute in California. They are non-fruiting male forms recommended for street planting, the former having particularly good autumn color. For more columnar selections, look for 'Princeton Sentry' from the famous Princeton nurseries in New Jersey, and 'Tremonia', a 1930s find from the botanic garden in Dortmund, Germany. There are prostrate forms, sometimes top-

A relatively young Ginkgo biloba *in Strybing Arboretum, San Francisco, in autumn.*

grafted on to a standard as in the wide-spreading 'Horizontalis'; this looks less natural than 'Pendula', but both live up to their descriptive names, though variations may occur in the latter. For the smaller garden, 'Tit' makes a bushy, heavily twigged specimen, slow but not a dwarf. Some cultivars, mostly under the name 'Variegata', have intermittent gold leaves or stripes. Many more varieties are available from specialists. Except for 'Tit', growth rates, once established, might be 6–18in (15–45cm) a year, but growth can be very variable according to situation.

All Z 4–9

JUNIPERUS

Junipers are among the most valuable and versatile groups of conifers for garden use. The sixty or more species in the genus, covering most of the northern hemisphere, have given us a multitude of selections with a variety of shapes, forms and colors to suit almost any garden and any climate. Many are among the hardiest of plants, adapting to a wide range of soils including chalk and lime; in nature they can cling to rock crevices almost without soil. Some Junipers have juvenile, prickly leaves, others scale-like foliage similar to Cupressus; some, like *J. chinensis*, have both on the same plant. There are columnar forms, much hardier than Chamaecyparis or Cupressus; and semi-prostrate and prostrate forms, widely used for ground cover particularly in North America – these are attractive when young but later they often suffer die-back and become overgrown. In garden situations most prostrate and semi-prostrate Junipers will benefit from early pruning to improve density and restrict size.

Most prefer sunny positions with good drainage, but some species such as *J. communis*, will tolerate wet conditions, and others light shade. Some species are susceptible to Juniper blight and a number of insect pests. Many Junipers have pungent aromatic oils and foliage; others have berries which are an important ingredient in oils, medicines and culinary flavorings including gin.

JUNIPERUS CHINENSIS

The Chinese Juniper, native to Japan and Mongolia as well as China, is variable in the wild from columnar to shrubby, growing in its tallest forms to over 50ft (15m). Most cultivars have a mixture of foliage – smooth adult and prickly juvenile – but some have only one kind; the various forms and foliage types lead to considerable confusion in identification and naming. As long as taxonomists disagree, many of the same prostrate and semi-prostrate forms will be listed under *J. chinensis* in North America, and under *J.* × *pfitzeriana* (syn. *J.* × *media*) in Europe. The species, particularly in its shrubby forms, is widely used for bonsai.

***Juniperus chinensis* 'Aurea'** (also called 'Young's Golden Juniper'). The Golden Chinese Juniper was discovered in 1860 as a sport or seedling at Young's Nursery near Godalming, Surrey. Despite some difficulty in propagation and initial slow growth, it is one of the finest golden columnar forms available. Its

This 15-year-old Juniperus chinensis *'Blue Alps' in Norfolk, England, is pruned regularly. Its solid structure and blue foliage make a good contrast to perennials and grasses, such as the golden* Rudbeckia fulgida *var.* sullivantii *'Goldsturm' in the foreground.*

prickly juvenile foliage in the early years develops into stronger adult growth, and it ends up with a mixture of both, with light yellow and deep golden-yellow textures as bright in winter as in summer. In exposed areas it may need early protection from cold winds and extreme summer sun.

Sometimes G

H 4–5ft (1.2–1.5m), W 18–24in (45–60cm)

UH 33–50ft (10–15m), UW 3–4ft (90cm–1.2m), Z 5–9

***Juniperus chinensis* 'Blaauw'** (syn. *J.* × *pfitzeriana* 'Blaauw'). This distinctive conifer apparently originated in Japan, and was introduced by the nursery Blaauw and Company, Boskoop, Holland. It makes a vase-shaped bush of completely adult deep blue-green foliage, rough but not prickly to the touch. Of similar foliage are ***J. c.* 'Plumosa Aurea'** and ***J. c.* 'Plumosa**

Aureovariegata', both slower-growing, lower and wider-spreading, the former gray-green to old gold in color, the latter deep green splashed with gold. The blue-green slow-growing dwarf ***J. c.* 'Shimpaku'** is widely used for bonsai. Plants on their own roots are best if available.

Generally G

H 4–5ft (1.2–1.5m), W 30–36in (75–90cm)

UH 10–16ft (3–5m), UW 6–10ft (1.8–3m), Z 4–9

***Juniperus chinensis* 'Blue Alps'.** A vigorous Juniper which makes a bushy plant with a single leading shoot (but sometimes several), nodding at the tips. The extremely prickly foliage is a deep blue in winter, and a bright steel-blue in summer. This is a good accent plant, and can be used among perennials and grasses to provide contrast and structure. Pruning is advisable at an early age. Also blue

with a more erect, eventually conical, form is *J. c.* 'Blue Point'; a good architectural plant is *J. c.* 'Obelisk', more of a gray-blue, making a tight but slightly curving column of prickly juvenile foliage.

H 5–6ft (1.5–1.8m), W 3–4ft (90cm–1.2m)
UH 20–33ft (6–10m), UW 13–16ft (4–5m), Z 5–8

Juniperus chinensis 'Kaizuka' (syn. 'Torulosa'). Known as the Hollywood Juniper because of its popularity in southern California, this superb architectural plant originated in Japan where it is still widely used for

planting against walls, as free-standing specimens and for bonsai. Without pruning or training it will make an irregular upright bush with a few upward leading shoots that spread and twist in different directions. The branches are clothed with almost totally adult, scale-like foliage of a deep rich green, the color held but a little darker in winter. Comfortable with both heat and frost, it is deservedly popular. It takes well to pruning and shaping. and makes a good focal point. An attractive form with mid-green foliage and irregular

creamy-white tips is offered in Britain under the name *J. c.* 'Japonica Variegata' (also *J. c.* 'Variegated Kaizuka'). In the US, another form from Japan listed as *J. c.* ' Variegated Kaizuka' (or *J. c.* 'Torulosa Variegata') has creamy-yellow variations on deep green foliage; it is undoubtedly the true plant.

H 5–6ft (1.5–1.8m), W 4–5ft (1.2–1.5m)
UH 16–26ft (5–8m), UW 10–16ft (3–5m), Z 4–9

Juniperus chinensis 'Keteleeri'. One of several cultivars of *J. chinensis* that make conical trees of some size and attraction, which can be used where *Chamaecyparis lawsoniana* selections, similar in appearance, would not be sufficiently hardy; all are rugged in outline with mostly adult blue or green foliage and upswept branches.

TOP *An unpruned 25-year-old* Juniperus chinensis *'Kaizuka' in Bedgebury Pinetum, England, in winter.*
LEFT *In the Miller garden in Seattle, vertical conifers show a range of sizes and colors. The* Juniperus chinensis *'Blue Point' (right) and the three dwarfer* Juniperus communis *'Gold Cone' are 10 years old; behind the variegated cordyline are 25-year-old specimens of* Tsuga mertensiana.

All are hardy and tolerant of drought, best planted in open, sunny situations. *J. c.* 'Keteleeri' has dark gray-green foliage but its most remarkable attribute is the mass of green-blue bloomed fruits it bears in autumn and winter on quite young plants. *J. c.* **'Olympia'** is broader and more pyramidal with blue-green foliage; *J. c.* **'Monarch'** has gray-green foliage on erect twisted branches; both fruit well.

H 8–10ft (2.5–3m), W 3ft (90cm)

UH 33–50ft (10–15m), UW 7–10ft (2–3m), Z 5–9

Juniperus chinensis **'Pyramidalis'**. Columnar in habit (despite its name), this has blue-green leaves, relatively soft to the touch, on erectly held branches that form a dense column. It was introduced from Japan in 1845 and is a good, easy garden plant. Another form, **J. c. 'Stricta'**, looks similar when young but has more prickly juvenile leaves – the two plants may be confused by nurserymen.

H 5–6ft (1.5–1.8m), W 18–24in (45–60cm)

UH 16–26ft (5–8m), UW 6–8ft (1.8–2.5m), Z 5–9

Juniperus chinensis **'Spartan'**. One of the best cultivars, which should be more widely used, this was introduced in 1961 by Monrovia Nurseries in California (and was for some time listed under *J. c. virginiana* 'Helle'). It is easy to grow across many climates, making a striking column of dark rich green, with mostly adult foliage and attractive blue-bloomed fruits on older plants in autumn. A good accent plant, it is trouble-free, takes well to pruning, and would probably make an

Hardy columnar junipers in the Mediterranean-style garden at Wave Hill, New York, summer: Juniperus chinensis 'Spartan' (left) is naturally narrow, while J. virginiana 'Burkii' (see page 123) is broader. Both are about 16 years old.

excellent hedge in cold and hot climates alike. *J. c.* **'Fairview'** is rather more open, of a similar color and free-fruiting.

H 10–13ft (3–4m), W 12–18in (30–45cm)

UH 33–50ft (10–15m), UW 3–4ft (90cm–1.2m), Z 4–9

JUNIPERUS COMMUNIS

The Common Juniper probably has the widest distribution of any conifer, spreading through the northern hemisphere from Japan, across Asia, through Europe and also the north of North America. It is native to high alpine regions as well as lowland, sandy plains, acid peat bogs and well-drained chalky soils – it is an amazingly adaptable species, though it prefers cool to warm temperate regions. The species varies so widely in habit, from narrowly columnar to bushy and prostrate, that a great many garden cultivars have been collected from the wild. Dwarf, slow-growing and miniature forms exist, some with golden foliage and some variegated, but few of these reach more than 33ft (10m) in height. All have short, prickly, juvenile leaves with a silver band above. Male and female flowers

appear on different plants. The female bears oval fruits, green with a bluish-gray bloom, turning black as they ripen in the second or third year – picked in their green state, these are used for medicinal purposes and gin.

Juniperus communis 'Berkshire'.

A true miniature, named after the Berkshire mountains in Massachusetts, discovered by noted plantsman Alfred Fordham of the Arnold Arboretum, Boston. It forms a dense bun-shaped mound, green in summer, bronzing in winter, with silvery highlights at all seasons. It is ideal for troughs and miniature gardens, and best in full sun.

H 6–8in (15–20cm), W 8–12in (20–30cm)

UH 12–18in (30–45cm), UW 24–30in (60–75cm), Z 3–8

Juniperus communis 'Compressa'.

The Noah's Ark Juniper is a desirable conifer forming a tightly compressed miniature column of light green. The

true cultivar is narrow, a rather weak grower, with occasional die-back from extreme weather conditions; it can be prone to red spider mite damage. Often sold under the same name is the fatter, cone-shaped *J. c.* '**Suecica Nana**', a much healthier plant with bright green foliage. On stronger soils in particular, stronger, reverting shoots will often develop and should be cut away when seen. Look out also for *J. c.* '**Miniatur**', a tight form with softer foliage, and *J. c.* '**Brynhyfryd Gold**', whose new spring foliage turns to soft gold in sunny positions, gray-green in winter. All are excellent for troughs, sinks and alpine gardens.

H 12–18in (30–45cm), W 4–6in (10–15cm)

UH 3–4ft (90cm–1.2m), UW 6–12in (15–30cm), Z 4–7

Juniperus communis 'Gold Cone'.

The name is descriptive of this slow-growing conifer, which is like a miniature Irish Juniper (*J. c.*

LEFT *A perfect, tight column of* Juniperus communis *'Compressa', 10 years old, in Boskoop, Holland, summer.*

BELOW *The spreading* Juniperus communis *'Green Carpet', in Norfolk, England, summer.*

'Hibernica'), with tightly compressed branches. Foliage in winter is greenish-yellow and sometimes bronze-tinted; late spring growth transforms to a warm, golden-yellow in summer. Much more vigorous is *J. c.* '**Schneverdingen Goldmachangel**' (syn. 'Golden Showers'), found in Germany by the late Gunter Horstmann. It is broader and more open, the outer branches terminating in nodding branch tips, the new shoots tipped with gold that suffuses the whole plant. Both tend to open up when older, and need tying in for support.

H 3–4ft (90cm–1.2m), W 6–12in (15–30cm)

UH 10–16ft (3–5m), UW 18–24in (45–60cm), Z 4–7

Juniperus communis 'Green Carpet'.

Perhaps the best prostrate cultivar of the species, discovered growing across an enormous rock in a fjord by Arne Bryne of Stavanger, Norway. Blooms of Bressingham, Norfolk, introduced it to England in 1984, and it has since found its way across the world. It forms a tight, rigidly branched mat of bright green foliage, darker green in winter; it is good on a bank or over a rock or wall, and excellent as a container plant. Many other prostrate

variations have been found in the wild; worth recommending is **J. c. 'Corielagen'** from Scotland, with longer, more flexible branches that follow the contours of the ground.

H 4in (10cm), W 24–36in (75–90cm)

UH 6–12in (15–30cm), UW 10–16ft (3–5m), Z 3–7

Juniperus communis 'Hibernica'. The Irish Juniper is the common name for this narrow, upright form of the Common Juniper; there are several similar types both in the wild and as cultivars, and all make attractive pillar-like trees, effective singly or in groups. Light green with silvery bands on the upper leaves giving a bluish-green cast, it is brighter in summer than winter. Much tighter, with a narrower habit and slower-growing, are **J. c. 'Sentinel'** (also known as 'Pencil Point') and **J. c. 'Arnold'**.

H 6–8ft (1.8–2.5m), W 10–12in (25–30cm)

UH 20–26ft (6–8m), UW 18–24in (45–60cm), Z 3–7

Juniperus communis 'Horstmann'. Thought by some to be grotesque, I think it is a great product of nature. Found by Gunter Horstmann in Germany as a sprawling, irregular bush with weeping foliage, light bluish-green and quite prickly, it offers itself to training upwards so that branchlets cascade down, but is also effective if permitted to create its own shape as a living sculpture. Allow space for it to develop as a specimen in a lawn or among low-growing plants. Once established, it will make 6–12in (15–30cm) of growth a year, but it can be controlled by pruning.

Juniperus communis 'Repanda'. This older cultivar is much used for ground cover. Rather dull bronze-green in winter, dark green with brownish stems in summer, its foliage is soft to the touch. It is vigorous, healthy and roots as it grows along. Similar in habit, low and spreading is **J. c. 'Spotty Spreader'**, with splashes of creamy-yellow on the foliage.

H 12in (30cm), W 6–8ft (1.8–2.5m)

UH 12–18in (30–45cm), UW 16–26ft (5–8m), Z 3–7

JUNIPERUS CONFERTA

The Shore Juniper originates from the coastal regions of Japan, and is particularly widespread on the northern island of Hokkaido where it grows among rocks and sand dunes, conditions that give a clue to its preference for good drainage and its tolerance of seaside planting. It is a vigorous grower, making a wide-

LEFT Juniperus communis *'Sentinel', 17 years old, in southern Holland, summer; this is a good accent plant for the smaller garden.*
RIGHT Juniperus conferta *'Blue Lagoon' makes excellent ground cover at the National Arboretum (Gotelli Collection), Washington D.C., summer.*

spreading mat of apple-green overlapping branches and prickly foliage. Some of the selected cultivars are lower-growing and less vigorous, but all can be used as effective ground cover, ideally in full sun on well-drained, sandy soil, though they do need some moisture at the roots. They will suffer die-back on heavy, poorly drained soils. **J. c. 'Blue Pacific'** and **'Blue Lagoon'** are hardly blue, but rather green with a bluish cast. **J. c. 'Blue Tosho'** from Japan is slow-growing, silver-blue in summer, green in winter. **J. c. 'Blue Ice'** is similar but has better winter color.

H 6–12in (15–30cm), W 6–8ft (1.8–2.5m)

UH 12–18in (30–45cm), UW 16–26ft (5–8m), Z 6–8

JUNIPERUS DEPPEANA (syn. J. deppeana var. pachyphlaea)

Originating from the south-western United States and northern Mexico, its picturesque common name of Alligator Juniper describes the appearance of the chequered bark on older trees. There are various forms, from columnar to shrubby, some exhibiting amazingly silver or blue foliage; they do best in hot, dry conditions and are less vigorous and

colorful in cooler zones. All have fine, mostly adult foliage. A few selections are available, such as **J. d. 'McPhetter'**, a dense bush of bright silver-blue, and **J. d. 'Silver Spire'**, columnar and very silver-blue.

H 5–6ft (1.5–1.8m), W 18–30in (45–75cm)

UH 26–33ft (8–10m), UW 6–10ft (1.8–3m)

Sizes approximate, Z 7–8

JUNIPERUS HORIZONTALIS

The common name of Creeping Juniper aptly describes this prostrate form of the species and its innumerable cultivars, many selected from the wild in its native North America. Found growing from rocky seashore to mountain regions, it is a hardy species which will take heat as well as cold. Nearly all forms have adult, scale-like leaves, soft to the touch. There are some very attractive cultivars for ground cover, for banks and slopes, and to hang over walls; and prostrate forms are now being top-grafted to make pendulous shrubs. In North America they have been widely used (in the past, undoubtedly over-used) for mass ground cover. Creeping Junipers grow well on a wide range of soils, rooting as they grow; they prefer sun and good drainage, but tolerate some shade. All benefit from pruning to increase density and restrict size, but the snaking habit of the leading branches is an attractive characteristic. They are susceptible to juniper blight (*phomopsis*) and spider mites (see Pests and Diseases, page 182).

ABOVE RIGHT Juniperus horizontalis *'Banff'* (syn. J. scopulorum *'Banff'*) *shows its bright blue summer color, in Holland; it was found near Banff in the Canadian Rockies.*
RIGHT Juniperus horizontalis *'Mother Lode', Norfolk, England, summer; it arose as a sport on J. h. 'Wiltonii' in Oregon.*

Juniperus horizontalis **'Andorra Compact'** (syn. 'Plumosa Compacta'). One of the best of a distinct group of Creeping Junipers with a more semi-prostrate habit and very feathery 'plumose' foliage. The first of these was **J. h. 'Plumosa'**, introduced by Andorra Nurseries in Pennsylvania in 1907; it is more vigorous, with gray-green leaves in summer, purplish in winter. 'Andorra Compact' and another good variety, **J. h. 'Youngstown'**, are similar, with branches angled at 45 degrees. Summer foliage is gray-green, turning purple-bronze in winter; they are more intensely colored in severe winters or when under stress. Both are good for ground cover, and tolerate some shade.

H 12–18in (30–45cm), W 24–36in (75–90cm)

UH 18–24in (45–60cm), UW 10–16ft (3–5m), Z 3–9

Juniperus horizontalis **'Blue Chip'**. One of the most attractive selections, it forms a dense, mounded carpet of blue-green, feathery foliage that turns a bright steel-blue in summer, with better winter color than most *J. h.* cultivars. *J. h.* **'Banff'** (now considered a *J. scopulorum* cultivar) is similar.

H 12in (30cm), W 4–5ft (1.2–1.5m)

UH 12–18in (30–45cm), UW 10–16ft (3–5m), Z 3–9

Juniperus horizontalis **'Blue Pygmy'**. Unusually for this species, this is a true miniature, not prostrate at all but

making a tiny ball of blue-green, with minute juvenile leaves which are bright silver-blue in summer. It is ideal for troughs, sinks and miniature gardens.

H 6–8in (15–20cm), W 6–8in (15–20cm)

UH 12–18in (30–45cm), UW 12–18in (30–45cm), Z 3–9

Juniperus horizontalis 'Mother Lode'. It often happens that two similar plants are introduced around the same time – 'Mother Lode' appeared in Oregon in 1982 at the famous Iseli nursery; **J. h. 'Golden Carpet'** in 1992 at the small Kruse nursery near Bad Zwischenahn in northern Germany. Each is becoming popular in its own continent. Both are flat like their

parent *J. h.* 'Wiltonii', but may vary according to location; both are best in sun with good drainage. If you grow them together you will see a difference, but not much. 'Mother Lode' is slightly more golden-yellow, even in winter (although their rather dirty bronze-yellow at that time of year is not their best attribute); both turn a bright yellow-gold in summer. They should be pruned to improve density.

H 2–4in (5–10cm), W 3–4ft (90cm–1.2m)

UH 6in (15cm), UW 10–16ft (3–5m), Z 3–7

Juniperus horizontalis 'Wiltonii'. A great many low-growing, mat-forming cultivars have vied for the top spot,

but none has yet improved on this one, the Blue Rug Juniper, introduced in 1914. In time it forms a perfect, flat-growing carpet of soft, feathery foliage, bright blue in summer, usually tinged purple in winter. For best effect, its vigorous, prostrate side branches should be pruned to encourage the plant to fill in the center. It needs good drainage. It makes an effective lawn, or a cover for banks or walls. Plants called **J. h. 'Blue Rug'** are usually synonymous.

H 4–6in (10–15cm), W 6–8ft (1.8–2.5m)

UH 4–8in (10–20cm), UW 16–26ft (5–8m), Z 3–9

JUNIPERUS × PFITZERIANA

This name now covers the mostly semi-prostrate cultivars that were previously listed under *J. × media* and, in the US, *J. chinensis* (see page 111). They are a very useful group of plants for the garden as specimens or ground cover, though some do get large in a fairly short space of time. Nearly all could be described as semi-prostrate in habit, with a mixture of prickly juvenile and smoother adult scale-like foliage. Nearly all benefit from pruning from an early age to improve density and restrict size, although doing so does increase height more quickly. They are tough, hardy, and will tolerate heat, cold and most soil conditions provided they are not too wet or badly drained. Their colors range from rich green to silver-gray and gray-blue to yellow and gold, as well as variegated. All are excellent for ground cover. Some dwarfer types exist, which are best selected for the smaller garden – en masse they can be

Juniperus horizontalis *'Wiltonii' (named after Wilton Nurseries in Connecticut), Seattle, autumn; it contrasts with fallen maple leaves and the grass* Stipa tenuissima *behind.*

overpowering, particularly if all golden foliage forms are used.

Juniperus × *pfitzeriana* '**Gold Coast**'. The Gold Coast Juniper, introduced by Monrovia nurseries in California, is among the best of a great many faster-growing semi-prostrate selections with yellow foliage. Rapidly forming a low, prostrate bush, it becomes more semi-prostrate with age. Its bright yellow, mostly adult, foliage holds its color in sunny situations well into winter. Many other selections have arisen, mostly from sports. *J.* × *p.* '**Gold Star**' from Canada has almost wholly juvenile foliage and is also flattish growing; it is bright golden-yellow in summer, much more green-gold in winter. Both *J.* × *p.* '**Carbery Gold**' from England and *J.* × *p.* '**Golden Saucer**' from Holland are low-spreading forms, with much juvenile foliage, bright yellow in summer and good in winter. All are best pruned.

H 24–36in (60–90cm), W 5–6ft (1.5–1.8m)
UH 4–6ft (120–180cm), UW 10–16ft (3–5m), all Z 4–9

Juniperus × *pfitzeriana* '**Gold Sovereign**'. Selected at Bressingham, Norfolk, this bright gold sport of *J.* × *p.* 'Old Gold' has proved to be not only a compact, slow-growing plant but one that maintains its bright yellow color in winter. Such compact forms are more suitable for the small garden, but may still need pruning after a few years. *J.* × *p.* '**Daub's Frosted**' has almost wholly juvenile yellow foliage with a bluish cast from the inner leaves in summer; this is less marked in winter, when young stems are more yellow than the leaves.

H 18–24in (45–60cm), W 30–36in (75–90cm)
UH 24–36in (60–90cm), UW 5–8ft (1.5–2.5m), all Z 4–9

Juniperus × *pfitzeriana* '**Hetzii**'. Too large for the smaller garden unless used as a hedge, this soon makes an imposing semi-prostrate bush with branches angled upwards and outwards, the foliage mostly adult and a pleasing gray-blue all year round. It is tough, hardy and adaptable to a wide range of soil conditions. It takes well to pruning, even topiary, but

beware – it can eventually grow high enough to walk under.

H 5–6ft (1.5–1.8m), W 6–8ft (180–240cm)
UH 16–26ft (5–8m), UW 13–20ft (4–6m), Z 4–9

Juniperus × *pfitzeriana* '**Mint Julep**'. Though vigorous, this is a valuable Juniper, not only for its ease of culture but for its upright form with pendulous branch tips, its mixture of juvenile and rich green, adult, 'minty' foliage, the color darker in winter. It can be used as a low hedge, as a background specimen to grasses and perennials or to clothe a bank, good of course in association with columnar forms or other J.× pfitzeriana cultivars. Preferable to the wider spreading J.× pfitzeriana.

H 3–4ft (90cm–1.2m), W 5–6ft (1.5–1.8m)
UH 10–16ft (3–5m), UW 10–16ft (3–5m), Z 4–9

Juniperus × *pfitzeriana* '**Wilhelm Pfitzer**'. The Pfitzer Juniper, first introduced in the 1870s, was the first of its type and widely planted as a specimen or for ground cover. It was often sold as a dwarf conifer to unsuspecting customers, but it is certainly not a dwarf: of the several forms in cultivation, most are wide-spreading, some low and some higher, with the latter eventually tree-like. The foliage is deep dullish green, part coarse adult, part prickly juvenile; branches are arching, and pendulous at the tips. It is not recommended for the average garden now that so many cultivars are easily available. The same goes for *J.* × *p.* '**Aurea**' – attractive though it is, it too makes a wide-spreading, very prickly plant, much

Juniperus × pfitzeriana 'Gold Sovereign' maintains bright year-round color. This 12-year-old plant in Norfolk, England, is making new growth in early summer among dwarf perennials and shrubs.

lower than *J. × pfitzeriana*, with bright yellow foliage on new growth, yellow green in winter. *J. × p.* **'Compacta'** is worth mentioning as a low-growing, flat-topped, densely foliaged plant, bright to mid-green, useful for ground cover.

H 3–4ft (90cm–1.2m), W 6–8ft (1.8–2.5cm)
UH 6–16ft (1.8–5m), UW 16–26ft (5–8m), Z 4–9

Juniperus × pfitzeriana **'Sulphur Spray'**. A unique color for Junipers, this arose at the Konijn nursery in Holland in 1962 as a sport on *J. × p.* 'Hetzii'. It has branches angled upwards and outwards and foliage of a light creamy-green in winter, bright sulphur-yellow on new shoots in summer. It is ideal as a specimen among heathers or low-growing contrasting shrubs or perennials – it would look good among green-leafed bergenias in summer, but it needs pruning if it is not to get too large. For best color, it needs sun.

H 4–5ft (1.2–1.5m), W 4–5ft (1.2–1.5m)
UH 10–16ft (3–5m), UW 10–16ft (3–5m), Z 4–9

JUNIPERUS PROCUMBENS

Juniperus procumbens **'Nana'**. The Dwarf Japanese Garden Juniper is believed to have originated in the wild, in the same habitat as the species – southern Japan along the coastal regions near Kyushu and the Bonin Isles. One of the most distinctive and attractive junipers, it is a popular plant in Japan for garden and bonsai. It makes a wide-spreading mat of

ABOVE RIGHT *Three 25-year-old plants of* Juniperus × pfitzeriana *'Aurea' conceal a manhole cover (rather too successfully!), Norfolk, England, late summer.*
RIGHT Juniperus procumbens *'Nana' in an ideal position, softening a wall and steps at Brookside Gardens, Maryland, summer.*

bright, apple green, prickly juvenile foliage, slightly purplish in exposed conditions in winter and with a bluish cast from the silver bands on the leaves. Its upward-raised branch tips are very attractive, arching up when the plant is hanging over a wall, down a slope or top-grafted on to a stem. With age, the plant can build in height from overlapping layers of foliage. It is hardy, but best with good drainage; older plants are susceptible to Juniper blight (*Phomopsis*) but less so in hotter climates than in cooler, wetter ones. *J. p.* **'Bonin Isles'**, often confused with 'Nana', is more vigorous.

H 6–12in (15–30cm), W 5–8ft (1.5–2.5m)
UH 12–24in (30–60cm), UW 16–26ft (5–8m), Z 5–9

Juniperus sabina *'Tamariscifolia', over 40 years old, Norfolk, England, early summer.*

JUNIPERUS RECURVA VAR. COXII
(syn. *J. r.* 'Coxii')
The common names Drooping Juniper, Himalayan Weeping Juniper and Coffin Juniper are all descriptive of the species, which is native to the higher regions of the eastern Himalayas. *J. r.* var. *coxii* was selected from seed collected by plant hunters E. H. M. Cox and Reginald Farrer in the 1920s. A slow-growing, eventually quite large tree of considerable character, it has orange-brown bark, bright green foliage in summer and bronze-green in winter, with slim, gracefully pendant branchlets. It is best in an open but sheltered position. As a garden plant it benefits from an annual light trim of the side branches to keep it narrow; this helps prevent it looking scruffy, since with age it tends to open up, revealing brown inner foliage. It can make quite a decorative plant and it is always a talking point.
H 6–8ft (1.8–2.5m), W 3–4ft (90cm–1.2m)
UH 26–40ft (8–12m), UW 16–23ft (5–7m), Z 7–10

JUNIPERUS SABINA
The Savin Juniper is native from southeastern Europe to Siberia. It varies considerably in habit, but most cultivars are bushy or spreading, with leaves that release a pungent aroma when crushed. All have both adult scale-like foliage and quite prickly juvenile needles on the same plant. Though hardy and adaptable to a wide range of soils and conditions including some shade, few are of outstanding garden merit. But they make excellent ground cover, arguably better than the more popular *J. horizontalis* types since they are better weed-suppressors. Some forms are susceptible to Juniper blight.

Juniperus sabina **'Buffalo'**. This is one of the best ground-cover Junipers, seemingly trouble-free. Along with two other spreading cultivars, *J. s.* **'Arcadia'** and *J. s.* **'Broadmoor'**, it was selected after lengthy trials of seedlings raised by the D. Hill nursery in Dundee, Illinois, from seed imported from Russia in 1933. All are resistant to Juniper blight and seem tolerant of coastal conditions. 'Buffalo' makes a carpet of bright green, its shorter branchlets raised at 45 degrees above the prostrate spreading branches; it is excellent for a bank or over a wall.
H 8–12in (20–30cm), W 4–5ft (1.2–1.5m)
UH 12–18in (30–45cm), UW 16–20ft (5–6m), All Z 4–7

Juniperus sabina 'Tamariscifolia'. This is far and away the best known and most popular form of the species, despite its susceptibility to Juniper blight and its extremely pungent foliage. It makes pleasing ground cover, gradually forming layers of overlapping branches densely furnished with green juvenile foliage, a brighter blue-green in summer. There may be more than one clone in cultivation. Monrovia nurseries in California have introduced a blight-resistant selection, *J. s.* 'New Blue', which offers a choice when available.

H 12–18in (30–45cm), W 4–5ft (1.2–1.5m)
UH 18–24in (45–60cm), UW 16–23ft (5–7m), Z 4–7

JUNIPERUS SCOPULORUM

The Rocky Mountain Juniper covers a wide natural area from Texas in the south to Alberta and British Columbia in the north where it is mostly found growing at about 5,000ft (1,500m). Though bushy, evenprostrate forms are found, it is mostly columnar or pyramidal, with trees reaching 50ft (15m); generally they have adult, scale-like foliage on thin branchlets. Some excellent cultivars have been selected. All are hardy, but do better in warmer, drier conditions, needing good drainage in cooler climates; whatever the temperature, they dislike moist air and humidity. Popular in California and the American Southwest, they should do well in Mediterranean climates; otherwise, plant them in sun with good drainage. They make good accent plants, some cultivars having an intense silver-blue summer color which is very striking. Some coarse-foliaged cultivars may be propagated by grafting.

Juniperus scopulorum 'Blue Heaven'.

A dependable columnar conifer with a mixture of horizontal and upward-curving branches, with adult scale-like foliage, rough to the touch. Blue-green in winter, it turns a bright silver-blue in summer, making a good background or accent plant, which will grow large in time. *J. s.* 'Wichita Blue', of a rather open pyramidal habit, is as intensely silver-blue as any cultivar in summer; it will also grow large but takes well to pruning.

H 8–10ft (2.5–3m), W 18–24in (45–60cm)
UH 33–50ft (10–15m), UW 5–6ft (1.5–1.8m), Z 3–7

Juniperus scopulorum 'Moonglow'.

One of the more reliable cultivars in cooler climates, this forms a broad, densely foliaged column with erect branches, bearing more semi-juvenile feathery foliage than most. It is a bright silver-blue in summer, more steel-blue in winter, and best in full sun. Another favorite, but not so easy to grow, is *J. s.* 'Gray Gleam'. It has much softer, thinner foliage, and grows to a narrow column of bluish-gray, brighter in summer but holding a better winter color than many cultivars. It is often grafted.

H 6–8ft (1.8–2.5m), W 12–18in (30–45cm)
UH 26–33ft (8–10m), UW 24–36in (60–90cm), Z 4–7

Juniperus scopulorum 'Skyrocket'

(sometimes listed under *J. virginiana* 'Skyrocket'). This is considered to be the narrowest pencil-like form of almost any conifer species, although the width varies under different growing conditions; plants on thin soils with good drainage are likely to be narrower than on richer, moister types. The sturdy vertical branches carry blue-green leaves, brighter gray-blue in summer, darker in winter. It makes a superb accent plant, almost able to mimic the Italian Cypress (*Cupressus sempervirens*) in colder climates where that would not be hardy; a row or group are quite dramatic, but lack the stature of the Cypress. They need tying up against damage from snowfall, and can be susceptible to Juniper blight when older. *J. s.* 'Blue Arrow' would be an excellent substitute for the smaller garden: it is tighter in form, though probably less blue.

H 8–10ft (2.5–3m), W 12in (30cm)
UH 26–33ft (8–10m), UW 12–18in (30–45cm), Z 3–7

Juniperus scopulorum 'Tabletop'.

There are a few selections of the Rocky Mountain Juniper with a semi-prostrate habit. This is one of the brightest and best; it is, however, neither low enough nor flat enough to justify its name. It is strong-growing, with upward-spreading branches and primarily adult foliage of a brilliant silver-blue, particularly in summer. It needs annual pruning unless it is used as a background plant.

Juniperus scopulorum *'Blue Arrow', 7 years old, Norfolk, England, in autumn, standing out against the purple-leaved* Cotinus *'Grace'.*

H 3–4ft (90cm–1.2m), W 5–6ft (1.5–1.8m)
UH 6–10ft (1.8–3m), UW 16–23ft (5–7m), Z 3–7

JUNIPERUS SQUAMATA

The Flaky Juniper or Singleseed Juniper, though not itself grown as a garden plant, has produced some first-class cultivars, mostly selected in cultivation: *J. s.* 'Blue Star' is arguably the best dwarf conifer ever raised. In the wild, *J. squamata* spreads at high altitudes from Afghanistan to central China. It is variable but mostly shrubby in habit, hardy and tough, withstanding drought well but generally growing better in cooler, drier climates. The silver-blue on the upper leaves is very prominent on some cultivars, giving an intense summer color. Most have juvenile foliage and the nodding shoot tips characteristic of the species.

Juniperus squamata **'Blue Carpet'**. A vigorous, spreading plant that arose as a sport on *J. s.* 'Meyeri' in Boskoop, Holland, this is now one of the most popular ground-cover junipers. The outer branches, angled slightly upwards from the center, have attractively nodding branch tips. The foliage is quite variable according to situation – in winter it can be blue-green, steel-blue or purplish, but in summer this transforms to a striking silver-blue. It needs pruning from an early age, and grows easily on most soils given good drainage. From Sweden comes **J. s. 'Hunnetorp'** (also known as **J. s. 'Blue Swede'**), another good blue-foliaged cultivar, taller but denser than 'Blue Carpet'; it also gets large in time, so pruning is recommended.

H 18–24in (45–60cm), W 5–8ft (1.5–2.4m)
UH 24–30in (60–75cm), UW 16–23ft (5–7m), Z 4–8

Juniperus squamata **'Blue Star'**. This marvelous conifer was found as a witch's broom on *J. s.* 'Meyeri' in about 1950, at the Hoogeveen nursery in Reeuwijk, Holland, and introduced to great excitement in 1964. It has the blue-green leaves of its parent but remains a dense, flat-topped dome with no reversion. The upper silver-blue surfaces of the leaves add brilliant color and a star-like sparkle, and it is now deservedly one of the most popular garden conifers. Older plants can mound and spread irregularly. It needs sun and good drainage for best effect; it is good for troughs and miniature gardens, often grafted on to a stem. Forms with variegated shoots – mostly creamy-white, sometimes more yellow – are attractive but vulnerable to frost and sunburn.

H 12–18in (30–45cm), W 18–24in (45–60cm)
UH 24–30in (60–75cm), UW 4–5ft (1.2–1.5m), Z 4–8

Juniperus squamata **'Holger'**. Rather more prostrate, but otherwise similar in habit to *J. s.* 'Blue Carpet', 'Holger'

was named after Holger Jensen, who selected it from seedlings at his nursery in Sweden in the late 1940s. Reputedly a hybrid between *J. ×pfitzeriana* 'Pfitzeriana Aurea' and *J. s.* 'Meyeri', its foliage appears like the latter. It transforms from a rather light bluish-green in winter to a brilliant display of butter-yellow new shoots in late spring, soon spreading to a sulphur-yellow over the whole plant, before gradually toning down again in late summer. It needs a prominent, sunny position where it can show off.

H 12–18in (30–45cm), W 3–5ft (1.2–1.5m)
UH 24–30in (60–75cm), UW 10–16ft (3–5m), Z 4–8

Juniperus squamata **'Meyeri'**. This, the earliest cultivar of *J. squamata* to be introduced, was discovered growing not in the wild but in a garden in China by Frank Meyer, who brought it to the Arnold Arboretum in Boston in 1914. Though it becomes large in time, it has a distinctive habit, its branches erect and the upper parts arching in all directions, with nodding branch tips. Densely packed with prickly, steel-blue juvenile foliage at the base, it is more adpressed towards the tip. Summer color is intense silver-blue, winter tinged slightly purplish. It needs an open position and benefits from regular pruning; older plants look scruffy if allowed to hang on to their old, brown leaves.

H 5–6ft (1.5–1.8m), W 3–4ft (90cm–1.2m)
UH 16–25ft (5–8m), UW 8–10ft (2.5–3m), Z 4–8

JUNIPERUS VIRGINIANA

This North American species, reaching 50ft (15m), is commonly known as the Eastern Red Cedar or the Pencil

Juniperus squamata 'Blue Star', a deservedly popular dwarf, is shown here at about 20 years old in close-up at Longwood Gardens, Pennsylvania, in summer.

Juniperus squamata 'Holger' makes new summer growth in this 20-year-old plant in Norfolk, England. The creamy-yellow foliage contrasts with Picea pungens 'Prostrata' behind.

Cedar, although it is not a cedar at all. Native to the eastern USA from Florida to Canada, it is an adaptable and hardy species, mostly columnar or pyramidal in the wild, though some types are more bushy or spreading; all have thin, mostly adult scale-like foliage. Both the leaves and the wood (used for making pencils) are aromatic when crushed. It is a tough, adaptable tree with some good cultivars of ornamental value. These do well on a variety of soils, acid or alkaline, heavy or light, but are best where good drainage exists in sun or light shade. Blue-bloomed fruits are an attractive

enhancement on some cultivars. The upright forms are good for shelter or background, even as hedges; some make vertical accent plants, and the semi-prostrate forms are excellent for ground cover.

Juniperus virginiana 'Burkii'.
Once one of the most widely grown cultivars, although hardy and adaptable it has fallen out of fashion. It forms a broad column of thin, erect, densely intertwining stems, blue-green in summer and a steely purplish-blue in winter. Narrower in habit is *J. v.* 'Glauca', with bright silvery-blue summer foliage, gray-blue in winter, while the more blue-green *J. v.* 'Manhattan Blue' makes a compact pyramid. *J. v.* 'Canaertii', an old cultivar, has dark green foliage nicely

set off on older plants by purple-grayish bloomed fruits. *J. v.* '**Emerald Sentinel**' is narrow, conical and rich green. *J. v.* '**Hillspire**' is a conical male form with green foliage maintained all year round.

H 8–10ft (2.4–3m), W 24–36in (60–90cm)
UH 20–33ft (7–10m), UW 6–8ft (1.8–2.5m), Z 3–9

Juniperus virginiana 'Grey Owl'. One of the best ground-cover junipers, this has few faults, unless being vigorous is considered one. Possibly a hybrid between *J. v.* 'Glauca' and *J. ×* *pfitzeriana*, it makes a wide-spreading bush of adult scale-like foliage, the branches overlapping as it builds up with age. Smoky blue-gray in color, which it holds well in winter, it usually has an abundance of silvery-gray fruits as well. *J. v.* '**Blue Cloud**' is lower-

Juniperus virginiana 'Blue Cloud'. The foliage shimmers as autumn frost lifts on this 12-year-old specimen in Norfolk, England.

spreading, with twisted foliage of a slightly grayer blue; its branches are more snake-like and less graceful. Lower still, with somewhat coarse, thicker foliage, dullish gray-green in winter and brilliant silver-gray in summer, is the California-raised *J. v.* **'Silver Spreader'**. All of these prostrate cultivars make excellent, trouble-free ground cover, but do not hesitate to prune them as often as necessary.

H 18–24in (45–60cm), W 8–10ft (2.5–3m)

UH 5–10ft (1.5–3m), UW 16–26ft (5–8m), Z 3–9

LARIX

Larches – along with the ginkgo, metasequoia and taxodium – are among the few genera of deciduous conifers, consisting of about ten species spread widely across the cooler regions of the northern hemisphere, and often found in mountainous areas. Most of the species are fast-growing trees, eventually to 100ft (30m) or more, and widely used for their timber. Beautiful conifers with distinct seasons of change, most are too large for the average garden. However, in recent years a great number of dwarfer

witch's brooms have been discovered, propagated and introduced: some of these are of great garden value.

From bare winter twigs come swelling buds in spring, with new shoots of bright green leaves bursting out in shaving-brush type clusters. The needles darken with age to a deeper green, giving the tree a similar appearance to the evergreen cedar, but the larch has another season of glory when it turns to golden-yellow before the leaves fall in autumn. The twiggy formation of the branches makes a beautiful silhouette against the winter sky, particularly when enhanced by frost. On older plants, colorful male and female flowers appear in spring on the same tree, the females producing attractive, small, cylindrical cones. The larch does best on a reasonably moist but well-drained soil; it is generally unhappy on very dry, chalky soils and on very wet ones, although there are exceptions. Early shoots on dwarf cultivars can be susceptible to spring frosts.

The European or Common Larch (*Larix decidua*) is a rapid-growing,

mostly conical tree, its horizontal branches terminating in gracefully pendulous branchlets; it will eventually be large. It is now less widely grown in Europe than the Japanese Larch (*Larix kaempferi*), which was introduced to Europe from Japan by Robert Fortune in 1861 and soon proved more adaptable to lowland, damper areas, more suited to heavy soils and more disease-resistant than the native species. *L. decidua* has longer, light brown, straw-colored twigs with light green leaves or needles, while *L. kaempferi* has shorter, thicker stems, a waxy bark of deeper brown, even red-brown, and new needles of a slightly bluish green. In winter the reddish twigs of previous seasons stand out strongly on the Japanese Larch. Both have good autumn color and are highly ornamental, but are too large for most gardens. Both species have produced witch's brooms for the smaller garden. All dwarf larches are reproduced by grafting, often top-grafted onto a stem.

H 20–33ft (6–10m), W 10–16ft (3–5m)

UH 80–100ft (25–30m), UW 50–65ft (15–20m)

Growth rates approximate

L. decidua Z 3–7; L. kaempferi Z 4–7

LARIX DECIDUA

Larix decidua **'Corley'**. Found as a witch's broom by the noted collector R. S. Corley and introduced by the Hillier Nursery in England in 1971, this makes a low, densely branched bush with strong shoots going in all directions. Its light brown stems are attractive in winter, flushed with bright green shoots in spring and of a good golden color in autumn. As with all dwarf larches, dead leaves tend to get trapped inside the plant so it needs a winter clean every so often.

From Australia, *L. d.* 'Little Bogle' is a dwarf upright form with horizontal branches suitable for smaller gardens.
H 12in (30cm), W 24–36in (60–90cm)
UH 3–4ft (90cm–1.2m), UW 6–8ft (1.8–2.5m), Z 3–7

Larix decidua 'Pendula'. So wide is the variation of plants sold under this name that unless you see the mother plant you cannot be sure what you will get. Some are wide-spreading, some are narrow; all have some weeping branches. Some selections may produce a strong leading shoot and revert in time to normal trees.
Growth rate 8–18in (20–45cm) a year, Z 3–7

LARIX KAEMPFERI
Larix kaempferi 'Blue Dwarf'. Many more dwarf selections have been made from *L. kaempferi* than *L. decidua*. Some of the witch's brooms are slow but very ornamental, which makes them ideal for the smaller garden, and for rock and alpine gardens. Those top- grafted on to stems are

Larix kaempferi *'Nana', like all larches, has golden autumn foliage; Norfolk, England.*

particularly effective as container plants for the patio. 'Blue Dwarf' makes a stiff, twiggy bush, its nut-brown horizontal branches studded with brown winter buds upturned at the tips. In late spring, buds break into leaf; the clusters of leaves have a distinct bluish cast but become greener as they mature. Several other forms are worth searching for (though they are likely to be in short supply). *L. k.* 'Nana' makes a dense, twiggy bush, wider than it is high; *L. k.* 'Blue Ball' is a hummock-shaped bush, higher than it is wide. A highly rated selection from Germany, *L. k.* 'Wolterdingen', has long, blue-gray leaves, and its new twigs are orange-brown in winter.
H 12–18in (30–45cm), W 18–24in (45–60cm)
UH 24–30in (60–75cm), UW 4–5ft (1.2–1.5m)
All Z 4–7

Larix kaempferi 'Diane'. This is not a dwarf, but it can be slow-growing for some years. It makes an irregular spreading or upright plant, with strangely twisted and contorted branches, pendulous at the tips. It can be pruned or trained when young, bonsai fashion, and is effective top-grafted on to a standard; it may then remain compact for some years, until a leading shoot takes off, snaking skywards. It is good in a container, with year-round appeal. Narrow, columnar cultivars include a selection introduced by Danish nurseryman Arne Vagn Jakobsen, *L. k.* 'Jakobsen's Pyramid'. This is less pyramidal, more fastigiate, and relatively sparsely branched with bright green needles, growing at least 12–18in (30–45cm) per year once established.
H 5–8ft (1.5–2.5m), W 3–4ft (90cm–1.2m)
UH 25–50ft (8–15m), UW 10–16ft (3–5m), Z 4–7

Larix kaempferi 'Pendula'. There may be several forms under this name. Its general qualification is a weeping habit, but the type most often offered would be prostrate if it were not grafted on to a stem, usually about 6–8ft (1.8–2.5m) in height, from where long, sweeping branches fall in a curtain to the ground. A more natural look is achieved if plants are grafted nearer the ground, or if a stem is trained up a cane so that branches fall from different levels. These can be eye-catching in a frontal position, on their own or among other plants.
Growth rate approximately 12–18in (30–45cm) a year
Z 4–7

METASEQUOIA GLYPTOSTROBOIDES
The Dawn Redwood or Dawn Cypress created great excitement in the botanical world when it was discovered growing in the wild in China in 1941 – considered a *Sequoia*,

Larix kaempferi *'Pendula', an attractive, weeping 20-year-old plant in Dennis Groh's garden, Michigan, summer.*

it was known only through fossils and thought to be extinct. Here, then, was a fossil tree, alive, its origins dating back fifty million years: it was an overnight sensation. By 1948, seeds and plants had been distributed to botanic gardens all over the world and thence to gardeners, and it has since settled well into cultivation. It becomes a fast-growing and large tree, resembling the Swamp Cypress (*Taxodium distichum*), but differing in its narrower, more open habit, with larger, flatter leaves arranged in opposite pairs (on the Swamp Cypress they are alternate). It forms a broadly conical tree, with fresh vibrant green early summer foliage, deepening later before turning a deep golden-brown before leaf fall. Small rounded cones hang like cherries on short pendulous stems and ripen from green to brown in their first year. With age, the Dawn Redwood develops a broad, flanged trunk with orange to russet-brown bark. Though amenable to most soils it does not like dry chalky types, preferring moist, but not waterlogged, conditions. Narrower selections, **M. g. 'Sheridan Spire'** and **M. g. 'National'**, are sometimes available. **M. g. 'Gold Rush'** (syn. 'Ogon') is more spectacular – slower than the species with bright golden-yellow foliage, it is a beacon against a darker background. It may need shelter from spring frosts and summer heat. Two recent selections, **M. g. 'Spring Cream'** and **M. s. 'White Spot'** with variegated tips, are also of interest.

H 16–26ft (5–8m), W 5–6ft (1.5–1.8m)

UH 100–130ft (30–40m), UW 16–23ft (5–7m), Z 4–9

MICROBIOTA DECUSSATA
Found growing above the tree line in the mountains of eastern Siberia in 1921, this low-growing Juniper-like plant was not introduced to Europe and North America until 1957. A great twentieth-century find, it is now a popular and widely grown plant. It forms a spreading carpet of soft, lacy frond-like overlapping foliage, bright green in summer, turning a distinctive purple-bronze in winter. Some consider it dull, but used as a contrast to other winter interest plants – such as a golden-foliaged heather, *Euonymus fortunei*, or *Pinus mugo* 'Wintergold' – it makes a striking association. Very hardy, it grows well in full sun or partial shade, and is best with good drainage.

H 6–12in (15–30cm), W 4–5ft (1.2–1.5m)

UH 12–18in (30–45cm), UW 10–16ft (3–5m), Z 2–8

MICROCACHRYS TETRAGONA
A dwarf, slow-growing sprawling shrub, native to the mountains of Tasmania with snake-like branches densely clothed in minute scale-like deep green leaves, closely adpressed to

Metasequoia glyptostroboides 'Gold Rush', 4 years old, Holland, summer.

the stem. Male and female flowers appear on the same plant, the bright red ovoid fruits quite eye-catching when they occur. A species for milder climates, it is ideal for the rock garden where it would look natural tumbling over or between rocks. Alternatively it can be trained upwards to make a narrow cascading plant. It prefers cooler, moist conditions.

H 4–6in (10–15cm), W 3–4ft (90cm–1.2m)

UH 12–18in (30–45cm), UW 8–10ft (2.5–3m), Z 8–9

PICEA
The spruces are a large genus of about fifty species, spread across the northern hemisphere. Found in North America, Asia and Europe, they grow as far north as Alaska and as far south as southern China and the Himalayas. They include some of the tallest and most beautiful trees, but a great many species are too large for garden use. Though there are exceptions, most spruces prefer cooler, moister climates and often do not prosper in hot, dry conditions where they are also more prone to pests and diseases, such as red spider mites. Most species are unhappy on dry chalk soils, dislike salt spray and are intolerant of atmospheric pollution. In most cooler temperate gardens they will be relatively trouble-free. Literally hundreds of selected cultivars have arisen from seed, sports or mutations, with dwarf varieties from witch's brooms; many are propagated by grafting. All species and many cultivars have male and female flowers, the former generally yellow and cone-shaped, the latter sometimes brilliant crimson before they develop pendulous cones. The spruce, *Picea*, is sometimes confused with the fir, *Abies* (see page 84). The easiest way to differentiate mature trees is by the

cones: on *Picea*, the cones are cylindrical, hang beneath the branches, and fall intact when mature; on *Abies*, they stand upwards like candles, breaking up and falling apart on the tree as they ripen.

PICEA ABIES

The Norway Spruce is native from northern Scandinavia eastwards to Russia, south to the European Alps, and the Balkan and Carpathian mountains. Grown widely for timber and paper-making, it is best known in Britain as the standard Christmas tree (although the Nordmann Fir, *Abies nordmannia*, is becoming a popular alternative as it is less inclined to drop needles). Since *Picea abies* will become a large tree of 170ft (50m)in moist, cooler climates, the temptation to plant out an old Christmas tree is best avoided. The Norway Spruce forms a narrowly conical tree with pendulous branches, normally dark green in winter and lighter in summer. As with the firs and the pines, there is usually one flush of growth a year: all plants are transformed as winter buds burst into new growth in early summer. Male flowers are yellow and female flowers greenish and often red-tipped, developing into long cylindrical cones. There are innumerable selections of great value in the garden; the best and most distinct are described below. Most are easy to cultivate in cool, moist conditions.

Picea abies 'Acrocona'. Discovered in Sweden in 1890, this is slow-growing, broad-spreading and rather untidy; without pruning it needs some space. It is notable primarily for bright red flowers and cones in spring; the cones enlarge and mature to a pleasing buff color and hang on the branch-tips for

Picea abies 'Acrocona' is unremarkable until early spring, when red flowers and cones brighten up the plant. This is a 20-year-old specimen in Norfolk, England.

a further year. Unusually, a witch's broom arose on 'Acrocona' giving the truly dwarf plant **P. a. 'Pusch'**, a miniature of its parent but much more freely coning, with masses of tiny red cones fading to buff; it is unlikely to exceed a height or width of 24in (60cm) in ten years. Both are grafted.
G; H 5–6ft (1.5–1.8m), W 5–6ft (1.5–1.8m)
UH 16–26ft (5–8m), UW 16–26ft (5–8m), Z 2–8

Picea abies 'Aurea'. The fast-growing golden Norway Spruce has needles brushed with gold when young in an open sunny position, but as it gets older the yellow is less pronounced and it can be dull in winter. The slower-growing **P. a. 'Aurea Magnifica'** is a better choice for yellow foliage: light yellow-green in summer, it turns to deep golden-yellow in winter. Early pruning is advised to restrict its size. It should be protected from exposure, which can cause sunscorch. **P. a. 'Argenteospica'**, also large-growing, has new shoots of a startling creamy-

white. **P. a. 'Finedonensis'** has silvery-white leaves and pale yellow new growth; it needs a semi-shady position and protection from strong sun and spring frosts. A new golden form from Sweden, **P. a. 'Norrkoping'**, has a more compact, pyramidal shape and seldom burns even in full sun.
G; H 16–23ft (5–7m), W 3–4ft (90cm–1.2m)
UH 65–100ft (20–30m), UW 16–26ft (5–8m), Z 2–8

Picea abies 'Clanbrassilana'. One of the oldest (introduced in 1836) but still one of the most distinctive dwarf conifers, this slowly makes a broad mound of dark green, short-needled foliage with prominent cinnamon-brown winter buds. It was discovered as a witch's broom on a *Picea abies* in Northern Ireland, probably around 1780, and named after Lord Clanbrassil who planted the original bush (which is still growing in Tollymore Park, Co. Down, and is approximately 10ft (3m) in height). With age, growth becomes a little more irregular, but the tightly held foliage is always attractive, although moss and algae can be problems. An attractive columnar form is widely grown in North America under the name *P. a.* 'Clanbrassiliana Stricta'.

H 12in (30cm), W 12–18in (30–45cm)

UH 10ft (3m), UW 10ft (3m), Z 3–8

Picea abies 'Cupressina'. Found in a German forest in 1904, this is one of the few narrow columnar forms; cypress-like, as the name suggests, it is a good accent plant and does not take up too much space. It forms a strong leading stem with upward-sweeping side branches – an imposing, slender, pyramidal tree, it can be pruned when young to restrict its size. In areas of winter snowfall, it is advisable to tie in the branches when it is young. *P. a.* 'Columnaris' is narrower, but its branches tend to open up with age. *P. a.* 'Pyramidata', despite its name, is much more open in habit.

H 6–8ft (1.8–2.5m), W 12–18in (30–45cm)

UH 50–65ft (15–20m), UW 6–10ft (1.8–3m), Z 2–8

Picea abies 'Frohburg'. Together with *P. a.* 'Aarburg' and *P. a.* 'Wartburg', this was introduced by the Haller nursery in Switzerland in 1965; all three have prostrate or weeping branches. 'Frohburg' is perhaps the most garden-worthy, being smaller and slower in growth; it often makes its own upward-leading stem (a cane should be provided if not). The other two are much more vigorous and more wayward in growth. All have mid-green needles (those of 'Frohburg' are much smaller); the side branches should be trained upwards to a desired height, and will then sweep down to form a carpet at the base. All make excellent stand-alone specimens for viewing from a distance. As with

P.a. 'Inversa', *P.a.* 'Reflexa' and *P.a.* 'Pendula', they can be trained into many shapes and forms; without training, growth can be inconsistent.

'Frohburg' 6–12in (15–30cm) a year; 'Aarburg' and 'Wartburg' 12–18in (30–45cm) a year

Growth rates estimated, Z 3–7

Picea abies 'Gregoryana'. A very slow-growing miniature that makes a small hummock of fine, light green needles, with congested foliage and short stems that terminate in pinhead light brown buds; it is studded with bright green new shoots in late spring. Slower-growing than *P. a.* 'Gregoryana Veitchii', with a stiffer, more prickly feel, it is still not as prickly as the rarer *P. a.* 'Echiniformis', the Hedgehog Spruce, which produces stronger clusters of growths that break away from the compact bush with age. All are ideal for miniature gardens, troughs or sinks, but should not be allowed to dry out.

H 6–8in (15–20cm), W 6–8in (15–20cm)

UH 18–24in (45–60cm), UW 3–4ft (90cm–1.2m), Z 3–8

Picea abies 'Inversa'. This weeping form is almost identical to *P. a.* 'Reflexa' and is sometimes confused with it in the nursery trade: 'Inversa' has more flexible branches, with winter buds that are pointed and a dull brown; 'Reflexa' is a coarser and more vigorous plant with larger, darker green needles, and larger, light brown buds. Both are quite vigorous. Without training, they would remain prostrate to form an enormous carpet; trained upwards on a stake to the desired height, they will then cascade down. However, to confuse matters, it is said that 'Inversa' will behave like *P. a.* 'Pendula' (and may even be the same; see below), in time throwing up a leading shoot. Arresting specimens,

they can be very effective over walls or down banks; they lend themselves to training into mounds, cascades, unusual hedges and fantastical shapes. Both G

Growth rate estimated 6–12cm (15–30cm) in a year; Z 3–8

Picea abies 'Little Gem'. An apt name for this plant discovered around 1958 by the Grootendorst nursery in Boskoop, Holland, growing as a witch's broom on the popular Bird's Nest Spruce (*P. a.* 'Nidiformis'). Propagated easily from cuttings, it became a worldwide seller, a true dwarf forming a tight flattish dome of short crowded branchlets, with minute light green leaves soft to the touch. In spring it is one of the earliest to break into growth with bright green shoots which can be susceptible to spring frost. Unfortunately, it is susceptible to spider mites, particularly in hotter, drier climates. It is a good alpine garden plant, and can be grown on a patio, in sinks or troughs.

H 8–12in (20–30cm), W 12–18in (30–45cm)

UH 24–30in (60–75cm), UW 3–4ft (90cm–1.2m), Z 3–8

Picea abies 'Nidiformis'. The Bird's Nest Spruce gets its name from the indentation in the center of its otherwise flat top, more evident on younger plants. Found in Germany in 1904, it has become one of the most widely distributed plants. It has pleasing light green foliage, with slender branches radiating from the center, gradually building up height and eventually losing its bird's nest center. Like many dwarf forms of the Norway Spruce, it is rather dull in winter but transformed in spring with fresh bright green shoots.

H 12–18in (30–45cm), W 24–36in (60–90cm)

UH 10–16ft (3–5m), UW 10–16ft (3–5m), Z 3–7

Picea abies 'Nidiformis', 14 years old, makes a solid corner structure to summer perennial and shrub borders in Peter Wooster's garden in Connecticut.

Picea abies 'Pendula'. The Weeping Norway Spruce is a name that has attached itself to almost any selection with prostrate or pendulous branches, but in the US in particular it is still used to describe this vigorous form (which may be the same as *P. a.* 'Inversa'). It has dark green needles, which unless trained will be prostrate, though it may occasionally throw up shoots in all directions. It is most often seen trained upwards on a post to make a broad, multi-branched top with most leading shoots and all branches beneath cascading down to form a carpet at the base. See also *P. a.* 'Inversa'.

G; growth rate 12–18in (30–45cm) a year, Z 3–8

Picea abies 'Pygmaea'. Though several similar variants are available, if you can get the true 'Pygmaea' it is one of the best and oldest, introduced over two hundred years ago. It slowly makes a compact little bush of light to mid-green needles, with congested bunches of short-stemmed branches clustered irregularly over the plant, each terminating in a minute brown ovoid bud, very prominent in winter.

H 6–10in (15–25cm), W 6–10in (15–25cm)

UH 4–5ft (1.2–1.5m), UW 3–4ft (90cm–1.2m), Z 3–8

Picea abies 'Repens'. Truly a prostrate form, with flattened branches and branchlets angled upwards at 45 degrees and overlapping with age, this seldom builds much height in the center of the plant. The leaves are mid-green, slightly lighter than the similar *P. a.* 'Procumbens', which builds in the center with age. This can happen on all prostrate forms if horizontal spreading branches are continually pruned, forcing the remaining growth upwards. Neither has prominent winter buds. *P. a.* 'Formanek' is another flat, carpet-like type which can be trained into a weeping growth habit.

H 12–18in (30–45cm), W 4–5ft (1.2–1.5m)

UH 24–36in (60–90cm), UW 16–26ft (5–8m), Z 3–8

Picea abies 'Rubra Spicata'. Though larger-growing if left to its own devices this seemingly ordinary Norway Spruce becomes quite extraordinary when new shoots appear in late spring – it literally turns a startling scarlet-crimson for a brief period, before greening again. It is best kept pruned as a pyramid immediately after new growth has faded, so that next year's buds develop. On both this and the similar *P. a.* 'Rydal', new shoots can be susceptible to spring frost. They make good second-row feature plants, with a brief moment of glory before they disappear into the background for the rest of the year.

Both G; H 8–10ft (2.5–3m), W 3–4ft (90cm–1.2m)

UH 50–65ft (15–20m), Z 3–8

Picea abies 'Wills Zwerg'. Discovered and named in the famous Oldenburg nursery area in northern Germany around 1936, this distinctive conifer had to wait for twenty years to be introduced. Not just another dwarf Norway Spruce, 'Wills Dwarf' (as it translates) forms an irregular pyramid of bright green, with new growth illuminating its darker center. Stronger competing side growths can be pruned away for symmetry; prune overall to reduce size.

H 4–5ft (1.2–1.5m), W 24–36in (60–90cm)

UH 16–26ft (5–8m), UW 10–13ft (3–4m), Z 3–8

PICEA ALCOQUIANA
(syn. *Picea bicolor*)

Picea alcoquiana 'Howell's Dwarf' (also known as 'Howell's Dwarf Tigertail') is a spreading bush with a rigid, semi-prostrate branching habit and all the foliage attributes of the species; without pruning it will get large in time. Flowers and cones on this type are unlikely. Stronger shoots emerge when the plant is older; these should be cut away to prevent it from reverting to a tree-like form. Its foliage has a real sparkle from the blue-white lower leaf surfaces, particularly noticeable in winter. This is a good

Picea breweriana, *20 years old, on a frosty winter morning in Norfolk, England.*

plant among heathers or low-growing, contrasting plants.

H 3–4ft (90cm–1.2m), W 4–5ft (1.2–1.5m)

UH 5–8ft (1.5–2.5m), UW 16–26ft (5–8m), Z 4–7

PICEA BREWERIANA

Brewer's Weeping Spruce is one of the most beautiful of conifers; though frustratingly slow as a young plant, it will after a great many years become a large tree. It is native to a small area high up in the Siskiyou Mountains of northern California and Oregon, where it grows to well over 100ft (30m). When young it is not very preposessing; it takes a few years to form a leading shoot and the weeping branchlets that are so characteristic of the species. Plants grown from seed may take ten years to reach 4ft (1.2m), but the grafted plants more

usually offered will be considerably quicker and are often from selected forms. The foliage is a rather dark, somber green, the plant developing into a broad pyramid with wide-spreading side branches; eventually it becomes more conical and pendulous streamers weep down. It is best in cool temperate regions, in sun or partial shade, and will grow in full shade if reasonable moisture exists – it grows faster in areas of high rainfall than low. This is a conifer to plant for future generations to enjoy: give it a prominent position, cane up a leading shoot when planting, trim any competing side branches to allow the leader to develop, stand back and wait. It is probably best avoided for the smaller garden, as it will undoubtedly get too big but be hard to part with.

H 4–6ft (1.2–1.8m), W 3–5ft (90cm–1.5m)

UH 50–65ft (15–20m), UW 16–23ft (5–7m), Z 5–8

PICEA ENGELMANNII

The Engelmann Spruce, much less used than the Colorado Blue Spruce (*Picea pungens*), can in one or two of its forms compete on more than equal terms – and it is less susceptible to aphid and spider mite attack. Originating in the Rocky Mountains from Arizona and New Mexico in the south to British Columbia in the north, it is a hardy, adaptable tree, pyramidal when young, conical with age. The upper branches are ascending but become more horizontal with age, the side branches are pendulous though this varies with plants raised from seed. The needles are mostly blue-green, with silver-white bands beneath, and have a pungent, fragrant, camphor-like odor when crushed.

Picea engelmannii 'Glauca'. This name may represent good selections with long, soft needles, gray-blue in winter, with new growth a startling powder-blue. On older plants, reddish-green pendulous cones mature to beige. Slightly less colorful, but suitable for the smaller garden, are *P. e.* 'Compact', with a pyramidal habit and shorter, thinner needles; and *P. e.* 'Bush's Lace', a selection made by Dick Bush of Canby, Oregon, with an upright habit and pendulous branches which in time create a gray-blue skirt around the base. They prefer moist soils, and will not be happy on thin chalk, or in very dry soils.

H 8–10ft (2.5–3m), W 5–6ft (1.5–1.8m)

UH 50–80ft (15–25m), UW 16–26ft (5–8m), Z 2–7

PICEA GLAUCA

The White Spruce spreads widely across northern North America from New England to South Dakota and up to Alaska, making a conical tree up to 80ft (25m). The species, though used relatively little as an ornamental or garden conifer, has given us some first-class cultivars selected from seed or witch's brooms. One of these, the Dwarf Alberta Spruce (*Picea glauca* var. 'Albertiana Conica'), is probably the largest-selling dwarf conifer in the world, and some of its many selections are listed below. Generally *Picea glauca* is of easy culture in cooler temperate zones and the cultivars are all hardy, though some are susceptible to spring frost on emerging shoots and some are prone to red spider mite damage, especially in warmer climates.

Picea glauca var. *albertiana* 'Alberta Blue'. Found by Ike Bos and his son Richard in Surrey, this was named by me and seems to be the bluest selection to date. It is difficult to be sure which is the most stable, reliable or desirable of these – all vary somewhat in their habit and intensity

Picea engelmannii *'Compact', 20 years old, brightened up by new summer growth, Norfolk, England.*

of summer color, which on new growth can be vividly blue, and in their prevalence to revert to green; all are similar in habit, pyramidal to conical, and any shoots reverting to green should be trimmed away. It was preceded by *P. g.* 'Sanders Blue', which has a bluish cast; *P. g.* 'Arneson's Blue Variegated', with light powder-blue patches often reverting to green; and the smaller-growing *P .g.* 'Blue Wonder', introduced by the young plant nursery at Kordes, Germany, which is less intensely blue but also has less reversion to green. Since all of these are not available in every country, your choice may be limited.

H 24–30in (60–75cm), W 12in (30cm)

UH 10–16ft (3–5m), UW 3–4ft (90cm–1.2m), Z 2–7

Picea glauca var. *albertiana* 'Alberta Globe'. One of a great many sports or mutations to arise on *P. g.* var. *albertiana* 'Conica', this distinctive dense, rounded bush was found as

a witch's broom in Holland. It has short green needles and rigid brown winter buds that invite a pat. In spring, brown buds burst open as new bright green shoots emerge. This is a splendid and readily available cultivar for alpine gardens, troughs or miniature gardens. Less common, and unlike the *P. g.* var. *albertiana* 'Conica' type, is another globular miniature form, *P. g.* 'Cecilia', a witch's broom found in the USA on *P. glauca* with blue-gray needles. Even more compact is *P. g.* 'Blue Planet', a tennis ball of a plant with tiny, deep blue-green leaves, dotted with minute brown winter buds. Another minute green form is aptly called *P. g.* var. *albertiana* 'Tiny'.

H 12in (30cm), W 12–18in (30–45cm)

UH 3–4ft (90cm–1.2m), UW 3–4ft (90cm–1.2m), Z 2–7

Picea glauca var. *albertiana* 'Conica'. The Dwarf Alberta Spruce, sold by the million perhaps because it looks so like a forest tree in miniature, is used not only as a garden plant but decked out each winter as a tiny Christmas tree. It was discovered in 1904 as a young seedling growing near Lake Laggan, Alberta, in the Canadian Rockies, by Professor J. G. Jack and Alfred Rehder of the Arnold Arboretum while they were waiting for a train; they brought it back to Boston with other similar seedlings. It makes a perfect dwarf pyramid, with soft, light green foliage with two or more tiny brown winter buds at the end of each shoot. In late spring these swell, then burst open with bright green new shoots that transform the whole plant; the needles mature to a duller green as the summer progresses. The metamorphosis is bewitching to gardeners, but unfortunately the plant is also irresistible to red spider mite, particularly in warm dry periods in spring and summer; preventive action must be taken if its appearance is not to be ruined.

H 3–4ft (90cm–1.2m), W 18–24in (45–60cm)

UH 10–16ft (3–5m), UW 6–8ft (1.8–2.5m), Z 2–7

Picea glauca 'J. W. Daisy's White'. This quite spectacular dwarf arose as a sport in Belgium, and is becoming more widely known. It has the same form as its parent var. *albertiana* 'Conica' but is slower-growing. From late summer through to winter it has pale yellow-green foliage; in late spring the first buds begin to break into creamy-white shoots, and soon this Cinderella is the belle of the ball as the whole plant becomes a pyramid of creamy-white foliage, toning down over the next several weeks. Often further flushes of growth occur later in the summer. The new shoots can be susceptible to spring frosts, so they need protection from early morning sun. Other sports from *P. g.* var. *albertiana* 'Conica' with gold or yellow foliage include *P. g.* **'Rainbow's End'**, found by Don Howse when working at the Iseli nursery, which needs a warm climate and full sun to perform since only on the second flush in mid to late summer do the creamy-yellow shoots appear in contrast with the darker, older foliage.

H 24–36in (60–90cm), W 12–18in (30–45cm)

UH 6–10ft (1.8–3m), UW 3–4ft (90cm–1.2m), Z 2–7

Picea glauca 'Laurin'. One of the best of many recent introductions with green needles to originate from mutations or witch's brooms on *P. g.* var. *albertiana* 'Conica', this is a bud mutation found in Germany. It is a perfect miniature replica of its parent, with growth of less than 2in (5cm) a year and tiny needles of a rich, deeper

green. It is slower-growing than *P. g.* 'Jean's Dilly', which makes a narrow pyramid of deep green.

H 10–16in (25–40cm), W 6–10in (15–25cm)

UH 4–5ft (1.2–1.5m), UW 24–36in (60–90cm), Z 2–7

PICEA MARIANA

Picea mariana 'Ericoides'. A dwarf clone of the Black Spruce native to the northern part of North America, a hardy and adaptable species that does well in most soil conditions, this makes a low-spreading bush with tiny heather-like blue-green needles, dense but soft to the touch. Give it space to spread. It is often confused with *P. m.* 'Nana', which has deeper blue-green needles and is a true miniature, much more compact – after thirty years it will not be more than 12in (30cm) tall and 24in (60cm) wide, which makes it ideal for troughs and sinks.

H 12in (30cm), W 24–30in (60–75cm)

UH 12–18in (30–45cm), UW 5–6ft (1.5–1.8m), Z 3–7

PICEA MARIORIKA

Picea mariorika 'Machala'. An attractive conifer, considered a hybrid

between *P. mariana* and *P. omorika*, this makes a broad-spreading bush which builds height with age. The curved blue-gray needles give a two-tone effect, often appearing more silver-blue in summer, gray-green in winter. Older plants may develop more vigorous side and vertical shoots, which are best cut out to restrict size.

H 24–36in (60–90cm), W 3–4ft (90cm–1.2m)

UH 6–10ft (1.8–3m), UW 16–23ft (5–7m), Z 3–7

PICEA OMORIKA

The Serbian Spruce is one of the most handsome species – it is also very adaptable, which is strange in some ways because it originates from a very small area of limestone mountains along the upper Drina river in Bosnia and Serbia, where it attains narrow, spire-like crowns of 100ft (30m). In cultivation variation does occur from seed, but most make narrowly pyramidal trees, with older branches pendulous and curving up at the tips, exposing the silvery undersides of the otherwise somber dark green leaves. Deep purple cones lie in clusters on maturing trees. Always extensively grown and popular in Germany, it deserves to be more widely planted – it is of easy culture on almost any soil, will take dry or drought conditions better than most spruces, and is resistant to most pests and diseases. Attractive as a single specimen, it is magnificent in a group with deciduous trees as background.

H 10–16ft (3–5m), W 4–5ft (1.2–1.5m)

UH 65–80ft (20–25m), UW 10–16ft (3–5m), Z 5–8

Picea glauca *'Laurin', a 15-year-old plant in early summer in Norfolk, England, contrasting with the creamy-white dwarf broom,* Cytisus ardoinoi, *behind.*

Picea omorika 'Nana'. In early years the Dwarf Serbian Spruce makes a rounded dome of dense green foliage, the broad needles dark green above with two bright silver-white stripes beneath, some of which are exposed, adding sparkle to the plant. Sooner or later it will develop one or more leading shoots and eventually one will win; it then belies its name by making a dense pyramid of several yards (metres), displaying more and more of the silver sparkle as it is viewed from below. Being narrow, it makes a specimen plant suitable for the medium-sized garden.

G; H 3–4ft (90cm–1.2m), W 24–30in (60–75cm)

UH 23–33ft (7–10m), UW 6–10ft (1.8–3m), Z 5–8

Picea omorika 'Pendula'. This name undoubtedly covers many selections made over the years from seedlings of the Serbian Spruce. Some are extremely slender, perhaps less than 3ft (90cm)across and 33ft (10m) high, with side branches sweeping vertically down along the stem; others may be much wider with pendulous side branches. *P. o.* 'Pendula Bruns' is a selection to look for; its leading shoot needs training for a few years, then its branches cascade down the trunk, making an arresting narrow specimen.

Most pendulous forms G

H 6–10ft (1.8–3m), W 2–3ft (60–90cm)

UH 33–50ft (10–15m), UW 3–10ft (90cm–3m)

Sizes approximate, Z 5–8

Picea omorika 'Pimoko'. Found as a witch's broom on a *P. omorika* in Germany, this has a rounded compact habit, with congested branches and dark green forward-pointing needles that hide the stems. Some shoot tips push up at odd angles to the main branches, showing their bright silver needles, adding a sparkle to the plant.

Picea omorika *'Pendula Bruns', 10 years old, in Norfolk, England: its narrow form creates a focal point among lower-growing summer perennials.*

There have been several worthy dwarf and miniature additions to this range, mostly from the Horstmann nursery in Germany.

G; H 8–12in (20–30cm), 12–16in (30–40cm)

UH 3–4ft (90cm–1.2m), UW 4–6ft (1.2–1.8m), Z 4–8

PICEA ORIENTALIS

The Oriental Spruce or Caucasian Spruce comes from the Caucasian mountains of Georgia and north-eastern Turkey. The species makes a handsome pyramidal to columnar tree, up to 130ft (40m), typically with short, glossy, dark green needles shorter than on any other spruce. New growth occurs late, so it avoids spring frosts; generally, the species and cultivars are easy to grow on most soils and situations and will take drier conditions than most, but they can be prone to windburn in very cold, exposed situations. A usual bonus with mature plants is an abundance of bright red male flowers or cones in late spring, and cylindrical purple-brown female cones exuding resin as they ripen to brown.

H 10–16ft (3–5m), W 5–6ft (1.5–1.8m)

UH 65–100ft (20–30m), UW 16–26ft (5–8m), Z 4–7

Picea orientalis '**Aurea**' (formerly 'Aureospicata'). Seeing this large-growing conifer for most of the year, it is difficult to imagine anything yellow ('*aurea*') about it at all – like the species, it has short, dark green needles that hide the stems. But in early summer the buds burst, and new shoots of golden-yellow appear as if by magic all over the plant; the new leaves emerge to create a bright gold, enhanced by the dark green older foliage. Within six weeks or so the new growth becomes green, and is just a memory until the next year.

G; H 8–10ft (2.5–3m), W 4–6ft (1.2–1.8m)

UH 50–65ft (15–20m), UW 16–23ft (5–7m), Z 4–7

Picea orientalis '**Barnes**'. This is one of several varied dwarf selections for the smaller garden, making a spreading cushion of dark green foliage with a nest-like indentation in the center. Even flatter is *P. o.* '**Bergman's Gem**', but on both of these upward growths will occur with age. From Germany, *P. o.* '**Professor Langner**' is a similarly attractive miniature form, while a most desirable miniature is *P. o.* '**Tom Thumb**', a witch's broom from *P. o.* '**Skylands**' with tiny leaves of golden-yellow. The last three are all ideal for troughs or miniature gardens.

All G; H 12–18in (30–45cm), W 18–24in (45–60cm)

UH 3–4ft (90cm–1.2m), UW 4–6ft (1.2–1.8m), Z 4–7

Picea orientalis '**Skylands**' (syn. 'Aurea Compacta'). An outstanding ornamental conifer when in the right situation, this makes a narrow pyramid of golden-yellow foliage all year round. A great find in Skylands Farm, New Jersey (now Ringwood State Park), it is slow-growing when young; a leading shoot should be trained up a cane, and stronger side branches pruned as required. It needs a sunny situation but one sheltered from freezing winds; in hot climates it will grow in partial shade, though this will affect the intensity of color. When young it is prone to sunscorch. Early care will be rewarded, as it becomes a beacon of bright yellow with an amazing annual display of crimson-scarlet male flowers and pendulous purple-brown cones.

H 5–8ft (1.5–2.5m), W 3–4ft (90cm–1.2m)

UH 33–50ft (10–15m), UW 6–10ft (1.8–3m), Z 4–7

PICEA PUNGENS

The Colorado Blue Spruce – native not only to Colorado but also to New Mexico, Utah, Wyoming and Idaho – grows at high elevations to become a large conical tree of up to 100ft (30m). Mostly gray-green, with sharply pointed prickly leaves, its new growth is bluer and soft, but it varies considerably in color and form when grown from seed. From the wild and from selected seedlings come a wide range of gray-blue or silver-blue cultivars which, where they can be grown, add color and spectacle to the garden; most of these will be grafted. Seedling-raised plants are often sold as Christmas trees.

The Colorado Blue Spruce and its cultivars ideally need full sun. They are distinctive not only for their color but for their prominent light brown winter buds, which swell in late spring and burst into new growth of an intense silver-blue. Taller-growing cultivars of some age occasionally have bright red male flowers and pendulous pale green cylindrical cones ripening to light brown. An adaptable plant which can take drier conditions than most Spruce, it is prone to insect attack, particularly red spider mites and especially in hotter, drier conditions; a preventive systemic insecticide spray in spring should protect its appearance. There are so many cultivars, both old and new, and not all are readily available, so the following list must be restricted.

H 6–10ft (1.8–3m), W 4–5ft (1.2–1.5m)

UH 50–65ft (15–20m), UW 10–16ft (3–5m)

Growth rate approximate, Z 2–8

Picea pungens '**Fat Albert**'. In a few years this has become a widely grown and popular cultivar. Its unusually descriptive name was suggested by Don Howse, assistant to Jean Iseli in 1975, for a distinctive selection in their nursery. A symmetrical, pyramidal tree with a broad base, it is quite successfully (although not always) rooted from cuttings, which leads to uniformity and faster growth so that it has less need of staking or training. It has softer needles than some cultivars, blue with less silver or gray. It will become large in time.

H 8–10ft (2.5–3m), W 4–5ft (1.2–1.5m)

UH 50–65ft (15–20m), UW 16–23ft (5–7m), Z 2–8

Picea pungens '**Globosa**' (syn. 'Glauca Globosa'). The most popular dwarf Blue Spruce, this forms a neat irregular bush with closely set branches angled outwards and upwards from the center. The light brown stems are circled by stiff, rather prickly, blue-gray needles, brighter in the sunny positions it prefers than in shade, where it will not color or prosper. The light brown winter buds become larger through the late winter,

Picea pungens *'Globosa', 25 years old, in Norfolk, England, late summer; it is regularly pruned to keep it compact.*

Picea pungens *'Hoopsii', 18 years old, in Michigan, summer; it makes a vivid contrast to the orange* Lilium tigrinum.

and in spring bright silver-blue shoots break the membrane to produce a dazzling display of new soft growth, transforming the plant's color for the whole summer. Plants are seldom available grown from cuttings (which would keep them more reliably dwarf); grafted plants, after a number of years, tend to develop stronger leading shoots which, if not cut away, will lead to an attractive dense pyramid shape. *P. p.* **'Montgomery'**, widely grown in North America, is almost identical in its color, and early and late pyramidal habit; **'Glauca Compacta'** is also similar.

All mostly G

H 18–30in (45–75cm), W 24–30in (60–75cm)

UH 26–33ft (8–10m), UW 8–10ft (2.5–3m)

(without pruning), Z 2–8

Picea pungens **'Gloria'**. This is ideal for the smaller garden. Named by conifer nurseryman Don Hatch after his wife, it forms a low-spreading carpet of upright angled shoots with blue-gray needles, with an annual growth of no more than 2in (5cm). Like many selections of similar habit, it is likely to be a collector's item because of short supply. From the US, *P. p.* **'St Mary's Broom'** is a plant of similar proportions and color, although perhaps taller and more rounded with age.

Both G; H 4–6in (10–15cm), W 12in (30cm)

UH 12in (30cm), UW 5–6ft (1.5–1.8m), Z 2–8

Picea pungens **'Hoopsii'**. One of the most popular and spectacular of the large Blue Spruces, this was selected in

Holland for its bright silver-blue, almost silvery-white foliage; its long, curved, thick and quite sharp needles are larger than most other cultivars. Because they are pointed forward, almost hiding the light brown stems, the leaves appears much denser, adding to the plant's appeal. Also conical, with shorter, curved, silver-gray needles, is *P. p.* **'Thomsen'**, one of the most sought-after forms. Both of these are eventually large and make ideal specimens where space is available, although they can be regularly trimmed to keep them more compact. *P. p.* **'Hoto'** and **'Erich Frahm'** are other noteworthy selections.

All mostly G; H 6–8ft (1.8–2.5m), W 3–4ft (90cm–1.2m)

UH 50–65ft (15–20m), UW 10–16ft (3–5m), Z 2–8

Picea pungens 'Iseli Fastigiate'. Initially a narrowly columnar plant, this becomes broader and more conical with age, and is less blue than many selected cultivars. An attractive form, it needs an open sunny spot to maintain density and, like many fastigiate plants, may need tying in to prevent snowfall damage.

G; H 6–8ft (1.8–2.5m), W 18–24in (45–60cm)
UH 33–50ft (10–15m), UW 8–10ft (2.5–3m), Z 2–8

Picea pungens 'Koster'. Koster's Blue Spruce is undoubtedly a good blue form, although in early years it is somewhat wayward in habit, needing a leading shoot to be trained and side shoots to be pruned if it is to form a balanced specimen. It seems to cone more freely than some other cultivars, but this may depend on climate and soil conditions. *P. p.* 'Oldenburg' was selected not only for its color but also for its ability to form a leading shoot early and develop a regular habit, even when grafted. It is quite vigorous, making a dense, narrow pyramid with long, blue-gray needles.

H 6–10ft (1.8–3m), W 4–5ft (1.2–1.5m)
UH 33–50ft (10–15m), UW 10–16ft (3–5m), Z 2–8

Picea pungens 'Pendula' (also known as 'Glauca Pendula'). This is likely to be a very variable tree, and there are probably several forms in cultivation. All exhibit a tendency to sprawl along the ground unless they are trained up a strong stake for some years – the leading shoot always wants to follow an inclination downwards. It can make quite an arresting and spectacular specimen, with branches and branchlets sweeping to the

Picea pungens *'Procumbens', 25 years old, in the Miller garden, Seattle; it shows up brilliantly among the fiery autumn tints of an* Acer japonicum *'Aconitifolium'.*

ground, in time creating a silver-blue carpet at the base. Use it as a specimen in a bed or a lawn, and allow it space. It is not always readily available.

G; 4–8in (10–20cm) a year (estimated), Z 2–8

Picea pungens 'Prostrata' (often listed as 'Glauca Prostrata'). This and *P. p.* 'Procumbens' (often listed as 'Glauca Procumbens' and in the UK *Plant Finder* as Glauca Group prostrate) are essentially the same type of plant – selections made with a prostrate or procumbent habit which can be undeniably attractive planted on a slope, over a rock, or among other contrasting plants. Often grafted from horizontal side shoots, while they may remain largely prostrate for a few years, they will inevitably develop vertical or upward-angled shoots which, if not pruned, will cause the plant to revert to a tree-like form. Even if there is a reliably prostrate form, the very fact of grafting it on to a normally tree-like seedling understock will mean increased vigor which eventually will produce an upward shoot. But such spreading

specimens can be of great beauty and character, so keep the pruning shears ready. Plants on poorer, thinner soils may remain prostrate for longer. Perhaps more reliable, but with green needles, horizontal branches and gradually mounding, is *P. p.* 'Mesa Verde', from Iseli Nurseries. All these will become large in time.

Growth rate 6–12in (15–30cm) a year, Z 2–8

Picea pungens 'Walnut Glen' (formerly 'Goldie'). Several selections of the Blue Spruce are now available with variegated shoots or golden-tinged foliage. From the US, this makes a typical pyramidal Blue Spruce with gray-blue needles, but its new growth is a startling creamy-yellow in late spring, toning down in summer. *P. p.* 'Maigold', from the Hachmann nursery in northern Germany, has blue-green foliage as dark background to its creamy-gold new growth, which is effective for several weeks. Selections with both golden-yellow growth and needles are *P. p.* 'Aurea', with its best color in winter; *P. p.* 'Lutea', deeper yellow, with gold on

the needles only if exposed to light, and the compact *P. p.* **'Stanley Gold'**, with a good year-round color. Many of these golden and variegated selections are rather prone to spring frost damage and sunscorch so they are not always satisfactory garden plants, but this should not put off keener gardeners. All need good light, but shelter from early morning sun.

H 5–6ft (1.5–1.8m), W 3–4ft (90cm–1.2m)

UH 23–33ft (7–10m), UW 8–10ft (2.5–3m), Z 2–7

PICEA SITCHENSIS

Picea sitchensis 'Papoose'. The Sitka Spruce, native to north-western North America from Alaska to northern California, is an important timber tree, now grown in other parts of the world as well. It is strange, then, that this adaptable conifer has not given more selections and cultivars of garden merit. 'Papoose' and its sister plant *P. s.* **'Tenas'** both originated as witch's brooms in Vancouver Island; they are so similar that they are confusing to gardeners and nurserymen alike. Both make rounded but flattish-topped bushes, with sharp, prickly needles. In a striking reversal of the normal foliage habit, it is the undersides that are dark green, while the upper sides are a distinct silver with a bluish cast. In time, 'Tenas' in particular becomes large, its growth rate at least a third faster than 'Papoose', but it is difficult to tell them apart when young.

H 18–24in (45–60cm), W 18–24in (45–60cm)

UH 5–8ft (1.5–2.5m), UW 8–10ft (2.5–3m), Z 4–8

PINUS

The pines are one of the most varied and valuable genera of evergreen conifers with over a hundred species, a few native to sub-tropical regions but most spread around the northern hemisphere reaching up to the Arctic Circle. Some will make trees of up to 200ft (60m) while others, normally found in high mountainous regions or tundra, are true dwarf forms. Most taller species are conical when young, often dropping their lower branches when old and becoming round or flat-topped, much more open and craggy. They are able to survive, even thrive, on very poor, thin soils from sand dunes to rock crevices, where they often look very picturesque. They are all distinctive in that their needles are mostly clustered in bunches of two to five, although at least one species has only one needle cluster, *Pinus monophylla*. When more mature, many species exhibit male cones in spring at the end of the shoots; often red, they turn brown then yellow as they expand and shed their pollen, fertilizing the female flowers which usually develop cones the following year or later. Cones on many species are an attractive feature, varying in size, shape and color – some pendulous, some clustered in the branches. The new needle growth on pines is one of their most striking features, emerging like erect candles of very soft tissue, often a different color from the rest of the foliage, and only later expanding to normal size and rigidity. Whereas many other conifers, such as *Chamaecyparis* and *Thuja*, continue to grow through the whole summer, pines make this flush of growth only once a year; when it is over, the tips of the new shoots develop a terminal bud in preparation for the following year's growth.

An enormous variety of cultivars is available to gardeners – selected from seedlings, plants in the wild and witch's brooms – with all sorts of colors, shapes and forms, some good for windbreaks, others as miniatures for troughs and sinks. Pines grow in most soils, but generally prefer good drainage and full sun, although many will grow in half shade. The lower branches will lose their needles and die if too little light is available, but

Picea sitchensis 'Papoose', 20 years old, in Norfolk, England, summer; it is surrounded by Spiraea japonica 'Magic Carpet'.

on some species and cultivars this is an advantage since the bark can be attractive. Many gardeners are reluctant to prune pines, partly because of lack of knowledge about their specific requirements (see page 176). Pines are not without their pests and diseases (see page 182), but for most gardeners they are unlikely to be a real problem. Nearly all cultivars are propagated by grafting.

PINUS ARISTATA

The Rocky Mountain Bristlecone Pine is distributed in the wild in western Colorado, northern Arizona and New Mexico, and gets its common name from the sharply tipped spikes or bristles on the cones of mature plants. Some specimens are recorded as being 2,400 or so years old, but these are young in comparison to the Great Basin Bristlecone Pine or Ancient Pine (*Pinus longaeva*), the oldest living plant, with specimens accurately recorded at well over 4,000 years old. Old, gnarled, picturesque specimens of the latter exist in the White Mountains, California, at elevations as high as 11,500ft (3,450m), nature and plants between them creating living sculptures to marvel at. *Pinus aristata* grows pretty well at lower elevations, however, soon making a conical tree with upswept branches, densely clothed with clusters of five needles, green on the outside and flecked with spots of white resin, silvery on the inside. The whole plant is rich in resin: developed cones exude the sticky substance and are fragrant with it. *Pinus longaeva* has no white flecks of resin on its foliage, which is one of the main ways to tell the two species apart. Jerry Morris, a noted conifer collector from Denver, Colorado, has collected several witch's brooms in the

Pinus longaeva *'Sherwood Compact', 15 years old, in Norfolk, England, making new growth in early summer.*

wild, all dwarf, which will no doubt be available from specialist nurseries in due course.

H 5–6ft (1.5–1.8m), W 4–5ft (1.2–1.5m)
UH 26–33ft (8–10m), UW 10–16ft (3–5m), Z 4–8

Pinus longaeva 'Sherwood Compact' (formerly *P. aristata*). A most attractive dwarf or slow-growing conifer, introduced by Andy Sherwood from Gresham, Oregon. It forms a dense pyramid of blue-green foliage, the clusters of needles pointing forwards, hiding the stems and buds until new growth emerges in late spring.

Cones may appear on older plants.

H 18–24in (45–60cm), W 8–12in (20–30cm)
UH 16–23ft (5–7m), UW 4–6ft (1.2–1.8m), Z 4–8

PINUS BUNGEANA

First seen by a Dr. Bunge in China in 1831, the Lacebark Pine was brought to the West by Robert Fortune in 1846. Arguably it has the most beautiful bark of any conifer in cultivation, in time competing with the best Paperbark Maple (*Acer griseum*) for interest and beauty. The biggest drawback is its early slowness of growth, although it seems to respond more quickly in regions with hot summers. It is a three-needled pine, forming a conical, often multi-stemmed tree, which can reach 65ft (20m) but is usually smaller. The long, mid-green needles are quite stiff and sharply pointed, the clusters quite widely spaced, giving the plant an open appearance. After ten years or so, glimpses of the treat to come appear on the main stems – the smooth gray-green bark develops flakes that peel away to reveal patches of silver-white, green, brown and even purple. There is a magnificent specimen at the US National Arboretum in Washington D.C., and a more compact one at the Rowe Arboretum in Ohio; from these and other good forms clones and cultivars have been grafted. These are the best plants, because you cannot always be sure of what you will eventually get if you buy from seed. All prefer a sunny, well-drained position and would make a magnificent specimen in any garden, given space and patience.

H 4–6ft (1.2–1.8m), W 24–30in (60–75cm)

UH 33–50ft (10–15m), UW 16–26ft (5–8m), Z 5–8

PINUS CEMBRA

The Arolla Pine or Swiss Stone Pine grows at high altitudes from the European Alps to the Carpathian Mountains of central Europe, and for garden and landscape use it is a very ornamental if slow-growing tree. A five-needle pine making a rather formal, mostly columnar, densely foliaged plant, it has blue-green needles, bright bluish-white inside, which stay on the tree for up to five years. Maturer specimens develop yellow to buff male flowers in spring and, later, blue or purplish cones ripening to brown (these seldom open). The species and cultivars are

Pinus cembra *‘Glauca’, 25 years old, Norfolk, England, contrasting in early summer with the gold of the shrub* Physocarpus opulifolius *‘Dart’s Gold’.*

fairly adaptable and hardy, but will be best in sun with reasonable drainage. Selections have been made with bluer foliage, mostly labeled as *P. c.* **‘Glauca’**; others have a narrower, more fastigiate, habit such as *P. c.* **‘Stricta’**. I am impressed every winter by *P. c.* **‘Aureovariegata’** (syn. ‘Aurea’), whose needles, which have a gentle yellowy cast in summer, turn to a deep golden-yellow in winter, providing a warm glow in a sunny position.

H 5–6ft (1.5–1.8m), W 24–30in (60–75cm)

UH 33–50ft (10–15m), UW 6–10ft (1.8–3m)

Average sizes, Z 4–7

PINUS CONTORTA

The two-needled Lodgepole Pine (the name comes from its use as the main support for Native American tepees) is a variable species, with three distinct geographical varieties spreading from the Californian coastline to the Rocky Mountains, north through British Columbia to Alaska. The two main forms are the Coastal Lodgepole Pine or Shore Pine (*Pinus contorta* var. *contorta*) and the Rocky Mountain Lodgepole Pine (*Pinus contorta* var. *latifolia*). The first is a fast-growing, mainly coastal plant with bright green to yellowish-green twisted needles. It will grow on sandy or peaty, acid soils, and is quite variable in the wild where it has to battle with salt-laden winds; it is widely used for forestry in coastal areas. The second originates from inland regions, often at high elevations, and is a very hardy tree with dark green needles. The salt tolerance of the one and the greater hardiness of the other give a choice to foresters and gardeners looking for species or cultivars for a particular region. The species are not much used in gardens, though they would make good shelter or windbreaks, but there are a few excellent cultivars.

Pinus contorta var. contorta 'Frisian Gold'. This was an amazing find at the Jeddeloh nursery in northern Germany in 1962, when a golden witch's broom was spotted growing on a green-needled Beach Pine. It makes a low-growing mound of golden needles whose color is maintained all year

round; although it is a brilliant golden-yellow in full sun, light shade is preferable to prevent sunscorch. A choice plant, never in plentiful supply, it is a real gem where it can be grown. A recent selection of the Rocky Mountain Lodgepole Pine, **Pinus contorta var. latifolia 'Chief Joseph'**, is a hardier alternative and equally attractive – very slow-growing with golden-yellow, twisted needles, brighter in winter than summer. Neither are easy to propagate.
Both G; H 12–18in (30–45cm), W 18–24in (45–60cm)
UH 3–4ft (90cm–1.2m), UW 5–6ft (1.5–1.8m), Z 6–8

Pinus contorta var. contorta 'Spaan's Dwarf'. A pine of some character, named after the nurseryman who found it near Longbeach, Washington, this makes an irregular bush with upward-sweeping, somewhat contorted, thickish branches closely set with short, dark green needles, the shoots tipped with round, brown purple winter buds. Although the branches are not overly congested, thinning of inner branches bestows a more picturesque outline on this plant. It is ideal for the rock or alpine garden, and also excellent for bonsai.
H 18–24in (45–60cm), W 18–24in (45–60cm)
UH 4–5ft (1.2–1.5m), UW 6–8ft (1.8–2.5m), Z 5–8

PINUS DENSIFLORA
The Japanese Red Pine is native not only to Japan but to Korea, northeast China and north-eastern Russia; it gets its common name from the orange-brown flaking bark on older trees. Although this two-needled pine reaches 65–100ft (20–30cm) in its native habitat, it is usually much

Pinus contorta var. contorta 'Spaan's Dwarf' in early spring, showing clusters of male flowers and dark green needles.

shorter in cultivation, making a rather irregular tree with a wide-spreading and often lax habit, its main trunk often leaning. The branches are clothed in long, quite bright green needles, which differentiate it from the somewhat similar Scotch Pine (*Pinus sylvestris*), whose needles are a distinct blue-green. This species is generally of easier cultivation and hardier than *Pinus thunbergii*.
H 8–10ft (2.5–3m), W 5–6ft (1.5–1.8m)
UH 50–65ft (15–20m), UW 23–33ft (7–10m), Z 3–8

Pinus densiflora 'Alice Verkade'. A seedling selected by the Verkade nursery in New Jersey and introduced in 1972, this has a broad-spreading dome-like form, the bright green needles very densely held on upward-curving branches. Like many of the *Pinus densiflora* cultivars, it will get large in time. Also slow-growing is **P. d. 'Jane Kluis'**, considered to be a hybrid between *P. densiflora* and *P. thunbergii* mostly on account of its striking white winter buds, its light green needles and its habit of making a rounded, rather flat-topped bush; it is an attractive garden plant in general plantings. Also gaining popularity in the US is **P. d. 'Low Glow'**, a seedling from a witch's broom introduced by Sydney Waxman of the University of Connecticut, a low mound of bright, almost yellow-green needles.
H 24–36in (60–90cm), W 3–4ft (90cm–1.2m)
UH 5–8ft (1.5–2.5m), UW 10–16ft (3–5m), Z 3–8

Pinus densiflora 'Pendula'. Like most pendulous forms, this selection would be prostrate if not trained up a stake to the required height so that the branches cascade downwards. It is also very effective tumbling over a rock or a wall, with its long, dark green needles and eventually reddish

Pinus densiflora *'Pendula'* trained to tumble downwards at Brookside Gardens, Maryland, summer.

emerge like silvery-white candles to cover the tree, a most attractive feature. The Bosnian Pine is very free-coning from early on: dense clusters of yellow male flowers are displayed in late spring to shed their pollen; female flowers, red at the tips of the new shoots, soon develop into tight cones of a deep cobalt blue, a color maintained as they enlarge into the second year, but maturing to light brown as they open. This is an adaptable tree, which grows happily on alkaline and acid soils, including those that are quite dry. Some taller-growing selections have been made, such as **P. h.** '**Satellit**' which has a narrower habit, particularly when young, and glossy, deep green needles that curve tightly towards the stem.

H 8–10ft (2.5–3m), W 4–5ft (1.2–1.5m)
UH 50–65ft (15–20m), UW 16–23ft (5–7m), Z 5–8

Pinus heldreichii '**Compact Gem**'.
This has dark, densely held, glossy green needles, curving to hug the stem

bark. Initially slow-growing, it needs training when it is a young plant as older branches become brittle, and it will be quite open in habit unless the side branches are pruned.

Growth rate 6–10in (15–25cm) a year, Z 3–8

Pinus densiflora '**Umbraculifera**'.
The Japanese Umbrella Pine (a common name also given to *Sciadopitys verticillata*), called Tanyosho or Tagyosho in the US, is a famous selection: the maturer tree much resembles an umbrella, its multi-stemmed branches supporting a broad, rounded crown of deep green foliage. It often cones very freely, with cones smaller than the species. With age its crowning glory is not the umbrella, but the trunks that are supporting it – they develop beautiful orange-brown

flaking bark which makes this a specimen to treasure.

H 4–5ft (1.2–1.5m), W 5–6ft (1.5–1.8m)
UH 16–23ft (5–7m), UW 16–26ft (5–8m), Z 3–8

PINUS HELDREICHII

The Bosnian Pine – once considered to be a form of the closely related *Pinus leucodermis* – is distributed in the wild in the Balkans including Greece, Albania and Bulgaria, making an attractive, eventually large, conical tree with dark green foliage. It is a wonderful background plant, with upswept branches and dark, lustrous, forward-pointing green needles borne in pairs, which hide the large brown buds. In early summer the new shoots

Pinus koraensis *'Silveray', 10 years old, Norfolk, England; a close look at the foliage and cones in late summer.*

at the branch tips. Like the species, it will eventually have bright yellow clusters of male flowers and blue cones. Consider the site carefully when planting, or be prepared to move it before it gets too large. It is a real gem both as a young and an older plant, and an ideal contrast to other conifers, shrubs, grasses and perennials. More recent introductions **P. h. 'Malink'** and a Horstmann selection, **P. h. 'Zwerg Schneverdingen'**, both slow-growing, would appear to be similar.

All G; H 3–4ft (90cm–1.2m), W 24–36in (60–90cm)

UH 26–50ft (8–15m), UW 16–26ft (5–8m), Z 5–8

Pinus heldreichii 'Smidtii' (formerly 'Schmidtii'). If *P. h.* 'Compact Gem' may be a little too large for the smaller garden, this is a perfect alternative, a miniature Bosnian Pine. It was found by Eugene Smidt in 1926 in the mountains near Sarajevo, Yugoslavia, not as a witch's broom but as a hundred-year-old broadly conical bush 10ft (3m) high and wide. He took grafts for reproduction, and the

original plant is still where he found it. He is honored for this marvelous find, so it is a pity that for many years the plant's name was wrongly spelled! This is in the top ten of conifers. It forms a tight hummock of lustrous, short, sharp, dark green needles, and will be even more compact on thinner, poorer soils. It is best in sun with good drainage. A cultivar called **P. h. 'Pygmy'** appears to be identical.

H 8–12in (20–30cm), W 8–12in (20–30cm)

UH (after 100 years!) 10ft (3m), UW 10ft (3m), Z 5–8

PINUS KORAENSIS

Pinus koraensis 'Silveray' (formerly 'Glauca'). This may be the best form of the little-known and underused five-needled Korean Pine, a very hardy tree resembling a somewhat more open Arolla Pine (*Pinus cembra*), the columnar pine native to Europe. It is relatively slow in early years, forming a rather open-branched column of gray-green branches with clusters of deep green needles showing bright silver-white bands on the reverse. It,

and the species, are notable for often producing cones on quite young plants, starting with red male and female flowers in late spring, followed by clusters of olive-green stem-hugging cones, which ripen to light brown and are tipped with white resin. *P. k.* **'Winton'** is slow-growing but in time makes a beautiful rounded shrub, with luxuriant blue-green needles.

All G; H 6–8ft (1.8–2.5m), W 3–4ft (90cm–1.2m)

UH 26–33ft (8–10m), UW 5–6ft (1.5–1.8m), Z 4–7

PINUS MONOPHYLLA

The common name of Single-Leaf Pinyon Pine pretty much describes this slow-growing species from the south-western US and northern Mexico, one of the nut pines. This is a group of eleven species known as the Pinyon Pines, all originating from the same region, and including the Rocky Mountain Pinyon *(P. edulis)* and the Mexican Pinyon *(P. cembroides)*. Most species have edible seeds, much appreciated by birds, animals and humans; they were a staple food for Native Americans. These species, including *P. monophylla*, are adaptable to hot, dry conditions and poor, well-drained soils, but they will grow well enough in other conditions given good drainage. *P. monophylla* is a curiosity, albeit an attractive one, with a conical habit, and upright branches clothed in curved gray-green mostly single needles, which become more bluish-green in summer on new growth; ovoid cones occur on older plants. A selection found in the wild, *P. m.* **'Tioga Pass'**, with bluer needles than the species, is best in full sun.

H 4–5ft (1.2–1.5m), W 24–30in (60–75cm)

UH 33ft (10m), UW 13–16ft (4–5m), Z 7–8

Pinus heldreichii *'Smidtii', 20 years old, Norfolk, England, winter.*

PINUS MUGO

The two-needled European Mountain Pine or Dwarf Mountain Pine is very variable in its native central European mountains – from sprawling prostrate shrubs to small trees – with several geographical forms from the mountains of western Spain to Romania in the East. With some notable exceptions, all have well-spaced green needles and quite prominent winter buds, with ovoid cones on older plants. The species and its cultivars are very hardy, and succeed in most soils including alkaline types where good drainage exists; they can withstand drought and the dry, inhospitable conditions of their natural environment. There is a wide range of excellent garden cultivars found as seedlings, sports and witch's brooms, some rather similar to each other, and several invaluable selections whose needles turn from green in summer to golden-yellow in winter. Some will therefore be ideal for a winter garden feature, others perfect for the smaller garden, for troughs or sinks. Many *P. mugo* cultivars can be rooted from cuttings; these are preferable to grafted forms though they will be slower-growing. More vigorous plants take well to pruning, which is best done when new growth emerges in the spring.

Species growth variable, most Z 3–8

Pinus mugo 'Corley's Mat'. Named after Ronald Corley, an avid collector in England who found it in a nursery seedling bed, this is one of a few prostrate or creeping forms of the European Mountain Pine. It has quite long, twisted, light to medium green needles, the branches upturned but spreading along the ground. It makes excellent ground cover, and is a good

Pinus mugo *'Humpy', 20 years old, Norfolk, England, makes new growth in early summer.*

choice for the rock or alpine garden or to hang over a rock or wall. *P. m.* 'Jeddeloh' from northern Germany is similar. Another German variety, *P. m.* 'Krauskopf', seems reliably prostrate, naturally compact and slower-growing with more densely held, brighter green needles.

All mostly G; H 12in (30cm), W 3–4ft (90cm–1.2m)
UH 18–24in (45–60cm), UW 10–16ft (3–5m), Z 3–8

Pinus mugo 'Mops'. Perhaps the most widely grown European Mountain Pine, this has a neat mounded habit, light green needles and brown winter buds; it is compact in early years, but shoots open up from the dense cushion with age. There are other excellent choices of similar habit, some much slower-growing. These include the popular *P. m.* 'Humpy', with dark green needles and prominent winter buds; *P. m.* 'Sherwood Compact', which makes a compact neat hummock of bright green needles, evenly arranged on erectly pointed stems; *P. m.* 'Teeny',

a shorter-needled compact globe, and – one of the smallest – *P. m.* 'Minimops', a tight ball of deep green, extremely short needles clustered around miniature winter buds, a real gem for troughs or the miniature garden, growing perhaps 10in (25cm) high and wide in ten years.

H 18–24in (45–60cm), W 24–36in (60–90cm)
UH 5–6ft (1.5–1.8m), UW 10–16ft (3–5m), Z 3–8

Pinus mugo var. *pumilio*. This form from the European mountains has come to represent the main prostrate selections raised from seed – and they will, unless pruned, vary considerably. Though usually making attractive spreading dwarf pines, they are a cheap and eventually unreliable substitute for selected cultivars: once the nursery-pruned plants are put out in the landscape, it will be pot luck what they may become without pruning, and they may perhaps turn into much more open, shrubby bushes.

Growth rates are not easy to estimate, Z 3–8

Pinus mugo 'Winter Gold', a group of 15-year-old plants in Norfolk, England, winter. They show how colorful conifers can be in association with heathers and other shrubs and trees. On the right are the fiery stems of Cornus sanguinea 'Winter Beauty'.

Pinus mugo 'Winter Gold'. Aptly named, this is an easy and excellent garden plant for the winter garden – its quite long, dark green summer needles change in late autumn and winter to a deep golden-yellow. Plant it with early bulbs such as blue Muscari or with contrasting foliage plants such as *Ophiopogon planiscapus* 'Nigrescens'. Initially low-growing, with age it starts to put on vertical growth of up to 6in (15cm) a year, so it should be pruned early (see page 174). With so many selections being raised with gold winter needles, the jury is still out on which is the best. Other contenders include *P. m.* 'Ophir', a bright light yellow in winter, and *P. m.* 'Zundert', a broad bush, golden-yellow in winter, dark green in summer. More compact is *P. m.* 'Carsten' (syn. 'Carsten's Wintergold'), with shorter needles, more compact, and deep almost orange-gold in winter. In the US, Iseli nurseries have introduced *P. m.* 'Pot of Gold', like a slightly more vigorous *P. m.* 'Mops' but a clear yellow in winter. *P. m.* 'Kokarde' is an unusual variant, a dwarf with golden bands across dark green needles. All of them will brighten winter days.

All mostly G

H 18–24in (45–60cm), W 3–4ft (90cm–1.2m)
UH 10–13ft (3–4m), UW 10–16ft (3–5m), Z 3–8

PINUS NIGRA

The European Black Pine is a group of closely related geographical subspecies of two-needled pines which have differing characteristics; the two most common are the Austrian Pine (*Pinus nigra* subsp. *nigra*) and the Corsican Pine (*Pinus nigra* subsp. *laricio*), the latter widely grown for its fast growth and timber. Both have dark green foliage and grow well on chalk soils; they make good windbreaks but get very large with age, well over 100ft (30m), with massive trunks and broad crowns. The Corsican Pine, spreading to southern Italy and Sicily, a handsome landscape tree, is less hardy than the Austrian Pine, but will take more heat and drought, though both are adapted to coastal conditions and able to grow in a wide range of soils. Unfortunately, in North America in particular, *Pinus nigra* suffers from tip blight (*diplodia*); often the whole plant can die, so advice from local experts prior to planting is advisable.

Austrian Pine Z 4–7, Corsican Pine Z 6–8

***Pinus nigra* 'Aurea'.** This looks like any conical, dark green Austrian Pine in winter and spring, somewhat open in habit – but in early summer the new growths resemble golden candles as they emerge from their buds, creating a dramatic contrast to the remainder of the tree. The needles gradually fade back to green through the summer. It is best planted in an open position and regularly pruned for greatest effect.

G; H 5–6ft (1.5–1.8m), W 3–4ft (90cm–1.2m)
UH 33–50ft (10–15m), UW 10–16ft (3–5m), Z 6–8

***Pinus nigra* 'Arnold Sentinel'.** Fastigiate or narrowly upright plants are always useful in the garden – they take up little space and create accent points either as individuals or to connect a visual line. This columnar Pine is one of many newer cultivars originally selected from the seed of *Pinus* f. *nigra* subsp. *pallasiana* var. *pyramidata*, from the Tavsanli region in Turkey. Raised by the Arnold Arboretum in Boston, it has erect branches clothed in long, glossy, green needles, the plant broadening with age. Quite similar is **P. n. 'Obelisk'**, raised in Germany, itself close to **P. n. 'Fastigiata'**. All have prominent resin-

Pinus nigra 'Black Prince', 20 years old, Norfolk, England. New candle-like shoots in early summer are a startling contrast to the dark green needles.

encrusted buds in winter. The best form for the smaller garden so far is probably **P. n. 'Frank'**, with dark green, shorter needles; it has half the growth rate of the others, and produces a dense column with striking white winter buds.

All G; H 8–10ft (2.5–3m), W 24–30in (60–75cm)
UH 33–50ft (10–15m), UW 5–6ft (1.5–1.8m), Z 5–8

***Pinus nigra* 'Hornibrookiana'.** Found as a witch's broom on an Austrian Pine in a park in Rochester, New York, before the Second World War, this was named after the author of the first book on dwarf conifers, Murray Hornibrook. It is a pleasing glossy, dark green with striking white-tipped winter buds that nestle in a circle of needles. It forms a broad, low-spreading bush, eventually of some size. **P. n. 'Black Prince'**, introduced by Don Hatch from Devon, England, is rather taller but an equally attractive mound of dark green. A more recent selection from Switzerland, **P. n. 'Pierrick Bregeon'**, a witch's broom of the Corsican Pine, makes a neat, cushion-shaped conifer of evenly spaced branches; it is often grafted

on to a stem as a patio plant.

All G; H 18–24in (45–60cm), W 24–36in (60–90cm)
UH 5–6ft (1.5–1.8m), UW 10–16ft (3–5m), Z 5–8

PINUS PARVIFLORA

The Japanese White Pine, as found in the wild in the mountains of Japan, is a rather upright, conical tree to 50–65ft (15–20m), eventually round-topped, its blue-green needles in bunches of fives, quite long, fairly straight and well spaced. But the species is seldom grown, even in Japan, and is represented there by cultivated selections. These forms are generally slower-growing with often a twisted or leaning trunk and wide-spreading branches; the tree is eventually as broad as it is high, adding an architectural and aged quality, a desirable ingredient in Japanese gardens. The needle length is normally shorter than in the wild species, curved or twisted, green above and bright silver-blue beneath, giving an overall effect of blue; the needles are retained for three to four years, so the branches appear well clothed. Most types cone freely when quite young, with up to eight cones clinging together round the stem about an inch (a few centimetres) behind the current season's growth. The ovoid blue-green cones mature to brown and remain on the tree, even when open, for several years (not always an increasing attraction!). Though tolerant of a wide range of soil conditions, they dislike poor drainage. There are innumerable cultivars and now an increasing number of attractive dwarf forms.

H 8–10ft (2.5–3m), W 6–8ft (1.8–2.5m)
UH 50ft (15m), UW 10–16ft (3–5m)
Sizes estimated Z 5–8

***Pinus parviflora* 'Adcock's Dwarf'.** A true dwarf Japanese White Pine,

named after Graham Adcock, head propagator of the Hillier Nursery in Hampshire, England, who found it in a bed of seedlings in 1961. It makes a compact bush of slender, congested branches, the tips clothed in short green needles, silver-gray beneath. Without pruning, it will with age have extending branches like a miniature of the species; it will be more compact in the open than if grown in partial shade and it must have good drainage. It is ideal for troughs, miniature gardens and bonsai. Even slower-growing and denser in habit is the cushion-shaped *P. p.* **'Hagoromo'**, a true miniature – in ten years probably 12in (30cm) high and the same across, with soft, blue-green needles.
Both G; H 12in (30cm), W 12–18in (30–45cm)
UH 3–4ft (90cm–1.2m), UW 3–4ft (90cm–1.2m), Z 5–8

Pinus parviflora **'Bonnie Bergman'**. One of several selections made by the Raraflora Nurseries in Feasterville, Pennsylvania, bearing the Bergman name and one of the best – a dwarf, columnar, dense, bushy plant with twisted silver-blue needles hugging the stems near the growing tips. Once it is a few years old, every year in late spring it gives a marvelous display of crimson male flowers at the tips of the leading shoots. Twisted needles are a main feature of another selection made at the same nursery, *P. p.* **'Bergman'**, which has a more spreading habit, needles a glossy blue-green surrounding prominent, long, brown winter buds; this also excels in spring with a colorful display of crimson male flowers, and in ten years perhaps makes 18in (45cm) in height and 3ft (90cm) in width.
Both G; H 3–4ft (90cm–1.2m), W 12–18in (30–45cm)
UH 10–16ft (3–5m), UW 4–5ft (1.2–1.5m), Z 5–8

Pinus parviflora *'Glauca', a beautiful 12-year-old specimen with considerable character, in the Miller garden, Seattle, autumn; its spreading form is typical of those used in Japanese gardens. In the foreground, and making a contrast to the conifer's architectural forms, is the waving golden grass* Hakonechloa macra *'Alboaurea', also originating from Japan.*

Pinus parviflora **'Glauca'**. The most commonly grown form of the species, usually with an upright, broadly conical habit, with spreading branches, the ends clustered with bunches of twisted blue-green needles whose silver undersides give a much deeper blue cast to the plant, particularly in summer. It cones freely, the cones remaining on the branches for some years. It becomes more wide-spreading with age but takes to pruning well – shorten side shoots in a restricted space, or thin out branches to create an aged bonsai effect. Another excellent, slightly slower-growing form is the broad, bushy, short blue-needled *P. p.* **'Negishi'** (formerly *P. p.* 'Bonsai' because it was such a favorite of the Japanese for that purpose).

All G; H 6–10ft (1.8–3m), W 6–8ft (1.8–2.5m)

UH 33–40ft (10–12m), UW 16–26ft (5–8m), Z 5–8

Pinus parviflora 'Ogon-Janome'.

A very striking golden variegated selection from Japan, certain to be popular once it is more widely available. Slow-growing, once established it will become quite a vigorous open plant unless it is regularly pruned. It has slender blue-green needles, banded with bright golden-yellow, and is most effective if planted against a darker background; it maintains its bright color all year round, making a beacon in the winter garden. It is vulnerable to sunscorch in exposed positions. It may be the same as *Pinus parviflora* 'Oculus Draconis'.

H 6–8ft (1.8–2.5m), W 3–4ft (90cm–1.2m)

UH 33–40ft (10–12m), UW 10–16ft (3–5m), Z 5–8

PINUS PINEA

The Stone Pine or Umbrella Pine is as much a part of the landscape of central and northern Italy as the Mediterranean Cypress (*Cupressus sempervirens*), and its strong single trunk and round umbrella-like crown is equally picturesque. As a young seedling, the foliage is blue and entirely juvenile; nursery-raised plants take some time to make a recognizable specimen, the lower side branches being removed to encourage top growth. The adult dark green needles, held in twos, are long and twisted; the bark on older trees is a striking feature, fissured between orange-brown plates. It does well on sandy, well-drained soils, withstanding heat, drought and coastal conditions, but more unexpectedly it also does well in cooler latitudes; once through the seedling stage, it is reasonably hardy. Use it as a specimen, but it can be kept quite small by pruning for some years.

H 8–10ft (2.5–3m), W 3–4ft (90cm–1.2m)

UH 50–65ft (15–20m), UW 33–40ft (10–13m), Z 7–9

PINUS PUMILA

Pinus pumila 'Dwarf Blue'.

This is the most widely grown selection of the five-needled Japanese Stone Pine or Dwarf Siberian Pine, and represents a good form of the species which in the wild is mostly low-growing or shrubby and seldom over 16ft (5m) high. Closely related to *Pinus cembra*, it is native to Eastern Siberia, northeast China, Korea and northern Japan, and is very hardy. It makes a spreading but not prostrate bush, with short, upswept branches densely covered in bunches of green needles whose bright silver-white undersides give a bluish cast. Both species and cultivars need sun and good drainage.

G; H 18–24in (45–60cm), W 3–4ft (90cm–1.2m)

UH 4–5ft (1.2–1.5m), UW 16–23ft (5–7m), Z 3–8

PINUS RADIATA

Pinus radiata 'Aurea'.

The Golden Monterey Pine was discovered in New Zealand, a long way from the original native green-needled species which is restricted to just a few small coastal areas of California and Mexico. For gardeners looking for golden foliage, there can be few more brilliant sights than the selection 'Aurea'. It makes a broadly conical tree, whose needles are a clear golden-yellow through the year, though somewhat prone to windburn and scorch. Quite fast-growing, it is best used as a specimen plant against a dark background. Much dwarfer and more compact is an Australian introduction, *P. r.* 'Goldie'. There is a limit to the hardiness of *P. radiata*; cultivars prefer a moist climate but good drainage at the roots, though the species is more adaptable. They can be grafted or rooted from cuttings.

H 10–16ft (3–5m), W 8–10ft (2.5–3m)

UH 50–65ft (15–20m), UW 23–33ft (7–10m), Z 8–9

PINUS STROBUS

The Weymouth Pine or Eastern White Pine is native to a broad triangle from Newfoundland in Canada west to Manitoba, then southeast to Georgia; a giant tree of up to 180ft (50m), it is important for timber. Fast-growing and conical when young, it slows with age and becomes more round-topped, making a handsome tree with soft, blue-green needles in bunches of five up to 6in (15cm) long. These are not held on the branches longer than two years, which creates an open look to faster-growing trees; on all types, the late summer and autumn browning and shedding of older needles lead to concerns for the plant's health, but this is an entirely natural occurance. It has attractive, long, cylindrical, pendulous cones that exude white resin, maturing to brown in the autumn of their second year. The species prefers moist, well-drained soils and will not put up with waterlogging; it also grows in more inhospitable drier, rocky sites, but is not tolerant of atmospheric pollution nor of highly alkaline soils. A great number of seedling selections have been introduced, and even more from witch's brooms. Many dwarfs tend to pick up speed with age and will need pruning in the smaller garden.

H 16–26ft (5–8m), W 8–10ft (2.5–3m)

UH 65–100ft (20–30m), UW 16–26ft (5–8m), Z 3–8

Pinus strobus 'Winter Gold' (syn. 'Hillside Winter Gold').

Eventually large, and best pruned when young to improve density, this has long needles which are suffused with gold in winter,

Pinus strobus *'Nana', 10 years old, Australia, bursting into growth in late spring.*

particularly in an open position. Perhaps the most promising new selection is **P. s. 'Louie'**, found by the noted collector Greg Williams in Vermont; all its needles are deep gold throughout the year, and it is much slower than the species, perhaps making 6ft (1.8m) in ten years.

Both G; H 8–10ft (2.5–3m), W 3–4ft (90cm–1.2m)
UH 50–65ft (15–20m), UW 13–23ft (4–7m), Z 3–8

Pinus strobus 'Blue Shag'. An attractive slow-growing Eastern White Pine selected by Sydney Waxman of the University of Connecticut. In early years this makes a low, flattish-topped mound of blue-gray needles but, like many of its type, it will eventually put up more vigorous shoots. It provides further interest by a good display of slender, pendulous cones. Similar in growth is **P. s. 'Nana'**, one of the most popular forms, which makes a broad dense bush, wider than it is high, its 4in- (10cm-) needles green with bright silver-gray bands beneath. (Note that most plants sold under the name *P. s.* 'Nana' are actually *P. s.* 'Radiata'.)

H 3–4ft (90cm–1.2m), W 4–5ft (1.2–1.5m)
UH 10–16ft (3–5m), UW 16–23ft (5–7m), Z 3–8

Pinus strobus 'Pendula'. A strange but impressive weeping form of the Eastern White Pine, this is popular in North America but surprisingly rarely planted in Europe. It is a flexible plant when young, and without training up or along a stake it would be ungainly and sprawling. There may be more than one form in cultivation, but this mostly has long, blue-gray or blue-green needles, with side branches and needle-clusters pendulous and graceful. The leading shoot can have a mind of its own in later years, pushing upwards or outwards. Like many other pendulous conifers, it can be developed as a living sculpture. Not prostrate and making a large tree in time, *P. s.* **'Torulosa'**, with severely twisted blue-gray needles, provides something a bit different.

G; Growth rate perhaps 12–24in (30–60cm) a year, Z 3–8

Pinus strobus 'Sea Urchin'. An outstanding selection by Sidney Waxman of the University of Connecticut, this is a true miniature, found as a witch's broom, which makes a rounded, dense ball of bright silver-blue foliage, the long needles hiding the branches. It is ideal for a trough or a miniature garden. Other reliably miniature to dwarf forms are **P. s. 'Bergman's Mini'**, which makes a neat, flattish cushion with short blue-green needles, growing to perhaps less than 12in (30cm) high by 24in (60cm) wide in ten years, and **P. s. 'Greg'**, a more rounded bush, whose short needles are, for the species, an unusual light yellowish-green. Good drainage is essential. All dwarf forms should have old needles cleaned out from the center to allow air circulation.

All G; H 6–10in (15–25cm), W 6–10in (15–25cm)
UH 3–4ft (90cm–1.2m), UW 4–5ft (1.2–1.5m), Z 3–8

PINUS SYLVESTRIS

The Scotch Pine, the only pine native to the British Isles and in particular to Scotland, spreads across northern Europe from Spain north and east as far as Siberia, and as far south as Turkey. It generally has a conical habit when it is young and at its most vigorous, becoming more wide-spreading and rounded with age; it reaches as much as 100ft (30m). In woodland conditions, lower branches drop to reveal scaling bark from light to dark brown, reddish or cinnamon. The slightly twisted needles, held in pairs, are dark blue-gray, sometimes tinged yellow in winter and brighter blue in summer. Older trees have pale yellow male flowers; red female cones on new branch tips turn green later in the year and expand the following spring, still green but slowly maturing to brown later in summer. It is a hardy and adaptable plant which will grow in inhospitable places, succeeding on acid and alkaline soils where good drainage exists; there is a limit, however, to its tolerance of heat and humidity. The species has produced innumerable cultivars from sports, seed and witch's brooms, which are nearly all propagated by grafting.

H 10–16ft (3–5m), W 6–8ft (1.8–2.5m)
UH 50–65ft (15–20m), UW 26–33ft (8–10m)
Sizes from seed are variable, Z 3–7

Pinus sylvestris 'Albyns'. It is strange that this slowish, low-spreading dwarf Scotch Pine is not more widely grown as it is one of the most attractive forms of this type, arising as a chance seedling around 1960 on the Albyn Nursery in Ohio. It makes a dense, semi-prostrate bush with outward-pointed branches raised at the tips and well furnished with blue-green needles. More prostrate and wide-spreading is *P. s.* 'Hillside Creeper', ideal for growing over a rock or a wall, perhaps 18in (45cm) high by 7ft (2m) wide in ten years, with gray-green needles in summer, yellowish-green in winter.

Both G; H 12–18in (30–45cm), W 30in–4ft (75–120cm)
UH 24–30in (60–75cm), UW 10–16ft (3–5m), Z 3–7

Pinus sylvestris 'Aurea'. The Golden Scotch Pine is well worth garden space for the winter cheer it provides. There may be a reliable dwarf form, but most plants are grafted which induces more vigor – I have tried such supposedly dwarf cultivars as *P. s.* 'Gold Coin' and *P. s.* 'Gold Medal' and on fertile, moist soil they started to increase their rate of growth after a few years, soon putting on 6in (15cm) or more a year. *P. s.* 'Aurea' is a perfectly good alternative because it is easy to keep it small (see Pruning, page 174), and it therefore suits all sizes of garden. It is in all respects similar to the species, but has lighter gray-green needles in summer, turning a light gold in winter, and a much brighter, deeper gold in a sunny position. In late spring, before the new growth appears, the needles start turning back to yellow-green, then gray-green again. There may be some variations of 'Aurea' in cultivation, of a lighter yellow rather than gold. If pruned to keep it small, this can be a plant for the rock or alpine garden, even for a large trough or container for a number of years, perhaps underplanted with hardy cyclamen. In exposed positions, some scorching on needles might occur, but summer

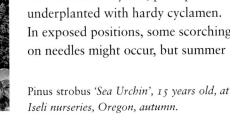

Pinus strobus *'Sea Urchin',* 15 *years old, at Iseli nurseries, Oregon, autumn.*

Pinus sylvestris 'Lodge Hill', 18 years old, Norfolk, England, late spring; it becomes large in time without pruning.

scorch is not a problem as needles are then green.

G; H 6–10ft (1.8–3m) , W 3–4ft (90cm–1.2m)

UH 33–50ft (10–15m), UW 16–26ft (5–8m)

Estimated growth without pruning, Z 4–7

Pinus sylvestris 'Beuvronensis'. This old standard is an example of the growth habit of many dwarf or slow-growing Scotch Pines that have arisen from witch's brooms – many of them are dwarf for ten years or more, but once their root systems get down to reliable moisture they can race ahead in all directions. *P. s.* 'Beuvronensis', discovered in France over a hundred years ago, is a compact broad globe when young, its shoots elongating with age, upward-angled and circled by short blue-gray needles, often paler in winter. Others that make similar dome-like bushes, much wider than high, include **P. s. 'Watereri'**, a popular, very old cultivar with quite long, blue-gray needles; it becomes almost tree-like in time, eventually 16ft (5m) or more. Slower and denser

in habit is *P. s.* **'Chantry Blue'** with intensely blue needles and contrasting orange candles in early summer; *P. s.* **'Lodge Hill'** has needles of a lighter gray-green, more blue in summer; it is a densely foliaged plant, perhaps 5ft (1.5m) high and 8ft (2.5m) wide in 20 years. *P. s.* **'Jeremy'**, whose many slender branches terminating in prominent brown winter buds make a dense hummock for many years, gradually increases in height and width so in 25 years it might be 3ft (90cm) high by 4ft (1.2m) wide.

A few cultural notes apply equally to all of these. It is best to clean out the dead needles that build up inside the plant to allow air circulation. The plants can be root-pruned every three or four years to keep growth down and enable them to be moved more successfully. More vigorous types can be pruned to keep them small, and all can have branches thinned out, bonsai fashion (see Pruning, page 174).

All G; H 24–30in (60–75cm), W 30in–4ft (75–1.2m)

UH 8–10ft (2.5–3m), UW 10–16ft (3–5m), Z 3–8

Pinus sylvestris 'Fastigiata'. A favorite of mine for its narrow, columnar habit, its vertical branches cling quite close to the main stem, with bright blue needles in summer, darker blue-green in winter; it is an excellent accent plant. It has a tendency to open up with age, and some branches fall out from wind or snowfall, but it remains attractive for many years, with small cones on older plants. It is best grown in an open position, perhaps tied in during winter in regions where snow is likely to occur. Some other selections have been made of similar habit. *P. s.* **'Sentinel'**, a blue-needled seedling from *P. s.* 'Fastigiata' found on Vancouver Island by William Goddard, appears slower and tighter in growth but broader in relation to its height. *P. s.* **'Spaan's Slow Column'**, also a seedling from *P. s.* 'Fastigiata', was found by Jon Spaan in Washington State; it has blue-green needles and more tightly held branches that afford better protection against snow damage.

H 6–8ft (1.8–2.5m), W 12–18in (30–45cm)

UH 26–40ft (8–12m), UW 3–4ft (90cm–1.2m), Z 3–8

PINUS THUNBERGII (syn. *Pinus thunbergiana*)

The Japanese Black Pine occurs in coastal and lowland Japan from Kyushu in the south to the island of Hokkaido in the north and into South Korea. It has been widely cultivated in Japan for centuries and is a feature in Japanese gardens where it is trained both to fit smaller garden areas, and also to create, bonsai fashion, a representation of old trees found in the wild. Its natural habit is conical when young, becoming open and irregularly round-topped with age; its trunk often leans picturesquely, exposing purplish-gray fissured bark.

Its needles, held in pairs, are deep gray-green, quite rigid and sharply pointed; each branch terminates in several pointed buds covered in silky white hairs, one of the most distinguishing features of the species. It is not always a long-lived tree, but though appreciating some moisture it thrives on sandy well-drained soils; it is extremely tolerant of salt spray either from the sea or from winter salted roads. The Japanese Black Pine prefers full sun and withstands heat and drought conditions better than the Scotch Pine (*Pinus sylvestris*). In Japan this is almost a revered tree – it is widely used for creating wonderful bonsai and it retains its needles even in dry conditions. *P. t.* '**Nishiki Tsukasa**', the cork-barked pine, is much sought after by bonsai specialists.

H 10–16ft (3–5m), W 7–10ft (2–3m)

UH 65–80ft (20–25m), UW 23–33ft (7–10m), Z 5–8

Pinus thunbergii '**Ogon**'. There are several selections of the Japanese Black Pine with golden or variegated foliage, though mostly they are available only from specialists. 'Ogon', which means gold in Japanese, is slow-growing but will eventually be quite large without pruning. Its long, well-spaced needles are golden-yellow and seldom scorch in full sun, less yellow in climates with less sun; it is brighter in winter. Pruning improves its density.

H 8–10ft (2.5–3m), W 6–8ft (1.8–2.5m)

UH 33–50ft (10–15m), UW 23–33ft (7–10m), Z 5–8

Pinus thunbergii '**Thunderhead**'. This is an outstanding plant, which impresses all who see it. Introduced by the Angelica nursery in Maryland, it is slow-growing but not dwarf, with a compact habit, stronger upright branches, dark, almost luminous rich green rigid needles, and sparkling central silky white winter buds. In late spring the buds start to emerge from their surround of dark green needles, pushing up spectacular bunches of long, slender white candles; the needles are green in the summer.

G; H 5–6ft (1.5–1.8m), W 5–6ft (1.5–1.8m)

UH 20–33ft (6–10m), UW 20–28ft (6–8m), Z 5–8

Pinus thunbergii '**Yatsubusa**'. Strictly speaking, 'Yatsubusa' (which means 'dwarf' in Japanese) should not be applied as a cultivar name, but this describes a form widely grown in North America. It forms a low spreading bush with long deep green needles, white winter buds and contrasting new shoots in summer. It is excellent for the larger rock garden. Taller and more open in habit is a selection renamed *P. t.* '**Sayonara**', formerly also labelled 'Yatsubusa'.

Both G; H 2–3ft (60–90cm), W 4–5ft (1.2–1.5m)

UH 4–6ft (1.2–1.8m), UW 26–33ft (8–10m), Z 5–8

PINUS WALLICHIANA (syn. *Pinus excelsa*, *Pinus griffithii*)

The five-needled Himalayan Pine or Blue Pine, given space and reasonable shelter from strong winds, makes a large and beautiful tree, eventually reaching 80ft (25m) or more. Conical when young, it becomes widely columnar with age; older trees retain their lower branches and needles when planted in an open position. The needles, in clusters at the end of the branches, are pendulous, giving the plant a graceful, open look. Some variation in color occurs, from gray-green to blue, the undersides silvery-blue. Long, cylindrical cones up to 12in (30cm) are shiny green when young, changing to purple, then maturing to brown. Vigorous when young, its whippy shoots grow as much as 3ft (90cm) a year. Though less seldom offered, *Pinus schwerinii* (a hybrid between *Pinus strobus* and *Pinus wallichiana*), is an attractive alternative, with needles of a darker blue-green but equally pendulous. *Pinus wallichiana* will grow on most soils with good drainage, but will not succeed on shallow chalk. In colder

Pinus thunbergii *'Yatsubusa', 45 years old, Doylestown, Pennsylvania, early summer.*

Pinus wallichiana 'Nana', 8 years old, in Don and Harriet Wild's garden in Ann Arbor, Michigan, summer.

areas, winter scorch or burn may occur, particularly on a form with variegated needles, *P. w.* 'Zebrina'.

H 16–26ft (5–8m), W 6–8ft (1.8–2.5m)

UH 65–80ft (20–25m), UW 16–23ft (5–7m), Z 5–8

Pinus wallichiana 'Nana'. A beautiful dwarf to slow-growing pine, making a broad, mounded bush, the branches evenly spaced and terminating in clusters of shining blue-green needles; silvery-blue undersides make the plant appear quite blue in summer. Branch tips appear a little like upturned mopheads, the needles gently pendulous.

G; H 24–36in (60–90cm), W 24–36in (60–90cm)

UH 10–13ft (3–4m), UW 10–16ft (3–5m), Z 5–8

PODOCARPUS

It may surprise many gardeners to know that the podocarp genus is the second largest of all the conifers after the pines. The majority of the species come from tropical or sub-tropical regions, so they cannot be grown widely in cooler temperate climates. Most of the hardier species are from New Zealand, Australia and Tasmania. They all have in common short, yew-like leaves, not opposite but alternately spaced along the shoots. They are dioecious, producing male and female flowers and fruits on different plants, unlike most conifers, which are monoecious. The male plants have erect small catkins which can be green, brown or pink; in late spring they shed their pollen to fertilize the female ovules, but male and female plants must be in close proximity for pollination to occur. The fertilized female flower attaches itself, strangely, to the outside of a red waxy fruit known as an aril. The species are hardier than is often thought and, with their small leaves, are well adjusted to tolerate poor soils, acid or alkaline. In recent years, much selection and hybridizing has produced some interesting and attractive slow-growing dwarf forms.

Podocarpus lawrencei (syn. *P. alpinus*). An Australian and Tasmanian species, the Mountain Plum Pine makes a variable shrubby plant. The needles are short and yew-like and vary in color from light to dark, gray- and even blue-green; new growth is light brown, cream or reddish. It makes good ground cover, but some selections can get large in time. A good female cultivar is *P. l.* 'Blue Gem' – not exactly blue, but with a distinct bluish cast to its green foliage, with new growth creamy-white and tinged purple; it makes perhaps 24in (60cm) high by 3ft (90cm) wide in 10 years. The species is variable, but all take well to pruning; most of the growth is spreading but it builds height with age.

Growth rate 6–12in (15–30cm) a year, Z 8–9

Podocarpus nivalis. The Alpine Totara is a New Zealand native growing in higher mountainous regions, fulfilling the same role as *P. lawrencei* does in Australia and similar to it in all respects, except that the leaf tips are mostly more sharply pointed, and basic green foliage colors are shaded from yellow to brown, more intense in winter. Bright red ovoid edible arils appear in autumn and winter on female plants when in close proximity to males. They are best in sun or light shade, with good drainage. *P. n.* 'Green Queen' is a vigorous, bright

green, freely fruiting female, up to 24in (60cm) high and 4ft (1.2m) wide in teb years. These and the hybrids can be pruned as necessary.
Z 8–9

Podocarpus hybrids between *P. lawrencei* and *P. nivalis*. The first three were raised by Graham Hutchins of County Park Nurseries in Essex, UK, a specialist in Australasian plants. '**County Park Fire**' is popular in England – a female form, low-spreading in habit, with bronze foliage in winter that contrasts with new shoots in spring that start cream, turn to salmon pink, and go green in summer; red fruits come in autumn. '**Spring Sunshine**', green to bronze in winter, has cream new foliage that turns to bright yellow. '**Young Rusty**', also female, has leaves that turn in exposed situations to a rusty bronze in winter. All are ideal for a bank or slope, or a larger alpine garden. *P.* '**Kilworth Cream**' is a compact male form, pale cream to light green with more pronounced cream in winter;

growth is perhaps to 18in (45cm) high and 24in (60cm) wide in ten years. Growth is variable but similar to that of the parents; prune as necessary.
Z 8–9

PSEUDOTSUGA MENZIESII

The Douglas Fir – in its coastal variety *P. m.* var. *menziesii* – is the world's second tallest conifer. It makes a tall, pyramidal tree to 300ft (90m) or more, more conical with age. Too tall to be considered for most gardens or landscapes, this fine tree was planted widely in parks and estates in Britain following its discovery by Archibald Menzies in the 1790s and its introduction by plant hunter David Douglas in 1827. The leaves vary somewhat in color according to the seed source, from yellow-green to bluish-green and glossy deep green, all with silver-white bands beneath. *P. m.* var. *glauca*, the inland Rocky Mountain Douglas Fir, tends to be bluer and hardier, so it is the best choice for colder regions; it is often sold as a Christmas tree in North America as it retains its needles well. The Douglas Firs prefer a moist, well-drained neutral or acid soil and full sun, and are unhappy on alkaline and dry soils. They are prone to some diseases, such as canker and insects. Growth varies from seed, but is slower in cultivation.
H 10–15ft (3–5m), W 5–6ft (1.5–1.8m)
UH 80–170ft (25–50m), UW 26–33ft (8–10m)
Estimated average size above
var. *menziesii* Z 6–8; var. *glauca* Z 4–8

Pseudotsuga menziesii '**Blue Wonder**'. Many excellent selections from the Douglas Fir, mostly from the Rocky Mountain Douglas Fir (*P. m.*var. *glauca*), have a foliage color to rival some of the Blue Spruces (*Picea pungens*). This old introduction from Holland is one of them, slow-growing for many years, forming a rather open pyramid with blue-gray needles and particularly vivid in summer. Older plants bear striking red male flowers and attractive pendulous cones. Seed-raised plants may at times be listed as a cultivar, *P. m.* 'Glauca', but good blue selections will also be offered as grafted plants under the same name – so if you cannot see the plant before purchase, enquire as to what is being offered. There is also a selection with yellow needles, *P. m.* '**Hillside Yellow**', perhaps a plant for collectors as it is prone to sunscorch; *P. m.* '**Glauca Pendula**' is also a choice plant.
All G; H 5–6ft (1.5–1.8m), W 4–5ft (1.2–1.5m)
UH 50–65ft (15–20m), UW 16–26ft (5–8m), Z 4–7

LEFT Podocarpus '*County Park Fire*', *10 years old, Norfolk, England, making new growth in late spring.*

RIGHT Pseudotsuga menziesii '*Fletcheri*', *about 12 years old, Michigan, summer.*

Sciadopytis verticillata, *a healthy and perfectly symmetrical specimen, 20 years old, Michigan, summer.*

***Pseudotsuga menziesii* 'Fletcheri'.** A pleasing, low-spreading conifer with luxuriant blue-gray needles with particularly attractive new growth in spring, this dense, bushy plant will get quite large over many years if it is not trimmed. More conical in habit, with soft, deep green needles, is ***P. m.* 'Little Jon'**, perhaps reaching 30in (75cm) in ten years. More compact, with small green leaves, are ***P. m.* 'Hillside Pride'** and ***P. m.* 'Idaho Gem'**, which both arose from witch's brooms; the latter will be less than 12in (30cm) high and the same in width in ten years.

All G; H 18–24in (45–60cm), W 3–4ft (90cm–1.2m)

UH 5–6ft (1.5–1.8m), UW 10–13ft (3–4m), Z 4–8

SCIADOPITYS VERTICILLATA

The Japanese Umbrella Pine is now native only to southern Japan, but fossils prove that this unique and ancient tree was once widespread in the northern hemisphere. The only species in the genus, it is narrowly pyramidal to conical, with upswept branches near the top of the plant, more horizontal below. Light brown stems bear clusters of twenty or more fairly rigid, glossy, dark green needles around the tips and hiding the buds, which resemble the spokes of an umbrella. The Umbrella Pine is very slow-growing for a number of years and ideally requires a position sheltered from strong winds, in full sun or light shade, on an acid, well-drained but moist soil; it will not succeed on alkaline or very dry soils. On established trees, dark green cones are a bonus, ripening to brown in their second year; on even more ancient trees, old enough to reveal their trunk, the bark is an attractive red-brown, which is shed in strips.

H 3–4ft (90cm–1.2m), W 24in (60cm)

UH 33–65ft (10–20m), UW 10–20ft (3–6m), Z 4–8

***Sciadopitys verticillata* 'Golden Rush'.** For many years there were few recognized or available selections of this monotypic genus, but we now have several choices, including dwarf types and several with golden-yellow needles. 'Golden Rush' makes a choice specimen in any garden – it is a good grower, pyramidal, with clear yellow needles. In the US, ***S. v.* 'Ossorio Gold'** is a good selection, while in Germany a cultivar has been introduced by Wittboldt Miller, ***S. v.* 'Firework'**, with green needles and gold tips.

H 30–36in (75–90cm), W 18–24in (45–60cm)

UH 23–33ft (7–10m), UW 8–10ft (2.5–3m), Z 4–7

SEQUOIA SEMPERVIRENS

The Coast Redwood or Californian Redwood is acknowledged to be the world's tallest tree, only a few yards (metres) short of 400ft (120m); in its native habitat of northern California some are well over 1,000 years old. That, of course, is a statement of awe and wonder, rather than a definite recommendation for its use as a garden conifer! This and its close relative, the Giant Tree (*Sequoia-dendron giganteum*), are magnificent trees which can still be seen in the wild and planted in parks, botanic gardens and larger gardens. *S. sempervirens* is a fast-growing, narrowly pyramidal tree, its side branches sweeping downwards and dropping on older trees to bare, reddish-brown, ridged, fibrous bark. The short, dark green

Sequoia sempervirens *'Adpressa', 20 years old, lit up by summer growth after pruning in spring (see page 175), Norfolk, England.*

leaves are silver-blue beneath and laid forward close to the stems; for such a large tree the cones are surprisingly small. It and its cultivars prefer moist, well-drained acid soils.

H 16–26ft (5–8m), W 7–10ft (2.1–3m)

UH 80–130ft (25–40m), UW 23–33ft (7–10m), Z 7–9

Sequoia sempervirens **'Adpressa'** (syn. 'Albospica'). For variegated foliage, this form of the Coast Redwood is a must – although left to itself it will make a sprawly medium to large tree of no particular attraction, with annual pruning it can be transformed into a densely foliaged mound of bright creamy-white. If pruned, the Coast Redwood freely puts out new shoots from old wood, even down to the trunk, and these put on rapid growth in one season. Prune the wayward branches of 'Adpressa' in late winter, and watch the creamy-white new shoots develop all over the plant making it look as if covered in snow; the foliage remains very bright in summer. Mostly rooted from cuttings, its height can be kept indefinitely at 3ft (90cm) if pruned; it will reach 50ft (15m) or more if not.

Growth rate 6–12in (15–30cm) a year, Z 7–9

SEQUOIADENDRON GIGANTEUM

This record-breaking tree has had several common names, of which Big Tree, Mammoth Tree, Wellingtonia and Sierra Redwood are among the most appropriate. Distributed in the Californian Sierra Nevada mountain range, it is in third place among conifers for height (after the Coast Redwood and Douglas Fir), reaching 300ft (90m) or more, but in first

place for its massive girth. The oldest specimens are recorded at over 3,000 years of age, second only to the

Sequoiadendron giganteum 'Glaucum', a selection of the Mammoth Tree with brighter foliage of silver-blue. Too large for most gardens, it is hardier and easier to grow than its close relative Sequoia sempervirens. *This stand of 5-year-old trees is in Nelis Kools' nursery, Holland, summer.*

Bristlecone Pines. It is attractive as a young tree with gray-green, rather coarse, scale-like leaves closely pointed forward along the stems, the main shoot pointing skyward, the lower branches horizontal then pendulous with age. These can be pruned away on older trees to reveal attractive reddish-brown spongy bark.

H 13–23ft (4–7m), W 8–10ft (2.5–3m)

UH 80–130ft (25–40m), UW 26–33ft (8–10m), Z 6–8

Sequoiadendron giganteum **'Glaucum'**. A slower-growing selection with a neat, pyramidal habit and brighter silver-blue foliage than the species, particularly in summer. *S. g.* **'Barabits Requiem'**, from Hungary, has pendulous branches and gray-green foliage; it is reliably hardy and makes an imposing stand-alone specimen. *S. g.* **'Blauer Eichzwerg'**, a new dwarf seedling from Austria, is a good blue in summer, gray-blue in

SOME OF THE BEST CONIFERS

winter, and perhaps 5ft (1.5m) in ten years. *S. g.* 'Little Stan', found by nurseryman and conifer collector Nelis Kools who holds the Dutch National Collection of Sequoiadendron, reaches only 20in (50cm) after seven years – a perfect miniature Mammoth Tree.

Most G; H 10–16ft (3–5m), W 6–8ft (1.5–2.5m)

UH 50–65ft (15–20m), UW 16–26ft (5–8m), Z 6–8

Sequoiadendron giganteum 'Pendulum'. This is an amazing tree, older specimens of which almost resemble prehistoric monsters from the age of the dinosaurs. Its upward branches are twisted and contorted, while the side branches cascade downwards. It can be wayward in habit, needing a leading shoot to be staked up for some years before it will make up its own mind to go upwards, outwards or downwards. A living sculpture, it needs space to develop.

G; Growth rate 6–12in (15–30cm) a year, Z 5–7

TAXODIUM DISTICHUM

The Swamp Cypress or common Bald Cypress is native to south-eastern USA and Mexico, a deciduous tree that thrives in moist conditions. Though large in time it has quite dramatic seasonal changes which add to its attraction; when growing in or beside water it develops unusual hollow aerial roots called "knees" which apparently assist the plant in breathing. A pyramidal to conical tree, growing to 80ft (25m) or more, with ascending branches, its tracery of branchlets when bare is most appealing when frosted or silhouetted against the winter sky; older trees develop a strong buttressed trunk with red-brown bark. In late spring, bright green new shoots appear, darkening in summer then usually giving a bold late display of rust-red autumn foliage,

falling before midwinter. Strangely enough, though happy in or near water, these plants often grow more quickly away from it, in a moist and preferably acid soil. Now considered a form of *T. distichum* rather than a distinct species, **T. d. var. imbricatum** (syn. *T. ascendens*), and the cultivar **T. d. var. imbricatum 'Nutans'** are slower-growing, more columnar in habit, with shorter horizontal side branches. 'Nutans' has pale green slender shoots, the leaves pointed forwards, later becoming pendulous.

H 13–20ft (4–6m), W 8–10ft (2.5–3m)

UH 65–80ft (20–25m), UW 13–20ft (4–6m), Z 4–9

Taxodium distichum 'Secrest'. This prostrate, slow-growing witch's broom found at the Secrest Arboretum in Ohio is gaining popularity as a flat-topped plant grafted onto a stem of the species at whatever height you choose. With short, bright green shoots in late spring, fresh green foliage most of the summer and good autumn color, it has definitely added to the range of conifers for the garden, whether used as a patio plant or among other plants. **T. d. 'Peve Minaret'** is a promising dwarf from Holland, more a miniature of the species, perhaps 4ft (1.2m) high by 30in (75cm) wide in ten years.

Both G; H 12in (30cm), W 3–4ft (90cm–1.2m)

UH 4–5ft (1.2–1.5m), UW 10–16ft (3–5m)

Approx. sizes if grafted at ground level, Z 4–8

TAXUS

The yews are one of the most valuable genera of conifers because of their diversity, their adaptability to a wide range of cultural conditions, and their ability to fit in informal as well as formal gardens, including hedges and topiary. The ten species are closely related, spreading across the northern

hemisphere from west to eastern North America, throughout Europe and Asia Minor and from the Himalayas north and east to China, Japan and Korea. All share certain characteristics in making trees or shrubs of variable shapes and sizes, from prostrate to tree-like, in nature more erect or bushy. The leaves are narrow, dark green above, lighter beneath; male flowers in spring are small, yellow and shedding pollen; the female fruits are borne on separate trees, the seed ripening in the center of a waxy, bright red aril. Their hardiness varies, but all are tolerant of acid and alkaline soils and some considerable shade; all have an intense dislike of, and will not succeed on, poorly drained or waterlogged soils and must not be planted deeper than the previous soil or pot level. All withstand clipping well, freely breaking from old wood. Almost all parts of the yews are poisonous; remember this when planting as they are dangerous to humans and animals.

TAXUS BACCATA

The Common Yew or English Yew is native to Europe, North Africa and to the Caucasus. It is the ancient, often somber, tree seen in British churchyards and countryside, where some specimens are recorded at around a thousand years old. Seedlings vary considerably, so hedging plants may need selecting for uniformity (see page 41). Growth rates on the species can be 6–12in (15–30cm) a year on established plants, not as slow as many people think. There have been a great many cultivars selected, from dwarf to

Taxodium distichum, 20 years old, Norfolk, England, showing late autumn color.

slow-growing, prostrate, pendulous and fastigiate, with needles or leaves of different colors. They grow well in shade as well as sun, but yellow or variegated types will lose color without good light. Here is a selection of the most distinct; some are grafted, but most are rooted from cuttings.

Taxus baccata 'Corley's Copper Tip'. A chance seedling from *T. b.* 'Dovastonii Aurea', discovered by Ron Corley and introduced by Don Hatch nurseries in Devon, this has turned out to be a popular semi-prostrate conifer in Britain. Its bright cream-variegated foliage and yellow-orange winter stems are enhanced by bright coppery-orange new growth in spring, still bright but toning down in summer. It takes happily to pruning to keep it a manageable size, but may get some leaf scorch in exposed positions.

H 18–24in (45–60cm), W 4–5ft (1.2–1.5m)

UH 4–5ft (1.2–1.5m), UW 16–23ft (5–7m), Z 5–8

Taxus baccata 'Dovastonii Aurea'. In my opinion, this is a far better form for general garden use than the rather large, wide-spreading, dark green-leafed *T. b.* 'Dovastoniana', a selection made in 1777. They have similar habits, often becoming sprawling, leaderless bushes; they are therefore often grafted, or cuttings are taken from leading shoots, to enable them to make a shapely form when young. These have erect, golden-yellow shoots in the center; the side branches are angled above the horizontal, with drooping tips and pendulous side branchlets. The leaves are margined yellow, brighter on younger stems and in sun. Regular pruning of the side branches with secateurs will keep the graceful habit, and maintain a form slender enough for the average garden.

H 6–8ft (1.8–2.5m), W 3–4ft (90cm–1.2m)

UH 26–33ft (8–10m), UW 16–26ft (5–8m), Z 5–8

Taxus baccata 'Fastigiata'. The Irish Yew makes a broad column of several erect branches with dark green foliage, gradually broadening with age; it is generally faster-growing and narrower in areas of high rainfall, reaching as much as 50ft (15m), but will be broader where drier. Plants may need tying in against snowfall. Useful though it is as a formal plant for garden use, I consider it has been surpassed by the hardier, much narrower column of *T. b.* 'Fastigiata Robusta', a seedling found in Switzerland that makes an excellent accent plant in smaller gardens. There are several fastigiate forms with gold, yellow or variegated leaves (see also *T. b.* 'Standishii') which are of similar habit. *T. b.* 'Fastigiata Aurea', the Golden Irish Yew, may be variable but usually has golden-yellow leaves on new shoots, later tinged yellow in a sunny situation. *T. b.* 'Fastigiata Aureomarginata' has a similar habit with clear yellow, not golden, variegated leaves. Both will get large and broader in time.

H 6–8ft (1.8–2.5m), W 18–24in (45–60cm)

UH 26–33ft (8–10m), UW (very variable) 10–23ft (3–7m), Z 6–8

Taxus baccata 'Repandens'. An extremely useful prostrate to semi-prostrate female form introduced from the US over a hundred years ago, this has dense, almost black-green foliage, particularly in shade, and is a richer green on new growth. It grows well in sun or shade, making excellent if somber ground-cover for difficult places, as long as the area is free of perennial weeds. As with all yews, it is made more compact with regular pruning. A selection of similar habit but variegated foliage, very bright on new growth in summer, is *T. b.* 'Repens Aurea' (sometimes called *T. b.* 'Repandens Aurea'). It is low-

Taxus baccata *'Corley's Copper Tip', 10 years old, Norfolk, England, showing winter color.*

Taxus baccata *'Fastigiata Robusta', 15 years old, is a striking accent plant among shrubs and perennials, Norfolk, England, summer.*

Taxus baccata *'Standishii', 25 years old, shows late autumn color, Norfolk, England. The red capsules are arils containing the seeds.*

spreading in early years, with wide-spreading branches close to the ground and raised at the tips, orange-yellow shoots in spring and older leaves variegated gold. *T. b.* 'Summergold', introduced from Holland, has more upward-spreading branches, darker green with narrow yellow margin in winter, bright yellow in summer. All plants will build up height with age, particularly if the side branches are regularly pruned. Their growth rates are similar.

H 12–18in (30–45cm), W 4–5ft (1.2–1.5m)

UH 24–30in (60–75cm), UW 16–26ft (5–8m), Z 6–8

Taxus baccata 'Semperaurea'. As the name suggests, this broad, bushy yew with erect branches maintains an excellent foliage color throughout the year, given a sunny situation; its leaves are golden-yellow even in winter. In late spring new growth is a startling orange-gold; the new shoots once the plant is established being quite vigorous. Pruning should perhaps start from an early age as it will get large in time; pruned, it will remain suitable for the smaller garden indefinitely.

H 4–5ft (1.2–1.5m), W 4–5ft (1.2–1.5m)

UH 16–26ft (5–8m), UW 16–26ft (5–8m), Z 6–8

Taxus baccata 'Standishii'. For those wanting a fastigiate or columnar form and golden-yellow foliage, this must be the best choice. It is slower-growing than *T. b.* 'Fastigiata Aurea' and *T. b.* 'Fastigiata Aureomarginata' and generally much narrower in habit, though it, too, will broaden with age. A female form, it is brighter in winter; older plants have bright red arils dotted among the foliage in autumn, until plucked by the birds. *T. b.* 'Ivory Tower' has tightly packed foliage on erect stems, creamy-white leaves particularly in winter, new shoots yellow in spring fading to cream, and will be perhaps 4ft (1.2m) high in ten years. All are best rooted from cuttings to reflect the habit of the parent plant, but 'Standishii' is often grafted because it is so slow. Some of these may burn in colder climates.

H 4–5ft (1.2–1.5m), W 12in (30cm)

UH 16–26ft (5–8m), UW 5–8ft (1.5–2.5m), Z 6–8

TAXUS CUSPIDATA

The Japanese Yew, native to Japan, Korea and eastern China, has been selected as a tougher species for use in the colder regions of North America, where the English Yew (*T. baccata*) would not be hardy. Similar in most respects, its dark green leaves are yellowish-green beneath, and the foliage in cold winter temperatures often tends to turn brown. Like all yews, it requires good drainage to thrive. There are fewer widely available selections with the golden or variegated foliage which is so popular in Britain; in North America it is mostly used for ground cover, formal hedges or foundation planting.
Z 4–8

Taxus cuspidata '**Aurescens**'. A low, bushy selection, very bright in summer when rich golden-yellow shoots appear all over the plant; these gradually fade to green, to be repeated again each year. Often used as a low hedge or edging plant, it has small needles and a compact habit. Two semi-prostrate forms of faster growth are *T. c.* '**Gold Queen**', with shorter, smaller leaves tipped yellow, and *T. c.* '**Low Boy**', somewhat similar to *T. baccata* 'Semperaurea'.
H 12–18in (30–45cm), W 3ft (90cm)
UH 4–5ft (1.2–1.5m), UW 8–10ft (2.5–3m), Z 4–8

Taxus cuspidata '**Cross Spreading**'. A very hardy, semi-prostrate selection from Cross Nurseries in Minnesota, with glossy, dark green leaves and wider-spreading habit, the foliage resistant to winter burn in extreme climates. The dark green *T. c.* '**Densa**' and *T. c.* '**Nana**' are widely used as specimens and foundation plants, while *T. c.* '**Capitata**', a vigorous pyramidal form, is often used for formal, densely pruned pyramids or topiary. All should be pruned as required.
H 3–4ft (90cm–1.2m), W 6–8ft (1.8–2.5m)
UH 5–8ft (1.5–2.5m), UW 16–26ft (5–8m), Z 4–8

TAXUS × MEDIA

A hybrid between the Japanese Yew (*Taxus cuspidata*) and the English Yew (*Taxus baccata*), this first arose in 1900 in the Hunnewell Pinetum at Wellesley, Massachusetts. From it a great many cultivars have been introduced, which have inherited the greater hardiness of the Japanese Yew, which in essence they resemble. As with most groups of conifers, there are too many similar plants which leads to confusion in naming, but the following form the backbone of traditional American foundation garden planting. When used in the landscape most end up being trimmed severely (into "meatballs", according to Professor Michael Dirr), so their original shape is often lost.
Z 4–8

Taxus × media '**Densiformis**'. A female semi-prostrate selection with a compact habit, its new and summer growth bright green, darkening in winter; the young previous season's shoots are brownish-green. It does not demand too much trimming, being naturally dense, and is very hardy.
H 3–4ft (90cm–1.2m), W 4–5ft (1.2–1.5m)
UH 7–10ft (2–3m), UW 16–23ft (5–7m), Z 4–8

Taxus × media '**Flushing**'. There are several fastigiate or columnar selections of the Anglo-Japanese hybrid Yews; this one, named after a town in Long Island, New York, is one of the most popular. It makes a narrow column of erect branches furnished with glossy dark green leaves, fruiting generously on older plants. It may need tying in in winter.

Taxus cuspidata *'Capitata', an old specimen pruned as a perfect pyramid, contrasts with the perennial* Aruncus dioicus, *in Longwood Gardens, Pennsylvania.*

Taxus × media *'Flushing'*, *10 years old, in excellent use as an accent plant in Berta Atwater's garden, Rhode Island, summer.*

THUJA

The thujas or arborvitaes are a small but very important group of six species of evergreens, related to the *Chamaecyparis*, which they resemble. Three main species, the Western Red Cedar (*T. plicata*), the Eastern Arborvitae or White Cedar (*T. occidentalis*), both from North America, and the Oriental Arborvitae (*T. orientalis*), from northeast Asia, rival the *Chamaecyparis* in the number of ornamental cultivars they have produced. Most have typical flattened foliage sprays with scale-like foliage which on some species and cultivars is pleasantly aromatic. *T. occidentalis*, in particular, is very hardy, enabling it to be used in place of *Chamaecyparis lawsoniana* in colder regions, while *T. orientalis* will take hotter, drier climates than the Lawsons, but it is the least hardy of the arborvitaes. The thujas grow successfully on most soils, including those containing lime, but they prefer moist, well-drained conditions, even though *T. occidentalis* is often seen growing in boggy areas. The range of shapes, sizes and colors in the cultivars – which have arisen from sports, mutations or seed – is enormous, although the color blue is not among them.

THUJA OCCIDENTALIS

The Eastern Arborvitae or White Cedar is native mainly to eastern North America from Nova Scotia as far west as Manitoba, south to Tennessee. It prefers moist but well drained soil, acid or alkaline; several selections are useful for shelter or hedging. Unlike *T. plicata* (the Western Red Cedar), it does not break into new growth from old wood, so pruning must be done regularly without going beyond the live foliage.

H 6–8ft (1.8–2.5m), W 12–18in (30–45cm)
UH 23–33ft (7–10m), UW 4–5ft (1.2–1.5m), Z 4–8

Taxus × media 'Hicksii'. The most widely used cultivar in North America for hedging but undoubtedly variable, this was originally a seedling raised at the former Parsons Nursery in Flushing, Long Island, selected and introduced by the nearby Henry Hicks Nursery in the 1920s. It makes a broad upright column, somewhat similar to the Irish Yew, with glossy dark green leaves; it also widens with age. The original plant is female. In Europe, *T. × m.* **'Straight Hedge'** is excellent for a narrow hedge, free-fruiting with dark green leaves.

H 6–8ft (1.8–2.5m), W 3–4ft (90cm–1.2m)
UH 33–50ft (10–15m), UW 16–23ft (5–7m), Z 4–8

All do best in sun. Most have foliage that is aromatic when pruned or rubbed; some, mostly dwarf, forms have feathery juvenile foliage like Chamaecyparis. From the vast range available, not surprisingly many are very similar, and these are linked in the descriptions below. Z 2–8

Thuja occidentalis 'Danica'. There are several rounded or globe-shaped dwarf cultivars of the Eastern Arborvitae, but some get large quite quickly and take up a lot of space. This seedling, selected in Denmark at Arne Jensen's nursery, grows quickly inot a neat, compact globe with erect, flattened foliage sprays. It is bright green in summer and bronze-tinged in winter – the colder the winter, the deeper the color.
H 12–18in (30–45cm), W 18–24in (45–60cm)
UH 3–4ft (90cm–1.2m), UW 8–10ft (2.5–3m), Z 2–8

Thuja occidentalis 'Degroot's Spire'. I was impressed with this Canadian introduction for its narrow columnar form and rich green twisted foliage; remaining attractive with age, it becomes much wider and its foliage turns bronze in winter. The closest to it in Europe, where it is as yet relatively unknown, is *T. o.* 'Spiralis', which is columnar but more open in habit, its spiral-like form made by acutely twisted stems and foliage.
H 4–5ft (1.2–1.5m), W 12–18in (30–45cm)
UH 33–40ft (10–12m), UW 7–10ft (2–3m), Z 2–8

Thuja occidentalis 'Hetz Midget'. A truly dwarf, cushion-shaped bush, this has small sprays of lacy, mid-green, tightly packed foliage which turns bronze or brown in winter. One of the few to be recommended for the smaller alpine or miniature garden, the original arose as a chance seedling at the Fairview Nurseries in Pennsylvania around 1940. Some new introductions offer good promise for those with smaller gardens. *T. o.* 'Mr Bowling Ball' (syn. *T. o.* 'Brabazon' and probably the same as *T. o.* 'Linesville') makes a broad globe-shaped light bluish-green bush, 24in (60cm) high and wide in ten years. Similar in size is *T. o.* 'Teddy', with fine juvenile feathery foliage, bright green in summer and bronze in winter.
H 6–10in (15–25cm), W 10–15in (25–35cm)
UH 12–18in (30–45cm), UW 24–36in (60–90cm), Z 2–8

Thuja occidentalis 'Holmstrup'. Another Danish introduction from a plant discovered by Asger Jensen from Holmstrup in 1951, this has become popular all over the world. Narrowly conical to pyramidal in habit, its flattened foliage sprays are slightly curved, bright green in summer, deeper green and tinged bronze in winter in colder climates. Older plants often bear masses of yellow flowers in spring and small cones in autumn. Becoming broader with age, it may need pruning or tying in. It makes an attractive stand-alone specimen, and can also be used for hedges (but see below, *T. o.* 'Smaragd').
H 4–5ft (1.2–1.5m), W 18–24in (45–60cm)
UH 16–26ft (5–8m), UW 8–10ft (2.5–3m), Z 2–8

Thuja occidentalis 'Danica': four 10-year-old plants form a distinctive feature in Holland, summer. They will soon need moving if they are not to spoil each other.

Thuja occidentalis 'Holmstrup's Yellow'. The foliage is yellow-green in summer, turning a brilliant yellow in winter in a sunny situation; it will be prone to scorching in exposed situations in colder climates. Prune it early to keep it more compact. *T. o.* 'Lutea Nana' is more yellow in summer, but almost orange-yellow in winter; it is not 'Nana' (i.e. dwarf), although it makes a good background plant. This is not to be confused with the taller *T. o.* 'Lutea' (formerly known as 'George Peabody'), another colorful background specimen.
H 5–6ft (1.5–1.8m), W 3–4ft (90cm–1.2m)
UH 16–26ft (5–8m); UW 10–16ft (3–5m), Z 3–8

Thuja occidentalis 'Rheingold'. Introduced in Germany, this has long been one of the most popular garden conifers in Britain, sold both as a very dwarf globose plant with wholly juvenile feathery foliage, and also as a faster-growing pyramidal plant with sprays of adult lacy foliage. To add to the confusion, juvenile and adult foliage can exist on the same plant, the former at the base, the latter from mid to top (see illustration, page 16). On stronger growing soils, the wholly juvenile type will often in time develop adult foliage. This plant has a winter color like no other conifer, particularly if planted in an exposed situation – it turns to a coppery-orange to bronze, excellent for the winter garden. Summer foliage is a more normal golden-yellow.

H 2–4ft (60–1.2m), W 30in–4ft (75cm–1.2m)
UH 10–14ft (3–4m), UW 8–10ft (2.5–3m)
Growth rate estimated, Z 2–8

Thuja occidentalis *'Rheingold', 8 years old, Yorkshire, England, in autumn; its foliage is nearly all adult.*

Thuja occidentalis 'Smaragd' (syn. 'Emerald'). Universally considered the brightest year-round green of all the Eastern Arborvitaes, this was introduced around 1950 by the D. T. Poulsen nursery in Denmark (famous for their roses). In France it is often listed as *T. o.* 'Emeraude' and in North America as *T. o.* 'Emerald', though both these translations are now officially invalid. Although mostly recommended as a hedging plant, it forms a narrow pyramidal to columnar conifer, able to be used as a solo accent plant or in a group or formal row. Its bright green lacy sprays of foliage are glossy and much finer than most – and not rough to the touch and dull, as are those of *T. o.* 'Holmstrup' and most pyramidal and columnar forms. It is a good hedging plant, particularly for the small garden, and needs little early trimming, but it is necessary to keep its sides in shape later. It is hardy and heat-tolerant. Other selections of a columnar to pyramidal habit find it hard to compete: the older cultivars **T. o. 'Columna'** and **T. o. 'Pyramidalis Compacta'** are more broadly pyramidal and densely foliaged; **T. o. 'Nigra'**, a narrow pyramid with deep emerald green foliage, is widely used in the US.

H 6–8ft (1.8–2.5m), W 24–30in (60–75cm)
UH 26–33ft (8–10m), UW 6–8ft (1.8–2.5m), Z 2–8

Thuja occidentalis 'Sunkist'. It is difficult to recommend the 'best' yellow or golden columnar or pyramidal selections of the Eastern Arborvitae, because performance will vary according to climate, and appreciation is of course always a matter of personal taste. **T. o.** 'Holmstrup's Yellow' is the brightest yellow, ideal for Britain; **T. o.** 'Yellow

Thuja occidentalis *'Sunkist', 10 years old, near Leeds, England, autumn.*

Ribbon', a narrowly columnar, densely foliaged cultivar is a pleasing yellow in summer, yellow-green to bronze in winter, and popular in Germany. *T. o.* 'Sunkist' is somewhere in the middle – a slow-growing, bushy plant with several shoots when young, eventually making a broad column of some size, golden-yellow in summer, and a deeper gold in winter on foliage exposed to sunlight; its scale-like leaves are tipped bronze. All may be improved by shearing when older.

H 4–5ft (1.2–1.5m), W 24–36in (60–90cm)
UH 16–26ft (5–8m), UW 10–13ft (3–4m), Z 2–8

Thuja occidentalis 'Wansdyke Silver'. Variegated conifers, and those with creamy to white foliage, are not to everyone's taste. But they are popular in Britain, which has a wider range to choose from than elsewhere; unfortunately, many of them are prone to scorch or winter burn in more extreme climates. They vary in size and color. *T. o.* 'Wansdyke Silver' rightly honors the work done by Humphrey Welch, a conifer expert who ran Wansdyke Nurseries in Devizes, Wiltshire, and named this cultivar. It is a slow-growing, compact pyramid with foliage tips splashed white, as bright in winter as summer. Rather finer, with lacy creamy-yellow foliage, is *T. o.* '**Marrisens's Sulphur**'. Both of these are easier to grow than some of the *Chamaecyparis lawsoniana* cultivars with similar-colored foliage. I also recommend the brightly variegated *T. o.* '**Perk Vlanderen**', a Dutch introduction apparently named after the director of parks in Utrecht; it is striking in winter with splashes of creamy-yellow glowing among dark green foliage. *T. o.* '**Sherwood Frost**', from Sherwood Nurseries in Oregon, is narrowly columnar, similar to *T. o.* '**Smaragd**' but with foliage tipped white.

H 3–4ft (90cm–1.2m), W 24–30in (60–75cm)

UH 10–16ft (3–5m), UW 4–6ft (1.2–1.8m), Z 3–8

THUJA ORIENTALIS (PLATYCLADUS ORIENTALIS)

The Oriental Arborvitae is considered by leading taxonomists to be a separate genus – either *Platycladus orientalis* or *Biota orientalis* – but in most books, catalogs and practical references it is still listed as *Thuja*. Differences reside in its cones, which are distinct from those of the thuja, and in its foliage and sap, which are almost scentless. Native to China, Manchuria and Korea, it has long been widely cultivated in China and Japan, making a tree to 50ft (15m). It grows well on most soils, acid or alkaline, and is more adapted to drier soils than other thujas; the cultivars lend themselves well to container or patio growing. The species is seldom used as a garden plant, but it has

produced some first-class cultivars, attractive in color and form. The branches are often thin so they can open up in snowfall, and may need tying in. The species and many cultivars are less hardy than the Eastern Arborvitae (*T. occidentalis*).

Mostly Z 6–9

Thuja orientalis '**Aurea Nana**'. One of the most popular dwarf conifers, this quickly forms an attractive oval bush with flattened sprays of soft fern-like foliage, light greeny-yellow in winter and sometimes tinged brown, turning to a bright golden-yellow on new growth in early summer which is held until autumn. It is ideal in the garden or in a container on the patio, since even in 50 years it will seldom exceed 10ft (3m). It is often wrongly listed by nurserymen in the US as Berckmans Golden Arborvitae, a name that correctly applies to *T. o.* '**Conspicua**'. Several other similar selections have been introduced, often with slightly varying shapes and rates of growth. These include the very similar (if not identical) *T. o.* '**Semperaurea**', while *T. o.* '**Golden Ball**', an introduction from New Zealand, is considered an improvement as its foliage is more fully furnished to the ground. *T. o.* '**Westmont**' seems to be the most widely grown dwarf cultivar in the US, its growth rate half that of *T. o.* '**Aurea Nana**'; it is a more rounded bush, with thicker, coarser foliage, green inside, gold-tipped all summer and bronze in winter. Slower-growing and more compact but with striking coppery-bronze winter color is *T. o.* '**Southport**'. Wansdyke Nurseries introduced *T. o.* '**Purple King**', also conical, green in summer and a deep almost black-purple in winter in colder temperatures.

H 24–36in (60–90cm), W 18–24in (45–60cm)

UH 10–16ft (3–5m), UW 5–6ft (1.5–1.8m), Z 5–9

Thuja orientalis '**Collen's Gold**'. One of several, somewhat similar, narrow columnar selections of golden-foliaged Oriental Arborvitaes. All make striking accent plants, bright golden-yellow in summer, some bronzing more than others in winter; the better drained the soil and the colder the temperatures the more intense their winter color will be. *T. o.* '**Collen's Gold**' makes a narrow spire when young, broadening with age with slightly twisted branches. *T. o.* '**Golden Sceptre**' is narrowly pyramidal, with slender, curved erect branches. Both are golden-yellow in summer, and neither noticeably bronze in winter unless under stress. An older selection from California, *T. o.* '**Beverleyensis**' is bright gold on young growth, green later in the season, then bronze in winter. All have similar growth rates.

H 6–8ft (1.8–2.5cm), W 24–30in (60–75cm)

UH 26–33ft (8–10m), UW 4–6ft (1.2–1.8m), Z 5–9

Thuja orientalis '**Pyramidalis Aurea**'. This is one of the hardiest selections of taller-growing, more pyramidal shaped Oriental Arborvitaes imported in recent years from Italy. It is now becoming widely planted in European gardens and parks, and enjoys the heat of an Italian summer as much as the cold of a German winter. It is less seen in Britain, where many similar cultivars already exist. It forms a compact pyramid with bright golden-yellow leaves in summer, turning greeny-yellow in winter but seldom bronze. Like most of the species, it thrives on summer heat and is tolerant of periods of drought. *T. o.* '**Elegantissima**' is another old variety, with a stiffer upright habit and usually

Thuja orientalis *'Golden Sceptre', 8 years old, Norfolk, England, summer, among* Geranium sanguineum *'Alan Bloom'.*

several leading shoots; the flattened foliage sprays are held on curving branchlets, and the foliage is a deep gold in summer and a striking bronze in winter. A recent introduction from Derek Spicer in England, *T. o.* 'Flame' is more narrowly pyramidal and has dramatic seasonal color variations – gold in summer, reddish bronze in winter in cold temperatures. *T. o.* 'Shirley Chilcott' is slower, with similar attributes. All are attractive, but not all are available in all countries.

H 6–8ft (1.8–2.5cm), W 24–36in (60–90cm)

UH 26–33ft (8–10m), UW 7–10ft (2–3m), Z 5–9

Thuja orientalis 'Rosedalis'. One of a few cultivars of Oriental Arborvitaes with wholly juvenile foliage, this is appealing for its dramatic seasonal color changes and compact, bushy, globe-like habit. Bronze-purple in winter, it is transformed in late spring by bright creamy-yellow shoots, toning down later in summer to a pale apple green. During the creamy spring period it can scorch in strong sun. It would make a good container plant.

H 18–24in (45–60cm), W 12–18in (30–45cm)

UH 4–5ft (1.2–1.5m), UW 3–4ft (90cm–1.2m), Z 6–9

THUJA PLICATA

The Western Red Cedar (not a cedar at all) has long been an important timber tree, reaching to 165ft (50m) in the high rainfall area of its native Pacific Northwest. Native Americans used it for totem poles, hollowed out its trunks for canoes, and used its stringy fibrous bark for weaving; its aromatic wood remains a staple of the present-day building industry. The species and cultivars are adaptable plants, growing in most situations and on most soils where not too dry. The species and particularly its form *T. p.* 'Atrovirens' make excellent hedging on moister soils, freely breaking into new growth from old wood; their foliage is very aromatic. There are several attractive dwarfer cultivars for garden use, while the larger types can be used as background and shelter plants, retaining their lower foliage in open positions.

H 16–26ft (5–8m), W 7–10ft (2–3m)

UH 65–100ft (20–30m), UW 33–50ft (10–15m), Z 5–8

Thuja plicata 'Atrovirens'. This is the best selection for hedging, and has a narrow pyramidal outline as a specimen tree; it has glossy, deep rich green foliage with pale green and silvery-white undersides, the color held well the year round. Plants from cuttings offer uniformity for a hedge and quickly make a dense wall of foliage; because it breaks freely from old wood, this selection is often more suitable for the purpose than *T. occidentalis* or *Cupressocyparis leylandii*, particularly on heavier, moister soils. *T. p.* 'Excelsa' is a somewhat similar, very hardy, form from Germany.

H 13–20ft (4–6m), W 3–4ft (90cm–1.2m)

UH 50–65ft (15–20m), UW 16–26ft (5–8m), Z 5–8

Thuja plicata 'Stoneham Gold', 20 years old, showing bright winter colors, Norfolk, England.

Thuja plicata 'Rogersii'. A dwarf selection which, together with *T. p.* 'Cuprea', was raised from seed of *T. p.* 'Aurea' at the W. H. Rogers Nursery in Hampshire, England, around 1930. It can be a slightly unstable plant, its habit and even its color depending on where the cuttings were taken, but normally it is a rounded, globular bush of densely congested foliage. The inner leaves are deep green, those exposed to sunlight deep golden-yellow to bronze; stronger growths sometimes appear which should be cut away if they are distorting the habit of the plant. It gives good year-round color, and is ideal for the alpine or miniature garden. *T. p.* 'Cuprea' has a mixture of creamy-yellow and coppery foliage; it is broader and more open in habit. Both it and the somewhat similar *T. p.* 'Copper Kettle' are more striking in winter than in summer.

H 12–18in (30–45cm), W 12in (30cm)

UH 3–5ft (90cm–1.2m), UW 24–36in (60–90cm), Z 6–8

Thuja plicata 'Stoneham Gold'. Long a favorite of mine for its colorful array of winter colors, this was raised in 1948 by the W. H. Rogers Nursery in Hampshire, England. It is very slow to form a broad conical shape, with several rather thick leading shoots bearing luxuriant scale-like foliage. With reddish-brown shoots and outer leaves a true gold-tipped bronze, the color is enhanced in open, sunny positions. It benefits from an occasional trim.

H 24–36in (60–90cm), W 18–24in (45–60cm)

UH 10–16ft (3–5m), UW 8–10ft (2.5–3m), Z 6–8

Thuja plicata 'Zebrina'. Eventually large-growing, this is a beautiful tree for backgrounds and large gardens – qualities that apply to several of these faster-growing selections with yellow or variegated foliage. Similar in habit to the species, it has light green foliage, the leaves splashed with creamy-yellow, brighter in full sun but even in shade retaining variegation. A brighter, deeper yellow but inclined to sun scorch is *T. p.* 'Irish Gold', which is possibly the same as *T. o.* 'Zebrina Extra Gold'.

H 10–16ft (3–5m), W 4–5ft (1.2–1.5m)

UH 50–65ft (15–20m), UW 26–40ft (8–12m), Z 6–8

THUJOPSIS DOLABRATA

The Hiba Arborvitae or False Arborvitae, with just one species in the genus, is a native of central Japan and is closely related to the thujas. A specimen observed from afar would resemble a broader *T. p.* 'Atrovirens', its foliage of a similar dark green, but looked at more closely it has stems that are more densely foliaged, not brown but sheathed in overlapping shining green pointed leaves or scales. The flattened foliage sprays are glossy green above and beneath each green-margined leaf has a brilliant silvery-white center, fascinating in close-up (see illustration, page 24). It prefers a moist soil, growing well enough in sun where this can be provided, but it also does well in shade. There is only one dwarf *Thujopsis* widely available, appropriately called *T. d.* 'Nana', which will seldom grow above 12in (30cm) in height, its thickened and wholly green-stemmed branchlets clothed in mid-green, slightly glossy, scale-like leaves. The plant slowly spreads with age to make a thick carpet-like cushion of green; ideal for the miniature garden.

H 5–6ft (1.5–1.8m), W 4–5ft (1.2–1.5m)

UH 50–65ft (15–20m), UW 26–33ft (8–10m), Z 5–7

TSUGA

The hemlocks are a genus of evergreen conifers containing nine species, four native to North America, the rest to Asia from the Himalayas eastwards. The main species used in gardens is the Canadian Hemlock (*T. canadensis*) and its innumerable cultivars, but some generalization can be made for all the species with regard to their cultural requirements. The Hemlocks prefer a well drained but moist soil, and will tolerate extreme acid to neutral types, even slightly alkaline where it is not too dry. Susceptible to drought, they dislike hot dry conditions, although they will be happy in sun where the soil is moist and the plants are protected from constant or extreme winds. They are shade-tolerant but prefer light, not dense, shade. There are variations among the species. Hemlocks are not always easy to grow in all locations, so giving them the most suitable conditions is vital for their success. *T. canadensis* in particular is under threat in the US from the woolly adelgid, which is having a devastating effect in some areas.

TSUGA CANADENSIS

The Canadian Hemlock or Eastern Hemlock is native to central and eastern North America, spreading from the Hudson Bay in the north to the southern Carolinas in the south. It makes a tall, graceful tree to 65ft (20m) or more, broadly pyramidal, often forked at the base. The horizontal side branches terminate in slender, pendulous stems, clothed in rows of soft, glossy, mid green leaves, each with two silvery bands beneath. General cultural remarks for *Tsuga* apply (see above), but the Canadian Hemlock is more lime-tolerant than the other species. It will be too large for most gardens, though it is widely used in North America as a hedge as it takes well to pruning. A multitude of cultivars have been introduced, most in the US, and a fascinating book is dedicated to the hemlocks (see page 186). Larger types can happily be pruned, which is best to do in early spring before new growth begins,

Tsuga canadensis 'Cole's Prostrate', a mature 15-year-old plant, effective over a wall, Holland, summer.

either with secateurs or shears, followed by a tidy-up if necessary in late summer. Only a limited selection can be described here.

H 13–20ft (4–6m), W 6–8ft (1.8–2.5m)

UH 50–65ft (15–20m), UW 20–33ft (6–10m), Z 3–8

Tsuga canadensis 'Betty Rose'. A choice but not difficult dwarf Hemlock, this is compact, bushy but irregularly branched, with mid to dark green leaves, the new growth in spring and summer cream-tipped, showing up well in a semi-shady position. Another dwarf, a chance find in woodland in New Hampshire, *T. c.* 'Watnong Star' makes a perfect globe of light green, its foliage tips almost white, at ten years perhaps 18in (45cm) high. Most hemlocks with white or variegated tips display this only on their second summer growth, but these two cultivars are white-tipped both with the first new shoots in late spring and again in summer.

H 12–18in (30–45cm), W 12–18in (30–45cm)

UH 6–10ft (1.8–3m), UW 4–6ft (1.2–1.8m), Z 3–8

Tsuga canadensis 'Cole's Prostrate' (syn. *T. c.* 'Cole'). One of the most popular and useful dwarf cultivars, this is suitable for the smallest gardens. It is best in shade and, because of its prostrate habit, can grow over a rock or a wall or tumble down a slope. It can even be quite effective trained up a cane when young, allowing the developing branches to form a dense column of cascading foliage. Older plants mound in the center, often exposing older stems.

H 4–6in (10–15cm), W 18–24in (45–60cm)

UH 12in (30cm), UW 5–8ft (1.5–2.5cm), Z 3–8

Tsuga canadensis 'Everitt Golden'. Very few Eastern Hemlocks have golden foliage – some of those classed as gold are often only a dirty yellow. However, this very slow-growing plant, found on a slope in the wild in New Hampshire by Samuel Everitt in 1918, has turned out to be a most desirable plant. It is also difficult, because its best color is in full sun

but it will get foliage burn; however, it colors quite well in light shade. Stiff upright branches carry small golden-yellow leaves, the color held throughout the year. Spring frost and drying winds can also damage the foliage but this is an outstanding plant when grown well. Faster-growing golden forms are *T. c.* '**Lutea**' and *T. c.* '**Vermeulen's Wintergold**'.

H 18–30in (45–75cm), W 12–18in (30–45cm)
UH 10–16ft (3–5m), UW 5–8ft (1.5–2.5cm), Z 3–8

Tsuga canadensis '**Gentsch White**'. Named after Otto Gentsch of Long Island who found it, this is one of the most reliable of selections with white-tipped or variegated foliage. Initially slow-growing but eventually tree-like, unless sheared regularly its foliage will be much less striking; the young, vigorous shoots color best. It will be rounded when young; upright shoots develop later, hastened by pruning of the side branches each spring, and it will then become pyramidal. The first flush of growth will be light green, the second in summer brilliant white, the color maintained well into winter. *T. c.* '**Frosty**' is whitish most of the year, with new shoots of pure white; it can burn in full sun, but the color is maintained well in shade.

H 24–36in (60–90cm), W 24–36in (60–90cm)
UH 16–26ft (5–8m), UW 16–23ft (5–7m), Z 3–8

Tsuga canadensis '**Jeddeloh**'. This has long been the most recognizable and popular dwarf Canadian Hemlock in Europe, now receiving recognition back in its native land of North America. It was apparently found in 1950 by Jan Dieter zu Jeddeloh as a chance seedling in a cemetery in Oldenburg, Germany, where dwarf conifers are widely used, and introduced by the Jeddeloh nursery

Tsuga canadensis '*Pendula*', *15 years old, trained up a stem in Norfolk, England, summer.*

in 1965. 'Jeddeloh' forms a low-spreading bush, with a nest-like indentation in the center in early years, globe-shaped with age, its outer shoots gracefully pendulous, the small leaves light to mid green. *T. c.* '**Bennett**' is similar.

H 12–18in (30–45cm), W 18–24in (45–60cm)
UH 4–5ft (1.2–1.5m), UW 8–10ft (2.5–3m), Z 3–8

Tsuga canadensis '**Minuta**'. Aptly named, this is one of the dwarfest of Hemlocks, a true miniature with a growth of less than 1in (2.5cm) a year. It forms a densely congested, irregular dome-shaped bush with short twiggy branches, each clothed in clusters of minute deep green leaves, terminating during autumn and winter in light brown buds, which flush bright green on new growth in spring. It is an ideal plant for miniature gardens, troughs and sinks, but must not be allowed to dry out. *T. c.* '**Abbotts Pygmy**' is of similar habit but even dwarfer, with mid to light green leaves and larger, more prominent, winter buds.

H 4–6in (10–15cm), W 4–6in (10–15cm)
UH 30–36in (75–90cm), UW 24–30in (60–75cm), Z 3–8

Tsuga canadensis '**Pendula**'. Without any training in early years, this popular cultivar will make a prostrate, undulating carpet, gradually building height with overlapping branches. Most nurseries training process by taking a strong shoot when young and training it up a cane; the gardener can continue this by taking it to the desired height. Eventually it will make a plant of some size, its long branches and mid green foliage cascading gracefully down to the ground. It is ideal to hang over a wall or a rock, but would also make a perfect specimen in a lawn or among other plants. Allow it space to develop, but it takes pruning well if needed.

Growth rate 6–8in (15–20cm) a year or more, Z 3–8

Tsuga canadensis '**Verkade Recurved**'. This distinctive, slow-growing cultivar is an appealing plant, though it is not always the easiest to grow and it is best in some shade. It has upward-spreading, slightly twisted, rigid branches which are brittle and easily broken. Its short branchlets are clothed in small, oval, glossy, deep green leaves, curved downwards, hiding their silver-white undersides. A stronger-growing selection, *T. c.* **'Curly'**, has similar foliage but is a lighter, duller green.

H 18–24in (45–60cm), W 12–18in (30–45cm)

UH 6–8ft (1.8–2.5m), UW 3–4ft (90cm–1.2m), Z 3–8

TSUGA CAROLINIANA

Tsuga caroliniana 'LaBar Weeping'. The Carolina Hemlock, a species inhabiting a relatively small area from the mountains of southwest Virginia to Georgia, is distinguished from the Eastern Hemlock by, among other things, its deep green, widely spaced needles and red-brown shoots. A popular prostrate or weeping selection, this was found at the LaBar Nursery in North Carolina and propagated by the noted collector Layne Ziegenfuss of Pennsylvania. It has similarities to *T. caroliniana* 'Pendula' but is more open in habit, with much darker green leaves; like most prostrate forms, it will need training upwards as a young plant. It needs some shade and a moist soil, and should be planted in a well-sheltered position.

Growth rate 6in (15cm) a year, Z 4–7

TSUGA HETEROPHYLLA

Tsuga heterophylla 'Iron Springs'. The Western Hemlock is a large and beautiful conifer, making 190ft (60m) or more in its native habitat, which spreads from northern California to Idaho, then north through British Columbia to Alaska. It has produced few garden cultivars, however, to compare with the Eastern or Canadian Hemlock. The species is a fast-growing and adaptable tree, pyramidal when young, more conical with age, but it could hardly be considered for the average garden except for hedging.

This selection was discovered growing near Iron Springs, a Pacific coastal resort in Washington State. It makes a slow-growing, narrow, upright but irregularly branched bush, with dense foliage. Its leaves are much smaller than the species, dark green with bright silvery-white undersides. *T. h.* 'Thorsens Weeping' is a new selection worth looking out for.

H 4–6ft (1.2–1.8m), W 2–3ft (60–90cm)

UH 23–40ft (7–12m); UW 26–33ft (8–10m), Z 4–8

TSUGA MERTENSIANA

To anyone who has seen it growing in the wild or well grown in a garden, the Mountain Hemlock never fails to impress – beautiful and graceful, it is a narrowly pyramidal to columnar tree with pendulous blue-gray foliage. The species, which can grow to 100ft (30m) but mostly less, is native to a large area at quite high altitudes from southern Alaska to central California and east to Montana and Idaho and most of British Columbia. It grows from close to sea level to the tree-line at over 9,000ft (2,700m) in the Sierra Nevadas, where it is seen as a shrubby, often stunted tree – a form that would encourage the gardener to believe it was hardy and widely adaptable. It is certainly hardy, but it dislikes heat and drought, growing better on moister, cooler soils in sun or light shade. Where it can be grown it will slowly develop to a slender, pyramidal to spire-like tree, its small gray-blue leaves clustered and pointed forward around the stems, the short branches and branchlets pendulous at the tips. Various selected forms with blue leaves are given the name *T. m.*

Tsuga mertensiana 'Elizabeth', 20 years old, among autumn foliage, Seattle.

'Glauca' and may be offered as seed strains or propagated from cuttings. An attractive, slender selection, made by Konijn Nurseries in Holland, is *T. m.* **'Blue Star'** with pale china-blue leaves – it may be available from specialists, sometimes grafted.

H 4–5ft (1.2–1.5m), W 24–30in (60–75cm)

UH 50–65ft (15–20m), UW 16–23ft (5–7m), Z 4–7

Tsuga mertensiana 'Elizabeth'. An impressive, initially spreading plant, found on Mount Rainier in Washington State around 1940. Quite dwarf for many years, it is later more upright and irregular in habit, with branches arching gracefully upwards and branchlets densely covered in deep blue-gray leaves pendulous at the tips, much brighter pale gray-blue in summer. It is an easy-growing plant in the garden once established, happy in full sun and succeeding in conditions drier than one would expect.

H 12–18in (30–45cm), W 24–36in (60–90cm)

UH 10–16ft (3–5m), UW 6–8ft (1.8–2.5m), Z 4–7

CARING FOR

CONIFERS

Before caring for conifers, the first thing to consider is what you should look for when you buy your plants. Ideally, it is always better to see and select them for yourself, but mail order can provide an important service to those not living near a good garden center or specialist grower. With conifers, as with most plants, you can generally expect to get what you pay for in the way of quality and trueness to name. Most companies will offer some guarantee of replacement or service if a problem occurs within a year or so of purchase.

When deciding what to buy, you need to take account of a conifer's ability to meet the demands of your location. Consider its hardiness, preference for sun or shade, drainage requirements and general adaptability to the conditions in your garden. Is your soil acid and peaty, sandy or heavy clay, alkaline or chalky? The particular likes and dislikes of specific conifers are covered in the Directory (see page 82), but use local knowledge to assist you too. Look around you: what grows well in your area?

You should always check that any plant you buy is healthy and well grown, with well established roots circling in the container. Avoid pot-bound plants with little soil left surrounding them.

Nurseries and garden centers mostly sell conifers as container-grown plants, though mid-size or larger plants which have been field-grown are also available sometimes. When these plants are lifted, burlap or some woven material will be wrapped around the rootball, in the case of larger plants secured by wire mesh. Rootballed plants will generally have had their roots regularly pruned and they will usually grow away well in garden soil – often better than pot-grown specimens. If in doubt, you can ask to inspect the rootball to ensure that no really large roots have been cut or torn. It is especially important that rootballed plants should not be allowed to dry out.

PREVIOUS PAGES
The author pruning the smaller branchlets of Tsuga canadensis *'Gentsch White' with shears (left) and using the extended pruner to cut larger upright stems on* Thuja occidentalis *'Holmstrup's Yellow' (right).*

PLANTING CONIFERS

On the whole, conifers are not fussy or difficult plants to grow. Planting is generally straightforward: there are just a few simple guidelines to remember. Most faster-growing conifers are best planted small so that roots become naturally well established in line with the plant's rate of growth. Spring or early autumn is generally recommended as the best time for planting, but provided sufficient water is available conifers can be planted all summer.

Before putting a conifer (or any other plant) into your garden, you should prepare the soil thoroughly, being especially careful to clear the planting area of perennial weeds. And it is always advisable, before planting, to immerse pot-grown plants in a tub or bucket for several minutes.

Dig a hole at least 12–18in (30–45cm) wider than the spread of the rootball and 6–12in (15–30cm) deeper. Mix some compost or well rotted manure into the excavated soil, and if your soil is poor the addition of a slow-release fertilizer can help.

Unless the specimens are very tall in relation to the rootball, or a site is particularly windy, staking is generally not necessary. With container-grown plants, it is best, when you remove the plant from its pot, to tease open circling roots; you can even cut some thick or large ones as long as there are plenty of younger fibrous roots left. Rootballed conifers can usually be planted with the wrapping still attached, provided the material is degradable (any non-degradable material must be completely removed, which may result in the rootball breaking up, so check when purchasing). Position the tree in the hole, spreading the roots out evenly and making sure that the base of the stem is level with the soil surface. Usually the old soil mark is a good guide. If you are planting a wrapped rootballed tree, you should now cut the top half or third of the wrapping from the trunk and rootball and either remove it or push it at least 6in (15cm) below the soil surface so that it will eventually rot. Backfill the hole around the plant with the compost and soil mixture: firm the soil as you go by treading it carefully. Water well.

If you are planting on a slope, or even on level ground if the soil is well drained, it is a good idea to build a circular ridge of soil about 2–3in (2.5–4cm) high around the plant; this saucer-like raised circle should be at least half-filled with a mulch of bark chippings or compost. This will prevent undue water loss and help retain the water that should be added in dry periods, especially during the first year, to help the tree establish. Mulching is all-important in retaining moisture, acting as insulation to the root system in hot and cold weather, and, of course, in keeping annual weeds down. Remember, both when planting and when adding mulch, that nearly all conifers dislike having their trunks or lower branches covered, so 2–3in (5–7.5cm) of mulch over the ground should taper to nothing at the trunk.

Conifers of course don't flag or droop when dry so, until new roots are firmly established, which might take several months, it is important to check regularly to make sure they have enough water.

MOVING CONIFERS

There are various reasons why a gardener might feel the need to move an established conifer: plants may be getting too close to each other; you might want to try a plant in another position; or you might want to move it to an entirely new location. Most conifers will move well from open ground soil, though it is usually advisable to call in professional skill and muscle power to help move large trees.

Some advance preparation may be needed to ensure success in transplanting. With a smaller plant you may be able just to cut round it with a sharp spade, lift it onto the spade or a wheelbarrow with the rootball intact and replant it immediately. But it is a good idea to prune the roots of older or larger conifers a year before they are to be moved. Root-pruning will enable a plant to make more young fibrous roots, which will hold the rootball together when it is moved and help the tree to grow away strongly. In my experience, the easiest conifers to move are *Chamaecyparis*, *Cryptomeria* and *Thuja*,

with *Taxus* and *Tsuga* not far behind. So long as they are less than about five years old, they should not need root-pruning. Most members of the *Picea* family are fairly shallow-rooting, but some species may put down tap roots which need to be pruned. *Juniperus*, *Cedrus*, *Cupressocyparis*, *Cupressus* and *Pinus* all need root-pruning a year ahead of moving. Root-pruning dwarf conifers every two or three years will not only help to control growth but also enable plants to be successfully moved at shorter notice.

Root-pruning is a straightforward but lengthy process. Dig a 6–12in (15–30cm) wide trench around the tree to a depth of 12–24in (30–60cm), with its outer circumference 18–30in (45–75cm) from the trunk, according to the size of the specimen. Use secateurs or a pruning saw to cut back the thick, woody shoots. Undercut some of the lower roots. Fill the trench with a peat or fine bark compost into which new roots will grow; water the filled circle regularly in dry periods. The following spring or early autumn, twelve months after pruning, you will be able to move the plant, now with new young fibrous roots, with almost certain success.

If the soil is dry, give it a thorough watering a few days before the move, so the plant can assimilate moisture and hold a better rootball.

When it comes to actually moving the tree, simply follow the stages pictured on page 174. Except for very small trees, lifting is usually a two-person job. The first step is to tie up the lower branches if necessary, to keep them out of the way. Then dig a trench around the base 12–24in (30–60cm) from the trunk, cutting through the roots (unless you have previously root-pruned, as above). This will create a plant on a pedestal. Ease a sheet of burlap in on one side, lean the rootball, sever the last roots and pull the burlap through. Then wrap the rootball tightly. Position another sheet of burlap underneath so that, holding it by the corners, you can lift the tree out. Move it in a wheelbarrow or, if it is very large, by tractor. A moved specimen may make little growth for one or two years, until it recovers from the shock of moving and new root systems develop. As long as it stays a healthy color, you shouldn't worry.

MOVING AND REPLANTING (*Athrotaxis laxifolia* shown, but the same principles apply to all)

Dig a trench 12–24in (30–60cm) around the trunk, severing the roots.

Sever the remaining roots and pull a sheet of burlap underneath. Wrap the rootball tightly.

Use another sheet of burlap to help you lift the wrapped rootball.

Drop the tree into a prepared planting hole. Remove or bury excess burlap.

Fill in the hole with compost or good garden soil, then mulch with composted bark or leaf mold.

Firm in and water thoroughly. Staking is not needed, but regular watering will be.

PRUNING

My views on pruning have changed since I started growing conifers at Foggy Bottom in Norfolk thirty-five years ago. Then, I felt it was wrong to prune conifers as it would spoil their natural shape. But the fact is that not all conifers improve as they age. They can become open and unbalanced, or they may just get too big. With almost every conifer there will come a time to prune, for shape or simply to keep it to a reasonable size.

Those with smaller gardens, especially, need to be prepared to prune as soon as need be. Even larger-growing trees, *Abies procera* 'Glauca' for example, can be kept to a reasonable size if you start pruning when they are young. With these, my preference is to accentuate the natural shape, by thinning branches.

With conifers of broadly columnar habit, for example *Chamaecyparis* or *Thuja*, it is a good idea, when a tree is young, to reduce the number of leading shoots, then trim all over. If this process is repeated every two or three years in spring or mid-summer, the width of the tree will be reduced and its density increased. (Even those narrow Italian cypresses are pruned regularly to prevent them opening up, as well as for aesthetic appeal.)

Pruning may also be required to balance a plant. Take, for example, a grafted plant of *Picea pungens*. Its leading shoot is usually tied up a cane at the nursery but the leader can be overtaken by one of the side-shoots, and some side-shoots on one side can be longer than those on the other. In such a case, the best course is to prune back the competing leading shoot half-way and shorten the longer side-shoots so that the plant is more pyramidal. This process should be repeated every year or two until the leading shoot takes over.

There are also plants that are much more effective or attractive if regularly pruned: *Sequoia sempervirens* 'Adpressa', for example, makes a rather scruffy-looking tree unless it is pruned annually, when it becomes a ball of cream-colored shoots. Some of the variegated *Tsuga canadensis*, such as

'Gentsch White', will lose their variegation in time without regular pruning. *Chamaecyparis pisifera* 'Squarrosa Intermedia', pruned annually, makes a dense pincushion mound of silver blue; unpruned, it becomes open and undistinguished.

Always make sure your pruning tools are of good quality. Good secateurs are essential, and shears, a small pruning saw and extended loppers are also useful. They should all be kept sharp and cleaned regularly with disinfectant. This is particularly important if diseased plants have been pruned.

CUTTING THE TOP AND SHORTENING BRANCHES (*Abies procera*)

PRUNING COLUMNAR CONIFERS

Using a saw, remove the top at the point where the growth becomes thin.

With secateurs, prune the side branches, keeping a natural shape.

Prune regularly, every two or three years, to restrict size.

PRUNING TO ACHIEVE BALANCE

PRUNING FOR EFFECT

This Picea pungens *has developed two leading shoots; one must be cut away.*

Early each spring, this 30-year-old Sequoia sempervirens *'Adpressa' is pruned with secateurs and shears. Its resulting new growth is creamy-white.*

Pruning semi-prostrate conifers With spreading conifers, such as the semi-prostrate junipers and yews, it is advisable to start pruning vigorous spreading shoots early, to increase the density of the plant, and, if necessary, to keep it from becoming too large. It is best to do this pruning in early spring before new growth begins. Use secateurs, and shears if need be.

Pruning mounded plants A plant like *Picea pungens* 'Globosa' normally makes a mound when young, but with age it will often develop leading shoots. You have a choice: you can either let the shoots go on

PRUNING SEMI-PROSTRATE CONIFERS (annual pruning in early spring of a 30-year-old *Juniperus* × *pfitzeriana* 'Aurea')

When pruning, it is important to keep the natural layered habit of the branching.

Use shears to tidy up the edges.

Cut the stems, but do not expose bare branches.

PRUNING MOUNDED PLANTS

Unpruned, this Picea pungens *'Globosa' would develop strong leading shoots.*

To keep the foliage dense and the size manageable, prune the side shoots and top growth in early spring.

Do not prune beyond the green (or blue or gold) shoots.

PRUNING PINES

In spring and early summer, pines develop new candle-like growths. If you want to restrict the size of the tree, you can nip or cut off these candles while they are still soft. When growth is pruned at this stage, new buds will still be able to form for winter and next season's growth. The plant shown here is a 20-year-old Pinus sylvestris *'Aurea' in my garden at Foggy Bottom, Norfolk.*

growing so that you have a pyramidal plant, or, using secateurs, you can cut out these and strong side-shoots to keep the plant compact. Prune in early spring before new growth begins.

Pruning pines Pines make one main flush of growth in summer. You can simply prune out the branch ends with secateurs or shears (making sure you leave enough side-shoots eventually to fill in any gaps). Or, if you want to keep your plants more compact, you can prune out the tips of the soft emerging candles when they reach 2in (5cm) or so in spring, shorter if the variety is slower-growing. Purists say that it is best to nip the shoot or candle tip by hand. For my part I use shears, which is much quicker, although there is a small risk that other needles may be damaged. I have kept a *Pinus sylvestris* 'Aurea' at 39in (1m) for twenty years and it still looks pretty natural, even though without pruning it would be in excess of 23ft (7m) by now.

Pruning large trees When a conifer gets large and a decision has to be made about whether it can be allowed to stay or really has to go, one alternative is to prune away the lower branches and thin out some of the others. While looking just as interesting, the tree will then allow the light through so that other plants can be grown under it. This can provide the ideal solution for broad-spreading pines, particularly those with attractive bark – forms of *Pinus densiflora* and *P. sylvestris*, for instance.

With larger plants particularly, it is a good idea to step back and walk around to judge each cut before and after, to make quite sure you are getting the effect you want.

Removing reverting shoots Sometimes on grafted plants, or even on plants (like *Picea abies* 'Gregoryana') that retain their juvenile foliage, strong reverting shoots occur; these should be cut away or eventually they will take over.

PRUNING LARGE CONIFERS

This Pinus sylvestris *'Lodge Hill' is growing into the side of a* Picea pungens.

Lower branches are removed or thinned, letting in light and air and creating a more mature-looking tree.

It is no longer competing with the Picea, *and other plants can fill around the base.*

REMOVING REVERTING SHOOTS
This 30-year-old Picea abies *'Gregoryana', a true mounded miniature conifer which arose as a witch's broom on a Norway Spruce, has thrown up a strong reverting shoot. Cut it out at the base, using secateurs (far right); if you do not, the whole plant will become a Norway Spruce.*

Use secateurs to cut out thick branches in the upper part of the hedge plants – here, Taxus × media *'Straight Hedge'.*

When you have thinned the hedge by taking out the more vigorous shoots, you can level the top by clipping the smaller shoots with shears.

An example of a perfectly trimmed 12-year-old × Cupressocyparis leylandii *hedge, treated with growth regulator.*

TOPPING TREES

If you have a tree, perhaps a × *Cupressocyparis leylandii* or a *Cedrus deodara*, which has become too tall, you may choose to cut the top off rather than chopping the whole tree down. You will almost certainly need to call in a tree surgeon to remove the top, but once this has been done, with the aid of a ladder and an extended lopper, you can prune the side branches, narrowing the tree toward the top, so that from the ground the main cut is hidden from view. Continue pruning the side-shoots for a couple of years until they begin to fill out the gaps. Making large cuts on tall tree trunks can lead to internal damage and decay, so be advised by a qualified tree surgeon. Painting wounds on trees is seldom recommended these days, the belief being that they will heal more naturally if left open to the air.

PRUNING HEDGES

Most people are well aware that hedges, once established, need pruning, and that the faster-growing they are the more regular pruning will be required. I find considerable satisfaction in clipping with old-fashioned hand shears, but for large or extensive hedges this is probably too time-consuming and, in the right hands, power-driven hedgecutters do an excellent and much quicker job.

Hedges are best planted small. Give the sides a light trim after the first year, and prune away the top once the desired height is reached (or even before), to encourage side-growth to fill in gaps between the plants. Narrow upright conifers such as *Thuja occidentalis* 'Smaragd' should be planted about 2ft (60cm) apart. Spacing of 3ft (90cm) is more appropriate for faster, broader-growing plants like × *Cupressocyparis leylandii*, which should be given an annual spring trim; it can be followed by a treatment of growth regulator to control any further growth for the rest of the season. Lower-growing spreading plants such as *Juniperus* × *pfitzeriana* 'Hetzii' could be planted even as wide apart as 4ft (1.2m).

The timing of pruning is not crucial, but mid-spring, just before the buds break, is a good time to prune hedges, the main growth for almost all conifers coming in late spring to early summer. Young plants can be pruned a second time in late summer, when the main growth has finished but there are still young growths coming through to cover the cuts by autumn. Most established hedges that are regularly pruned are cut only once a year, especially in big estates and gardens where hedge-clipping can be a massive undertaking. This cut is usually given in late summer, but can continue into autumn. Yews can of course be severely pruned back into old wood if a hedge is getting too wide since, so long as the hedge is growing vigorously and the climate is fairly mild, they will break into growth from older stems. Cut the top and the sunny side first, and leave the other side until two years later, giving the first half time to recover and make good growth.

PROPAGATION

Those who become interested in conifers will probably want to consider propagating their own at some stage but, as with most large groups of plants, while some are easy to propagate, others are extremely difficult. In this book, rather than going into great detail, I shall just give some general guidance on types of propagation. Gardeners who wish to know more should consult one of the specialist books listed on page 186.

The three main propagation methods that fall within the scope of the average gardener are raising from seed, taking cuttings and grafting. The micropropagation of conifers, a technique that is still in its infancy, is really a method for professionals.

RAISING CONIFERS FROM SEED

Most of the forestry industry use selected seed for raising the millions of plants they require of such conifers as *Pinus radiata*, *P. contorta* and *Pseudotsuga menziesii*. However, the amateur gardener is more likely to want to try raising seed from more unusual species or even cultivars, perhaps *Pinus bungeana* or *P. sylvestris* 'Aurea', *Chamaecyparis obtusa* 'Nana Gracilis' or *Cupressus sempervirens* 'Swane's Gold'. From these might come some interesting variations, since few plants raised from seed will be identical to the parent. (None, of course, should be given the parent's cultivar name.) Seed from golden or blue-foliaged conifers or from dwarf forms is likely to result in a variety of colors and shapes; some, if they are very distinct, may prove, when fully assessed, to be good enough to introduce as a new plant.

Collect cones as they ripen, normally in early autumn. Most cones will open up if kept for a while at room temperature. If they are very slow to open, you can speed the process by giving them some heat – up to 104–113°F (40–45°C). Shake out the seeds, keep them cool and moist in a container in a fridge for six weeks, then sow them in an open, acid compost in pots or in well-prepared open-ground beds. Cover with 1in (2.5cm) or so of peat or composted bark. Avoid sowing too thickly (this may lead to damping off), be careful not to compact the compost, and if the seeds are outside protect the pots or beds with chicken wire or something similar to keep out mice and squirrels. Once germination begins (and that may not happen for more than a year), leave seedlings two years before transplanting.

You will find more detailed advice on propagating specific types of conifer in some of the books listed on page 186.

ROOTING PLANTS FROM CUTTINGS

Many conifers, including dwarf and miniature types, can be rooted quite easily from semi-ripe or fully ripe (woody) cuttings taken from the current year's growth. Various forms of *Chamaecyparis*, *Juniperus*, *Thuja* and *Taxus* are among the most successful. There is no need for any particularly sophisticated equipment: you can get perfectly satisfactory results using no more than secateurs and a deep tray or pot filled with rooting compost.

Cuttings can be taken from early summer through to the following spring, usually avoiding the dullest six weeks of winter, though with artificial lighting and bottom heat even this time can be used. Cuttings from younger, more vigorous plants will generally root better. The resulting rooted cutting will make a plant identical to its parent.

Fill a deepish pot or tray with rooting compost. For most conifers, it is best to use a fairly fine composted bark or coarse peat or coir, with added perlite to improve aeration and drainage.

Using a sharp, clean pruning knife or secateurs, cut a short side-branched stem from the top two-thirds of your chosen plant. Choose your stem with care, to avoid spoiling the plant, and do not take any strong leading shoots. Cut or pull side-shoots carefully from the stem, retaining a heel (the actual woody core attached to the main branched stem). Cuttings of course will vary in length according to the size and growth habit of the parent – a cutting from a dwarf conifer may be only 1in (2.5cm) long, while one from a taller type may perhaps be 8in (20cm). Trim any small side-shoots from the bottom third of the cutting.

Dip the base of each cutting in a powder or liquid rooting hormone: choose the strength of the hormone depending on the woodiness of the cuttings, using stronger hormones for woodier cuttings. Push the cutting into the rooting compost. When you have positioned all your cuttings, spray with a fungicide to prevent rotting, then cover the tray with a sheet of thin polyethylene or a polyethylene bag. Place in half shade. In winter, some bottom heat (to 60°F (16°C)) will be beneficial.

Cuttings need good drainage but they must not be allowed to dry out. Automatic mist or irrigation systems directly onto the cuttings can preclude the need for daily attention but care must be taken not to overwater, particularly in autumn and winter. As the cuttings begin to root, start to wean them off. If under polyethylene, remove the covering to expose them and allow them to grow away, first under shade and, eventually, as they grow stronger, in the open.

In summer, cuttings under polyethylene should not be in direct light. In winter they will need more light and ideally bottom heat.

PROPAGATING BY GRAFTING

There are various reasons for grafting conifers. The first and most straightforward is that many species, and particularly cultivars, are pretty much impossible to root from cuttings. Trees that fall into this category include some *Abies*, *Cedrus*, *Picea* and *Pinus* (though in each genus there are some that will root from cuttings). Then there are plants that if grown on their own roots tend to lack vigor, or not be sufficiently hardy, or be susceptible to a particular disease. *Chamaecyparis lawsoniana*, for example, has a susceptibility to phytophora or root rot disease, but this tendency may be overcome if it is grafted on to an appropriate seedling understock of another species, such as *Chamaecyparis nootkatensis* or *Thuja orientalis*. Then come the economic reasons. Rooted cuttings of many plants grow very slowly, while grafted plants are much quicker: for example, a grafted *Chamaecyparis obtusa* 'Nana Gracilis' will in its first year make at least twice as much growth as a rooted cutting of the same plant. This, of course, means that grafting is often a more commercial proposition for the nurseryman. From the point of view of the purchaser, however, the story is not quite so good, as a grafted plant may well develop a much

GRAFTING (*Picea pungens* 'Hoopsii' shown, but the same principles apply to all)

1. *Take a cutting or scion from your chosen plant. Cut the needles from the base and remove a 1in (2.5cm) diagonal chip, cutting from the surface a third of the way into the stem.*

2. *Remove the branches on the lower third of the stock, then make a 1in (2.5cm) cut in the stem, to match the cut in the scion.*

3. *Align the two cut surfaces, so that the cambium layers fit snugly together.*

4. *Wind a grafting tie around the stem, binding stock and the scion firmly together.*

faster-growing and uncharacteristic habit. Unless there are sound reasons for grafting, plants grown on their own roots are preferable.

Grafting is a skill, but one that can be acquired by the amateur. If you are a collector of conifers and have friends with plants you covet, then exchanging cuttings or scion material will give you the opportunity to propagate your own.

Take, for example, a cultivar of the Blue Spruce, *Picea pungens* 'Hoopsii', which will not root from cuttings. In the photographs below left we show the process of grafting a cutting (called a scion) of this *Picea* onto a two- or three-year-old pot-grown seedling, called the understock, in this case a Norway Spruce, *P. abies*. The understock must be of a species that is compatible with the scion: usually a closely related species is best. The stock should also have a growth rate similar to that of the scion. Furthermore, there are right and wrong times for grafting different conifers. According to type, the right time may be late summer, autumn or mid-winter. Blue Spruces are usually best grafted in late summer or late winter.

Keep grafted plants in a cold frame or greenhouse, plunged in moist peat under thin polythene to retain moisture and protected from direct sunlight to prevent changes in temperature. In winter it will

be beneficial to have some heat – up to around 60°F (16°C). During the incubation period you will need to keep a close watch to make sure the plant is not subjected to excesses of heat or moisture or the risk of drying out, but after six weeks or so the scion should begin to callus and blend with the stock, and then more light and air can be introduced. After about three months the plants can be moved out.

Start gradually reducing the top stem of the stock once the scion has made 1–2in (2.5–5cm) of new growth. Don't be in a hurry to remove it entirely. Until the scion is fully growing and established (which may take up to a year), the stock's foliage is needed to feed the roots and to draw sap up to the graft.

The young plant will need handling with care until the union is fully secure, and for as long as the scion is still flexible the leading shoot will need training up a cane – as also will the leading shoot of a pendulous form if you wish to train it as a supporting stem.

Again, there is only room here for general advice. Specialist information can be sought from books on propagation and grafting (see page 186).

GENERAL MAINTENANCE

Keeping plants healthy is obviously important, but unless your soil is lacking in nutrients, it should seldom be necessary to add fertilizer. If you have any doubts about the ability of your soil to grow healthy plants, you can take a soil sample. If you simply want to test the pH you can use a home kit, or you can send the sample to a professional organization, who will be able to do more extensive tests and advise on how to correct any shortcomings.

Digging in well-rotted garden compost, then mulching, will improve virtually any soil.

To keep weeds down, you can lay down a sheet of thick black polyethylene and cover it with gravel. Both will help to retain moisture as well as reduce seedling weeds, but they do have disadvantages: the gravel may wash away, and the polyethylene may

The plants in the three small pots on the left show progress through the first winter after grafting. The following spring the plant is potted into a larger container, where a year later it has reached the size shown. Another year brings to the size shown on the far right.

In colder regions, such as here in New England, plants like Juniperus scopulorum *'Skyrocket' will need tying in before winter snowfall.*

retain too much moisture in winter; also, the extra layers make planting in between the conifers more difficult. Any perennial weeds need to be eradicated as soon as possible before they get hold: you can hand weed or dig them out with a fork, or, if all else fails, apply a systemic herbicide such as glyphosate, taking care not to splash any on the conifer foliage.

CLEANING DEAD FOLIAGE FROM OLD SPECIMENS

Many spruce and pines which have arisen from witch's brooms are very compact and densely branched and dead needles become trapped inside the plant. You need to clear them out every year or two or they will build up and restrict air circulation, which may ultimately lead to the loss of the plant.

TYING IN AGAINST SNOWFALL

In areas where there is snow most winters, it will pay to tie in branches on those conifers with an erect branching system, particularly if they have several leading shoots. Examples of plants that will probably

be safer tied in include upright cultivars of *Thuja orientalis, Cupressus sempervirens, Juniperus communis, J. chinensis, J. scopulorum* and some *Chamaecyparis lawsoniana.* You can tie up the plant for the winter by simply circling it with garden twine or polypropylene netting, though neither will look very sightly. The alternative is to use the twine or a stronger rope to tie the stronger upright branches together inside the plant, but it will need to be removed before additional growth cuts into the bark.

PESTS AND DISEASES

Pest and diseases rarely afflict conifers which are growing among other plants. On the other hand, those that do occur can appear a mystery, since the pests are so small and are not seen, and can sometimes disappear before the damage shows up.

The first rule is to keep plants healthy, with plenty of air circulating around them. Conifers, like other plants, are more likely to succumb to pests and diseases when under stress from drought or waterlogging. The second rule is to be aware of the most likely pests and diseases you are likely to come across in your region, and take preventive action against them. In North America pests and diseases may be more prevalent because of the wide range of native conifers, and extreme climatic conditions putting plants under stress.

A list that covered all eventualities and how to avoid or correct them would need a fair-sized book to itself. I have restricted the listing here to just a few guidelines, and would advise the interested (or concerned) reader to seek more detailed local knowledge in the literature listed on page 186.

SOME DISEASES

Some diseases are widespread under nursery conditions and in the garden and *Phytophthora* is one of them. The several species of *Phytophthora* attack the root systems of trees, causing them to collapse and rot. This occurs more commonly in

Chamaecyparis lawsoniana (see page 93), but also in *Taxus baccata* and some junipers. If you can ensure that your trees have good drainage, you should be able to keep *Phytophthora* out of your garden.

Honeyfungus or *Armillaria* is a devastating fungal disease that can attack a wide range of plants. It usually occurs initially in the stump of a dead tree but can spread by bootlace-type rhizomorphs or structures to nearby live trees. This is one of the reasons it is best to remove dead stumps and woody material as soon as possible after felling. Chemical soil treatments are unlikely to be effective.

Phomopsis juniperivora, commonly known as juniper twig blight, particularly affects low-growing junipers, and usually occurs where air circulation is poor, causing young growth to die back; *Kabatina juniperi* causes juniper blight dieback on older, larger branches. Affected branches should be pruned away. A similar effect can be caused by rodents and juniper twig girdler which ring the bark in winter, leading to shoot death later in spring when growth begins.

Diplodia or tip blight (now known as *Sphaeropsis* tip blight of pines) is a fungal disease occurring on a few pines, in particular *Pinus nigra* and *P. sylvestris*. Dead branches should be cut away in late summer and fungicidal sprays, where available, used at intervals in spring when growth begins.

The Italian Cypress, *Cupressus sempervirens*, is susceptible to *Cytospora* canker, and *Coryneum* canker can occur on other cypresses. Both occur in dry conditions and manifest themselves in the form of dead branches starting from the base of the plant. These branches should be rapidly removed. Where extreme heat and drought occur, *Seiridium* canker will attack × *Cupressocyparis leylandii*, killing most when they reach thirty years or more; this is an increasing problem in the US.

A FEW PESTS

This is one area where those gardening in cooler climates have the advantage, as pests are likely to be far more troublesome in regions with mild winters and hot or humid summers. Local knowledge and advice should be sought as to likely troublesome

predators; it is probably best to avoid planting highly susceptible species and cultivars in danger areas.

What follows is my personal pest selection.

Mites, aphids and adelgids are all sap-sucking insects, often so minute that they are not easily spotted without a magnifying glass. They suck the sap from conifer needles and stems, with a bad infestation causing all minor needles to turn brown before dropping. Detect them in early spring by using a magnifying glass or tapping a branch over a piece of white paper. If they are present you will see small crawling specks. Depending on your time and inclination and what you have available, as well as the size of the tree, spray with a strong jet of water to dislodge the insects, or with an insecticide which states that it covers these pests. It may be worth treating the more susceptible cultivars (such as *Picea glauca* var. *albertiana* 'Conica') with a preventive spray in spring and every few weeks in summer.

Scale insects, bagworms, hemlock woolly adelgids, pine bark beetles, tip moths and mealy bugs may also be a trial, but there is no need to become paranoid about such a list of bugs: in a general collection devastation is unlikely to occur. Seek local advice from reputable plant-oriented nurseries or garden centers, or from specialist information services.

ANIMAL PESTS

For some gardeners, rabbits and hares can be a real problem, chewing back even quite prickly junipers in winter when food is short, and nibbling on soft new shoots in spring. You may need to protect young trees with a circle of chicken wire or the whole garden with a rabbit-proof fence. Deer are harder to control, since they can jump quite high fences and will strip bark and foliage even from large trees. Few trees are completely deer-proof, and different deer in different regions will appreciate different delicacies. Even yew, which is poisonous to cattle and horses, appears not to trouble deer. You can try protecting your trees with wire. Electric fences will deter deer, but are not always practicable. But an electric fence used by the Dawes Arboretum in Newark, Ohio, has apparently been a great success: it is coated with peanut butter!

GARDENS AND SPECIALIST SUPPLIERS

The importation of live plants and plant materials across borders requires special arrangements, which will be detailed in suppliers' catalogs.

Canadians importing plant material must pay a fee and complete an application for permit to import from:
Plant Health and Production Division,
2nd Floor West, Permit Office, 59 Camelot Drive, Nepean, Ontario K1A OY9
Fax: 613 228 6605, Website: www.cfia-acia.agr.ca

Americans importing plant material should write to:
U.S. Department of Agriculture, APHIS,
Plant Protection and Quarantine, Permit Unit,
4700 River Road, Unit 136, Riverdale,
Maryland 20737-1236,
Toll-free tel.: 1 877 770 599
Website: www.aphis.usda.gov

CANADA
Royal Botanical Gardens, P.O. Box 399, Hamilton, Ontario L7T 4H4, Toll-free tel.: 905 825 5040
Tel.: 905 527 1158, Fax: 905 577 0375
Website: www.rgb.ca
Van Dusen Botanical Gardens, 5251 Oak Street, Vancouver, British Columbia V6M 4H1
Tel.: 604 257 8659
Niagara Parks Botanical Gardens and School of Horticulture, Box 150, Niagara Falls, Ontario L2E 6T2
Tel.: 905 356 8554
Jim and Simone Lounsbery, 4540 Martin Road, Beamsville, Ontario N0L 1B1
Nursery and display gardens
Tel.: 905 562 4836

USA
Public gardens are listed first; private gardens are open by arrangement.

California Mendocino Coast Botanical Gardens, 18220 North Highway One, Fort Bragg, California 95437
Moderate collection
Tel.: 707 964 4352, Fax: 707 964 3114
Strybing Arboretum, 9th Avenue at Lincoln Way, San Francisco, California 94122
Extensive conifer collection throughout
Tel.: 415 661 1514

Colorado Denver Botanic Gardens, 909 York Street, Denver, Colorado 80206
Moderate conifer collection in a rock garden

Connecticut Bethlehem Nursery, 66 Jackson Lane, Bethlehem, Connecticut 06751
Propagator of miniature conifers with an extensive collection
Contact: Dennis Dodge, Tel.: 203 266 7783
Twombly Nursery Inc., 163 Barn Hill Road, Monroe, Connecticut 06468
Contact: Ken Twombly
E-mail: info@twomblynursery.com

Georgia Atlantic Botanical Garden, 1345 Piedmont Avenue NE, Atlanta, Georgia
Moderate conifer collection
Tel.: 404 876 5859, Fax: 404 876 7472
Piccailly Farm, 1971 Whippoorwill Road, Bishop, Georgia 30621

Nursery and display gardens
Contact: Sam and Carleen Jones, Tel.: 706 769 6516
Illinois Anderson Gardens, 318 Spring Creek Road, Rockford, Illinois 61107
Authentic Japanese garden
Tel.: 815 229 9398, Fax: 815 229 9391
Heartland Gardens, 910 Middle Road, Fulton, Illinois 61252
Extensive collection of witch's brooms
Contact: Randy Dykstra, Tel.: 815 589 2004
Rich's Foxwillow Pines Nursery, 11618 McConnell Road, Woodstock, Illinois 60098
Specialists in garden conifers and rare trees
Contact: Richard and Susan Eyre
Tel.: 815 338 7442, Fax.: 815 338 7446
E-mail: coniflora@richsfoxwillowpines.com
Website: www.richsfoxwillowpines.com
Iowa Bickelhaupt Arboretum, 340 South 14th Street, Clinton, Iowa 52732
Extensive collection, more than 500 dwarf conifers
Tel.: 319 242 4771, E-mail: bickelarb@clinton.net
Dubuque Arboretum, 3800 Arboretum Drive, Dubuque, Iowa 52001
Moderate but expanding conifer collection
Tel.: 319 556 2100, Fax 319 556 2443
Dennis Hermsen, 11463 Jamesmeier Road, Farley, Iowa 52046
Nursery and display gardens
Tel.: 319 744 3991
Lasting Beauty Landscaping, P.O. Box 22, McCausland, Iowa 52758
Display gardens
Contact: Jeff and Lora Rathje, Tel.: 319 225 2670
Kansas Marvin and Emelie Snyder, 9107 Outlook Drive, Overland Park, Kansas 66207
E-mail: mksnyder@juno.com
Kentucky Jerry Baker, 4701 Morgantown Road, Bowling Green, Kentucky 42102
E-mail: jebaker318@aol.com
Michigan Hidden Lake Gardens, 6280 West Munger Road, Tipton, Michigan 49287
Extensive collection, more than 600 dwarf conifers
Tel.: 517 431 2060, Fax 517 431 9148
E-mail: myers@hlg.msu.edu
Gee Farms, 14928 Bunkerhill Road, Stockbridge, Michigan 49285
Extensive nursery and display gardens
Contact: Gary and Kay Gee, Tel.: 517 769 6772
Website: www.geefarms.com
Wavecrest Nursery, 2500 Lakeshore Drive, Fennville, Michigan 49408
Conifer display gardens
Contact: Robert Tomayer and Carol Hop, Tel.: 616 543 4175, Website: www.wavecrestnursery.com
Don and Harriet Wild, 3058 Cross Creek Court, Ann Arbor, Michigan 48108
Tel.: 734 662 6461, E-mail: louwild@aol.com
Jim and Sandy Wilkins, 7469 Hunters Ridge Road, Jackson, Michigan 49201
Tel.: 517 536 4304, E-mail: hostadocta@msms.org
Missouri Missouri Botanical Garden, P.O. Box 299, St Louis, Missouri 63166
Moderate conifer collection, authentic Japanese

garden
Tel.: 314 577 9400, Website: www.mobot.org
Lovett Pinetum, 2850 Versailles Avenue, Springfield, Missouri 65804
Private pinetum
Contact: Robert Lovett, Tel.: 417 887 9971
E-mail: lovettmo@cs.com / lovepine@u-n-i.net
New Jersey Blue Sterling Nursery, 372 Seeley Cohansey Road, Bridgeton, New Jersey 08302
Wholesale nursery; website lists retailers that sell stock
Contact: Jim and Barbara Smith
Toll-free tel: 1 800 5 CONIFER Tel.: 856 451 2259
Website: www.bluesterling.com
Watnong Gardens, 2379 Watnong Terrace, Morris Plains, New Jersey 07950
Contact: Helen Donn, Tel.: 973 538 8633
New Mexico Plants of the Southwest, Agua Fria Route 6, Box 11-A, Santa Fe, New Mexico 87501
Specialist collection of evergreens for high country and arid regions
Toll-free tel.: 1 800 788 7333
Tel.: 505 471 2212, Fax: 505 438 8800
Website www.plants of the southwest.com
New York Edward Rezek, 109 Slabey Avenue, Malverne, New York 11565
Tel.: 516 599 8555
North Carolina John Dilley, 9400 Sauls Road, Raleigh, North Carolina 27603
Tel.: 919 772 6761
E-mail: hobbitgarden@yahoo.com
Ohio Bill Barger, 3200 Rohrer Road, Wadsworth, Ohio 44281
Nursery-propagator and display gardens
Tel.: 330 336 9695, E-mail: billbarg@remprod.com
Wade and Gatton Nursery, 1288 Gatton Rocks Road, Bellville, Ohio 44813
Display gardens with conifers, alpines, hostas and perennials
Contact: Van and Shirley Wade, Tel.: 419 883 3191, Fax: 419 883 3677
Oregon The Oregon Garden, 879 West Main Street, Silverton, Oregon 97381
Premier conifer collection in Oregon, expanding
Tel.: 877 674 2733 (toll free), Fax: 503 874 8200
Website: www.oregongarden.com
Stanley & Son Nursery, 11740 S.E. Orient Drive, Boring, Oregon 97009
Contact: Larry and Marlene Stanley
Conifer display gardens
Pennsylvania Longwood Gardens, P.O. Box 501, Kennett Square, Philadelphia, Pennsylvania 19348
Extensive collection
Tel.: 610 388 6741
Marty Books, 235 Cherry Lane, Doylestown, Pennsylvania 18901
Nursery and private arboretum featuring mature specimens
Tel.: 215 348 4309
Washington, D.C. U.S. National Arboretum, 3501 New York Avenue NE, Washington, D.C.
Extensive collection
Tel.: 202 245 2726, Fax: 202 245 4575

Washington State Coenesium Gardens 4412 354th
Street East, Eatonville, Washington 98328
Rare and unusual conifers; primarily mail order
Contact: Robert Fincham, Tel./Fax: 360 832 8655
Email: bobfincham@mashell.com
Website: www.coenosium.com

Collectors' Nursery, 16804 N.E. 102nd Avenue, Battle
Ground, Washington 98604
Contact: Bill Jenssen and Diana Reeck, Tel.: 360 574
3832, Website: www.collectorsnursery.com

The American Conifer Society welcomes new members,
who don't have to be experts or American to join!
ACS National Office, P.O. Box 3422, Crofton,
MD 21114-0422
Tel.: 410 721 6611, Fax 710 721 9636
Website: www.conifersociety.org

If you are planning a trip to the US, you may contact
Charlene Harris, Tours and Events Planner and
member of the ACS, to help arrange your travel and
garden visits: Charlene Harris, P.O. Box 519,
Chelsea, Michigan 48118
Tel.: 734 433 9773, E-mail:conifer@coast.net

UK

An invaluable resource is the *RHS Plant Finder*,
published annually, which lists all conifers currently
offered by UK nurseries and details of where they can
be purchased. The publisher is:
Dorling Kindersley, 9 Henrietta Street,
London WC2E 8PS

Berkshire Savill and Valley Gardens, Crown Estate
Commissioners, Windsor Great Park, Windsor,
Berkshire, SL4 2HT
Contact: Mark Flanagan, Tel: 01753 860222

Devonshire Kenwith Nursery, Blinsham, Torrington,
Beaford, Winkleigh, Devonshire, EX19 8NT
Contact: Gordon Haddow, Tel.: 01805 603274
Fax: 01805 603663
E-mail: conifers@kenwith63.freeserve.co.uk

East Sussex Wakehurst Place Garden, Ardingly,
Haywards Heath, East Sussex, RH17 6TN
Tel.: 01444 894000 / 894066

Gloucestershire Westonbirt Arboretum, Tetbury,
Gloucestershire, GL8 8QS
Tel.: 01666 880220, Fax: 01666 880559
E-mail: curator.westonbirt@forestry.gov.uk
Website: www.westonbirtarboretum.com

Hampshire The Sir Harold Hillier Gardens and
Arboretum, Jermyns Lane, Ampfield, Romsey,
Hampshire, SO51 0QA
Tel.: 01794 368787, Fax: 01794 368027

Kent Bedgebury National Pinetum, Park Lane,
Goudhurst, Cranbrook, Kent, TN17 2SL
Holds several national collections of conifers
Curator: Colin Morgan, Tel.: 01580 211044
Fax: 01580 212423
E-mail: curator.bedgebury@forestry.gov.uk
Website: http://www.forestry.gov.uk

Norfolk Foggy Bottom, Bressingham, Diss, Norfolk,
IP22 2AA
Foggy Bottom is open with the Dell garden at
standard opening times; outside of those and for
groups, by appointment only
Tel.: 01379 688 585
Website: www.bloomsofbressingham.co.uk
A good range of conifers is available at the nearby
Bloom's of Bressingham Garden Centre

Royal Botanic Gardens, Kew, Richmond, Surrey,
TW9 3AB
Tel.: 020 8940 1171

Royal Horticultural Society Garden, Wisley, Woking,
Surrey, GU23 6QB
Tel.: 01483 224234

Yorkshire David Ward, 3 Barnaby Cottages, Winn
Moor Lane, Shadwell, Leeds 17, Yorkshire,
LS17 8LU
Tel.: 01132 650769

Argyll and Bute Younger Botanic Garden Benmore,
Dunoon, Argyll, Argyll and Bute, PA23 8QU
Tel.: 01369 706 261, Fax: 01369 706369

Glasgow Colzium Estate, Kilsyth, Glasgow
Tel.: 01236 825070

Edinburgh Royal Botanic Garden Edinburgh, Inverleith
Row, Edinburgh, EH3 5LR
Tel.: 0131 552 7171, Fax: 0131 248 2901

Further information on National Collection holders
of various genera and species can be obtained from:
NCCPG National Office, The Stable Courtyard,
Wisley Garden, Woking, Surrey, GU23 6QP
Tel.: 01483 211 465, Fax: 01483 212 404
Website: www.nccpg.org.uk

The Association of British Conifer Growers may be
able to assist in recommending local retail outlets
for plants that are more difficult to find:
Website: www.conifers.org.uk

IRELAND

National Botanic Gardens, Glasnevin, Dublin 9,
Republic of Ireland
Tel.: 1 837 7596 / 4388, Fax: 1 836 0080

CZECH REPUBLIC

Jan Beran, Kozinova 22/4, 10200 Praha 15, Hostivar
Conifer collection
Tel.: 02 7175 1217, Fax: 02 7175 1215

FRANCE

Pépinières des Laurains, route d'Etrelles 22,
10170 Longueville sur Aube
Conifer nursery
Tel. and fax: 03 2539 1717

GERMANY

Baumschule H. Hachmann, Brunnenstraße 68,
D-25355, Barmstedt in Holstein (near Elmshorn)
Nursery and show garden of conifers and
rhododendrons
Tel.: 04123 2055 / 2056, Fax: 04123 6626
Website: www.hachmann.de

Baumschule Uwe Horstmann, Rotenburgerstraße 60,
D-29640, Schneverdingen (near Bremen)
Nursery and private collection of dawrf and
miniature conifers
Tel.: 05193 4468, Fax: 05193 2688

THE NETHERLANDS

Visitors welcome by arrangement

Baexem Weil Linssen, Rhijdstraat 11, 6095 BJ Baexem
National collection of *Sciadopitys*, nursery and show
garden with many dwarf and miniature conifers
Tel.: 0475 451265, Fax: 0475 453005

Deurne Nelis Kools, Beukenstraat 98,
5753 GD Deurne
National collection of *Picea glauca*, *Thuja orientalis*
and *Sequoiadendron*, display garden and nursery
Tel.and fax: 0493 314601, E-mail:
bkwkools@xs4all.nl, Website: www.awi.nl/bkwkools

Hilversum Pinetum Blijdenstein, Van de

Lindenlaan 125, 1217 PJ Hilversum
Collection of more than 520 conifers,
including 44 endangered species
Contact: Nico Schellevis, Tel.: 035 6232 1123
E-mail: Schellevis@dutch.nl
Website: www.bio.uva.nl/Pinetum/

Kerkrade Jos Flecken, Peschbeemdenstraat 19,
6462 RX Kerkrade
Collection with many heather cultivars in
combination with dwarf conifers
Tel.: 045 545 6398, E-mail: j.gflecken@freeler.nl

Leende Wim Rutten, Zevenhuizen 1, 5595 XE Leende
Nursery and private collection of magnolias and
conifers
Tel.: 040 206 3528, Fax: 040 206 3529

Rotterdam Arboretum Trompenburg, Honingerdijk 86,
3062 NX Rotterdam
National collection of *Fagus*, *Hosta*, *Quercus*, large
collection of older conifer species and dwarf cultivars
Contact: Gert Fortgens, Tel.: 010 233 0166
Fax: 010 233 0171
E-mail: arboretum@tromenburg.nl
Website: www.tromenburg.nl

Zoelen Ronald Vermeulen, Langesteeg 17,
4011 JS Zoelen (near Tiel)
Private collection of more than 500 *Abies*, *Cedrus*,
Picea and *Pinus* cultivars
Tel.: 0345 652290, Fax: 0345 650336
E-mail: RvermeulenNCV@cs.com
Contact address: Deilsedijk 30, 4158 CG Deil

For further information, contact the Dutch Conifer
Society (NCV)
Contact: Wil ten Dam, Grolweg 5, 6964 BL Hall
Tel.: 0313 619338, E-mail: w.t.dam@hccnet.nl

SWEDEN

Brita Johansson, Musselvägen 3, 46834 Vargön
Conifer collection
Tel.: 0521 221598

AUSTRALIA

Conifer Gardens Nursery, Mount Dandenong Tourist
Road, Ferny Creek 3786, Victoria
Contact: David H. Daly, Tel.: 03 9755 1793

Ross Conifers, Gemalla (via Bathurst), New South
Wales 2795
Tel. 02 6337 5555

Yamina Rare Plants, Monbulk, Victoria
Tel.: 03 9756 6335

NEW ZEALAND

Anderson's Arboretum, Glendonald, Cumberland
Road, RD16, Albury

Cedar Lodge Nurseries Ltd, 63 Egmont Road, RD2,
New Plymouth
Contact: David and Noeline Sampson
Tel.: 06 755 0369, Fax: 06 755 0319
E-mail: sampson@conifers.co.nz
Website: www.conifers.co.nz

Ian McKean's Arboretum, Rangiwahia, Kimbolton,
RD Feilding
Species collection founded in 1958
Contact: Ross Geary, Tel.: 06 328 2849

Conifer Pete's Nursery, 1999 Pakowhai Road, RD3,
Napier
Tel.: 06 878 2917

Wakanui Conifers, Kaimatawi Road, RD2, Taihape
Contact: Don and Vivian Tantrum
Tel. and fax: 06 388 0635

BIBLIOGRAPHY AND FURTHER READING

General

American Conifer Society Bulletin 1989–2001

Bailey, L. H., *The Cultivated Evergreens*, MacMillan, 1923

Bean, W. B., *Trees and Shrubs Hardy in the British Isles*, John Murray, 1991

Bloom, Adrian, *Conifers for Your Garden*, Floraprint, 1972

Cutler, Sandra M., *Dwarf & Unusual Conifers Coming of Age: A Guide to Mature Garden Conifers*, Barton Bradley Crossroads, 1997

Dallimore, W. and A. B. A. Jackson, *Handbook of Coniferae and Ginkgoaceae*, Edward Arnold, 1966

Dirr, Michael A., *Manual of Woody Landscape Plants: Their Identification, Ornamental Characteristics, Culture, Propagation and Uses*, Stipes Publishing Co., 1998 (the US nurseryman's bible!)

Gordon, George, *The Pinetum: being a synopsis of all the coniferous plants at present known, with descriptions, history and synonyms*, Henry G. Bohn, 1880

Growing Conifers, Brooklyn Botanic Garden, 1997

Hamilton, Bruce Taylor, *Human Nature: The Japanese Garden of Portland, Oregon*, Japanese Garden Society of Oregon, 1996

Harrison, Charles, *Ornamental Conifers*, Hafner, 1975

Hillier's Manual of Trees & Shrubs, David & Charles, 1988

Hornibrook, Murray, *Dwarf and Slow-Growing Conifers*, Country Life, 1938

Krussman, Gerd, *Manual of Cultivated Conifers*, Timber Press, 1985

Lanner, Ronald M., *Conifers of California*, Cachuma Press, 1999

Mitchell, A. F., *Conifers in the British Isles: a descriptive handbook*, Forestry Commission, 1972

RHS Plantfinder Dorling Kindersley, published annually

Rushforth, Keith, *Conifers*, Christopher Helm, 1987

Swartley, John, *The Cultivated Hemlocks*, Timber Press, 1984

Tomlinson, Harry, *DK Pocket Encyclopedia: Bonsai*, Dorling Kindersley, 2001 (recommended for beginners)

Van Gelderen, D. M. and van Hoey Smith, J.R.P., *Conifers, The Illustrated Encyclopedia*, 2 volumes, Timber Press, 1996

Welch, Humphrey J., *Manual of Dwarf Conifers*, Theophrastus, 1979

Welch, Humphrey J. and Gordon Haddow, *World Checklist of Conifers*, Landsmans Bookshop, 1993

Propagation

Browse, Philip McMillan, *RHS Plant Propagation*, Mitchell Beazley, 1979

Clarke, Graham and Toogood, Alan, *The Complete Book of Plant Propagation*, Ward Lock, 1992

Dirr, Michael A., *Manual of Woody Landscape Plants* (see under General)

Dirr, Michael A. and Charles W. Henser Jr, *The Reference Manual of Woody Plant Propagation*, Varsity Press, 1987

Pests and Diseases

Allen, E. A., D. Morrison and G. Wallis, *Common Tree Diseases of British Columbia*, Canadian Forest Service, 1996

Hansen, Everett M. and Katherine J. Lewis, *Compendium of Conifer Diseases*, The American Phytopathological Society, 1997

Johnson, Warren T. and Howard H. Lyon, *Insects that Feed on Trees and Shrubs*, Cornell University Press, 1991

Strouts, R. and T. G. Winter, *Diagnosis of Ill Health in Trees*, TSO (UK), 2000 (2nd edn)

Sinclair, Wayne. A., Howard H. Lyon and Warren T. Johnson, *Diseases of Trees and Shrubs*, Cornell University Press, 1987

HARDINESS ZONES

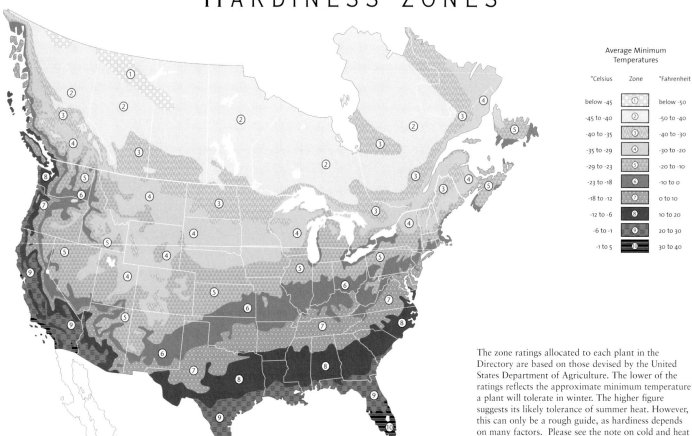

°Celsius	Zone	°Fahrenheit
below -45	1	below -50
-45 to -40	2	-50 to -40
-40 to -35	3	-40 to -30
-35 to -29	4	-30 to -20
-29 to -23	5	-20 to -10
-23 to -18	6	-10 to 0
-18 to -12	7	0 to 10
-12 to -6	8	10 to 20
-6 to -1	9	20 to 30
-1 to 5	10	30 to 40

Average Minimum Temperatures

The zone ratings allocated to each plant in the Directory are based on those devised by the United States Department of Agriculture. The lower of the ratings reflects the approximate minimum temperature a plant will tolerate in winter. The higher figure suggests its likely tolerance of summer heat. However, this can only be a rough guide, as hardiness depends on many factors. Please see the note on cold and heat tolerance on page 84.

INDEX

Growth regulator

Some conifers can be controlled after pruning in spring by the application of a growth regulator, which will not harm the hedge or fast-growing conifer, and is ideal if required for × *Cupressocyparis leylandii*. The product is available in most garden centres.

ACKNOWLEDGEMENTS

There are many people who made this book possible; Richard, my youngest son, with his superb close-up photography; my wife Rosemary, for her support and help with the manuscript; the publishers Frances Lincoln; Jo Christian, Jane Havell and Caroline Hillier; Tony Lord for his comments on nomenclature.

The book would lack its broad scope and authority without the detailed advice given to me on the Directory by expert contributors; in the USA, in particular, Don Howse, conifer specialist and co-owner of Porterhouse Farms, Oregon; Susan F. Martin, curator of conifer collections at the US National Arboretum, Washington D.C., and Ethan Johnson, plant records curator of the Holden Arboretum, Kirtland, Ohio. In New Zealand, Noeline Sampson gave additional information as a conifer specialist and co-owner of Cedar Lodge nurseries, New Plymouth, while Graham Hutchins from Essex, England, helped with up-to-date information on *Podocarpus*. Pests and Diseases is an important subject, and I couldn't have had better advice than from Scott Aker, integrated pest management coordinator at the US National Arboretum in Washington, D.C.; and, from RHS Wisley, Chris Prior, head of plant pathology, and Andrew Halstead, senior entomologist – to whom my thanks for giving detailed information at short notice. Thanks, too, to expert propagator Brian Humphrey and Pat Gray for the grafting sequence and other advice.

There is not room for too many details on each of the following except to thank them for information and support in giving specialist and general advice for the book: Charlene and Wade Harris, Chelsea, Michigan; Paul Halladin, propagating manager at Iseli nurseries; Colin Morgan, Curator, Bedgebury National Pinetum, Kent; Wiel Linssen, conifer specialist and nurseryman, Holland; Brita Johansson, Sweden, and collector Yoshimichi Hirose, Japan.

Richard and I took many photographs in the UK and on visits to the USA, Holland, Germany, Australia and Japan, as well as other countries. We would like to thank the following for allowing us to take photographs in their gardens:
UK David Ward, Leeds, pp. 59, 84, 95, 93, 101, 105,163; Colin Morgan, Bedgebury National Pinetum, Kent, p. 112; Maggie and Steve Putt, Roydon, p. 51; Richard Ayres, Cambridge, p. 54; David Howard, Roydon, p. 178; Arthur Hall, Barningham, p. 91; The Grimsthorpe and Drummond Castle Trust for use of my photograph taken at the Drummond Castle Gardens, Perthshire, Scotland, p. 13.
USA Bill Janssen and Diana Reeck, Oregon, p. 100; The Elisabeth C. Miller Botanical Garden, Seattle, pp.79, 101, 112, 117, 136, 146, 169; Nancy Britz, Ipswich, Massachusettes, p. 182; Dennis Groh, Dearborn Heights, Michigan, pp.103, 125, 135; Bob Fincham, Eatonville, Washington, p. 106; Phil Normandy, Brookside Gardens, Maryland, pp. 43, 119, 141; Bill Thomas, Longwood Gardens, Pennsylvania, pp. 35 (right), 52, 122, 160; Marco Polo Stufano,Wave Hill, New York, p.113; Peter Wooster, Roxbury, Connecticut, pp. 73 (bottom left), 129; Paul Halladin, Iseli nurseries, Oregon, pp.73 (bottom centre), 77, 81 (left and right), 149; Marty Brooks, Doylestown, Pennsylvania, p.151; Don and Harriet Wild, Ann Arbor, Michigan, pp. 34 (right), 152; Larry Mackles, Bloomfield Hills, Michigan, p.153; Ray Weigand nursery, Michigan, p.154; Berta and Nate Atwater, Rhode Island, pp. 39, 80,161; Susan Martin, US National Arboretum, Washington, D.C., p. 34 (left); Scot Medbury, Strybing Arboretum, San Francisco, p.110; Jenny Shattuck and Jim McDaniel, Ladew Topiary Gardens, Monkton, Maryland, p. 41 (middle); Russ

Morash, The Victory Garden, Boston, p. 50 (right); The Japanese Garden of Portland, p. 74.
Holland Gerd Fortgens and Dick van Hoey Smith, Trompenburg Arboretum, pp. 88, 116; Kas Koemans, Boskoop, pp.72 (bottom left), 90, 99,114; Wil ten Dam, Hall, p. 92; Nelis Kools, Deurne, pp. 98, 155, 162; Jos Flecken, Kerkrade, pp. 33, 102, 115, 167; Wiel Linssen, Baexem, p. 126; Tom de Lange, Nuenen, p. 70.
Germany Kurt Kramer, Edewecht, p. 48.
Spain Generalife Gardens, Alhambra Palace, Granada, p. 41 (top).
Australia Don and Jenny Allan, Victoria, p. 50 (left); Jeremy Francis, Cloudehill, Victoria, p.148; David W. Daly, Victoria, p.108; Lindsay Gray, Victoria, pp. 40, 41 (bottom), 72 (top),109; John and Connie McCabe, Victoria, p.58.
Japan Kuroishi Garden, Japan, pp.75,76.

Others who gave their assistance, either in allowing us to photograph their gardens or with help and advice were:
UK Hazel Jones, Kings Lynn, Norfolk; Mark Flanagan, Keeper of the Gardens at Savill and Valley Gardens, Berkshire; Peter Milner and Chris Crowder at Levens Hall, Cumbria; Jonathan Tate, Lime Cross Nursery, East Sussex; Gordon Haddow, Kenwith Nursery, Devonshire; Andrew Hart, Curator at Harlow Carr Botanical Gardens, North Yorkshire.
USA Landon Reeve, President of Chapel Valley Landscape Co., MD; Dean Linderman, Leesburg, VA; W. David Thompson, owner of Foxborough Nursery, Inc., MD; Gary Koller, Koller & Associates, MA; Diane Dalton, MA; Ellen McFarland, MA; Ellyn Meyers, Director of Hidden Lake Gardens (Harper Collection), Michigan State University, MI; Suzanne Thatcher-Johnson, MA; Wade and Charlene Harris, conifer specialists, MI; Richard and Raven Tuttle, Saguaro Rare Plant Nursery, MI; Jack Krasula, MI; Rich Owings, Curator, Mendocino Coast Botanic Gardens, and Tom Tillotson, CA; Judith and Robert Mathey, CA; Larry Stanley, Stanley & Son, Nursery, OR; Talon Buchholz, Buchholz & Buchholz Nursery, OR; Andre W. Iseli, OR.
Holland Wim Rutten, nurseryman; the Bomer family, ginkgo and conifer specialists; Ronald Vermeulen, Secretary of the Dutch Conifer Society.
Germany Jan-Dieter and Gertrude zu Jeddeloh.
Australia Dr Kingsley Dixon, Director of Plant Science, Kings Park and Botanic Gardens, Perth; David Daly Senior and David W. Daly, Conifer Garden Nursery, Vic.; Leo Koelewyn, Coolwyn Nurseries, Vic.

I also wish to acknowledge the assistance and information given by members of both the American and Dutch conifer societies before, during and after visits to the USA, The Netherlands and Germany.

Photographic credits

All photographs are by Adrian and Richard Bloom, except for that on page 8 which is by Jerry Morris, a noted Colorado conifer collector who scaled the heights to take this dramatic photograph, for which many thanks.